BRAZIL SOUTH

Its Conquest & Settlement

Translated from the Portuguese by

LINTON LOMAS BARRETT &

MARIE McDAVID BARRETT

BRAZIL SOUTH:

Its Conquest & Settlement

MOYSÉS VELLINHO

WITH A PREFACE BY

ERICO VERISSIMO

NEW YORK /

ALFRED · A · KNOPF   1968

To the memory of

OSWALDO ARANHA

and

OTHELO ROSA

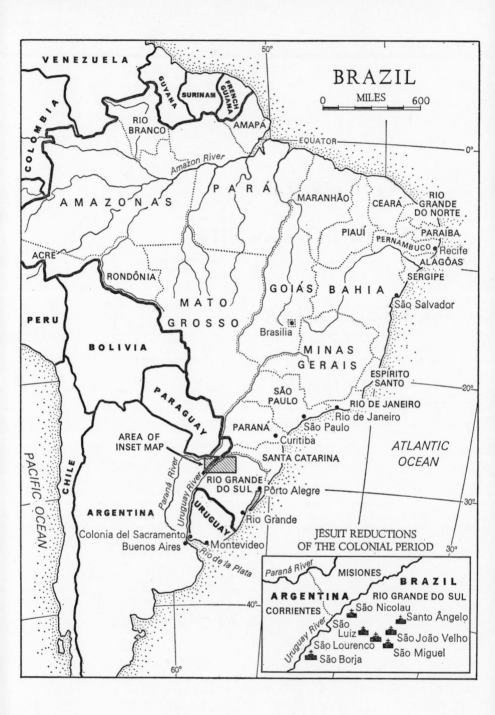

BRAZIL

0 MILES 600

VENEZUELA

GUYANA
SURINAM
FRENCH GUIANA
AMAPÁ

COLOMBIA

RIO BRANCO

EQUATOR 0°

Amazon River

PARÁ

AMAZONAS

MARANHÃO CEARÁ RIO GRANDE DO NORTE

PARAIBA

ACRE

PIAUÍ

PERNAMBUCO
Recife
ALAGÔAS

PERU

RONDÔNIA

SERGIPE

MATO

GOIÁS BAHIA

São Salvador

BOLIVIA

GROSSO

Brasilia

MINAS GERAIS

ESPÍRITO SANTO 20°

PARAGUAY

SÃO PAULO

RIO DE JANEIRO
Rio de Janeiro

AREA OF INSET MAP

PARANA
São Paulo
Curitiba

ATLANTIC OCEAN

PACIFIC OCEAN

CHILE

Paraná River
Uruguay River

SANTA CATARINA

RIO GRANDE DO SUL
Pôrto Alegre 30°

URUGUAY

ARGENTINA

Colonia del Sacramento
Buenos Aires

Montevideo

Rio Grande

Rio de la Plata

JESUIT REDUCTIONS
OF THE COLONIAL PERIOD 30°

40°

60°

JESUIT REDUCTIONS OF THE COLONIAL PERIOD

Paraná River MISIONES BRAZIL

ARGENTINA RIO GRANDE DO SUL

CORRIENTES São Nicolau Santo Ângelo

Uruguay River

São Luiz São João Velho

São Lourenco São Miguel

São Borja

PREFACE

IN ITS ORIGINAL BRAZILIAN EDITION this book dispensed with a preface, but it needs one for its English language version, although not necessarily written by myself.

Driven by an understandable urge for oversimplifications that save time and trouble, Americans usually designate all the countries below the Rio Grande under the general name of Latin America, forgetting or not knowing that there is both a Spanish and a Portuguese America. The latter is formed by Portuguese-speaking Brazil, a kind of empire in itself, with an area of nearly 3,300,000 square miles, and a population which by 1980 is expected to reach 100,000,000.

If I were asked to mention one single reason why I think Moysés Vellinho's book should interest the American reader, I would say that it explains the differences between these two so-called Latin Americas, and because, moreover, it describes and analyzes the territory where, the time when, and the acts and facts through which southern Brazilians struggled to remain under the domination of the Portuguese, resisting the soldiers of the kings of Spain. In brief, this book tells the dramatic story of a bloody frontier.

Being a southern Brazilian myself, I remember that in my school days we were compelled to study the history of our home state, Rio Grande do Sul, in tedious textbooks and in terms of lackluster myths and legends. It was a boring succession of wars against the Castilians (not only the Spaniards but also those who later were to be called Argentinians, Uruguayans, and Paraguayans). Of course the Brazilian armies won all the combats, all the battles, and all the wars. We memorized the names of many bemedalled generals with pompous sideburns and stern faces. What we were fed in school was mythology, not history. It was almost like attending a puppet show that we disliked: cardboard dolls moving stiffly against a background of painted paper simulating our prairies and green, rolling hills, while all the time the teacher repeated patriotic platitudes in a monotonous voice. Many years later, when as an adult I decided to write a kind of mural novel covering two hundred years in the life of my home state, from the original settlers, in the seventeen-thirties, up to Getúlio Vargas, in 1945—the first thing I had to do was forget the textbooks of my childhood and start debunking our history and our heroes. Beneath the dust of false gold that covered our myths I found a land, a people, and a saga much more lively and beautiful than all the "official" legends.

Honest historians like Moysés Vellinho and very few others helped me indirectly in the task of "giving names to the oxen," to use an old and realistic *gaúcho* saying. It is not easy for any writer to admit that some of his ancestors were horse thieves and slave traders, before becoming respectable ranch owners, and that most of the pioneers who crossed our wilderness, during almost two centuries, were not immaculate knights-errant or even plainsmen with hearts of gold, as incarnated by movie heroes like Gary Cooper and John Wayne. It is also rather embarrassing, in a Catholic country, to recognize publicly that the simple fact of a missionary wearing a cassock and holding a wooden cross in his hand does not necessarily make him a saint.

In my opinion *Capitania d'el Rei* is perhaps the first and certainly the best essay written in the extreme south of Brazil using modern historical methods, that is, an adult appraisal of our past and our origins in which facts are disentangled from myths.

THE FIRST CHAPTER of *Brazil South* deals with the southern expansion of Brazil in the seventeenth century, when the Portuguese crown decided to occupy once and for all the lands south of the Amazon and north of the River Plate. (Look at the map and see what a substantial piece of real estate that was!) The southernmost Portuguese settlement in America at that time was Laguna, beyond which lay what a French traveler and naturalist would later call "a frightening six-hundred-league desert." For that expansion the King of Portugal depended not only on missionary priests but also on soldiers and pioneers.

Mr. Vellinho tells the story of the *bandeirantes*, those groups of adventurers and explorers that periodically left the Captaincy of São Vicente (today the state of São Paulo) bound for the unknown backlands, in search of gold and silver mines and the fabulous "country of the emeralds." They also knew, less romantically, that there was good money in the traffic of Indian slaves.

One of these *bandeirantes*, a certain Raposo Tavares, left São Vicente bound for the Paraná River. His intention was to destroy the Jesuit missions, to dominate Paraguay, and later on to explore the legendary lands of Peru. According to some historians, having encountered strong armed resistance from the Indians commanded by the priests, Raposo Tavares and his men changed their itinerary only to take on a more ambitious one. They started out in small boats on the Tocantins River, reached the Amazon and braved its waters eastbound, and went up to Pará, whence they came back home. The trip lasted three years, and everybody thought they were lost or dead. Other chroniclers affirm that Tavares's prowess was still more fabulous, that he and his *bandeirantes* crossed the Andes and went up to Quito and probably later reached the shores of the Pacific.

Mr. Vellinho gives careful attention to the origins and the fate of Sacramento, the colony that Portugal founded on the north bank of the River Plate. Its failure led the Portuguese crown to establish in 1737, somewhere up north on the seaside of the land they wanted to hold, a military presidio with a garrison of dragoons, which is considered the first Portuguese settlement in that part of Brazil, later to be known as the Captaincy of São Pedro. In this chapter the reader is able to follow the many changes undergone by a movable border, the lines of which were periodically thrust forward up north or down south by the lances, the swords, and the breasts of the frontier warriors.

One of the most fascinating aspects of the history of the New World is the role played by the missionaries of the Society of Jesus during colonial times. I think that nowhere in the whole of the American continent did the issue become more bitter and controverted than in Paraguay and neighboring Brazil. Even to this day historians engage in endless and heated arguments over the matter.

The idea that the Portuguese Jesuits were faithful and obedient to the government of their home country seems to be generally accepted. But what about the Spanish? Did they work for Spain, in which case they were against the Portuguese interests in America, or did they work for themselves, that is, for the fulfillment of what could be called the "dream of a Theocratic Empire"?

The seven missions that the Spanish Jesuits instituted in Paraguay (the famous *Sete Povos*) and which later were incorporated into Brazil, induce us to sponsor the second theory, namely that those tenacious black-cassocked priests followed mainly religious ideals. They segregated the Indians in small "nations" established around a cathedral and under the totalitarian and at the same time paternalistic authority of the priests, who had spiritual, civil, and criminal jurisdiction over the natives. Economically it was, at least on the surface, a kind of communistic experiment. The priests taught the Indians how to read and write (Latin and Spanish, of course), music, the plastic arts, and a great number of crafts. The spirit of the Sete Povos, its organization, and practical results have been either praised or mercilessly attacked by historians through the centuries.

It seems to me that in this essay Moysés Vellinho has said the right word about the role of the Jesuits in southern Brazil, without a shadow of prejudice.

MR. VELLINHO debunks some of our traditionally accepted heroes and exalts those whom other historians have overlooked or underrated. Another sore point of controversy in the history of Rio Grande do Sul has as its central figure Sepé Tiaraju, a supposedly intelligent, wise, kind, and brave Indian chieftain, who was *correge-dor* at the Saint Michael Mission and who, through the greedy fantasy of poets and the carelessness of historians, has become not only a blameless hero but also a sort of saint. (Every country has the Pocahontas it deserves. . . .)

Mr. Vellinho roused the wrath of many a fellow historian when he voiced his doubts about the feats of Sepé Tiaraju, taking issue with those who consider him the first *gaúcho*—that is, Brazilian *gaúcho*-guerrilla leader. He proves with crystal clear arguments that the "noble savage" could not be a *national* hero since he fought for the Spaniards against the Portuguese.

The chapter in which Mr. Vellinho draws a parallel between the state of Rio Grande do Sul and the River Plate region is most illuminating. He thinks that it is a mistake to suppose that Brazilians, Argentinians, and Uruguayans resemble each other. This misconception arises from the fact that they are all conditioned by the same environment, the same type of activity—cattle raising—and that they all suffered, one way or the other, the influence of the working techniques of the native tribesmen.

Moysés Vellinho's study of caudillos goes from the first settlers in both regions—transient pioneers who became cattle ranchers, and eventually, in times of war, military leaders—up to urban political bosses of our day, like Pinheiro Machado and Getúlio Vargas.

The kind of Portuguese spoken by the Brazilian *Gaúchos,* that is, the inhabitants of Rio Grande do Sul, is generally accepted as the neatest in all the country. We do not mince the letters or the words, but sort of "bite" them as the good beef-eaters that we are, endowed with good teeth. Ours is a clean-cut, well sculptured Portuguese.

Mr. Vellinho thinks that we try to speak that way deliberately because, conscious of our role as guardians of a frontier, we feel the permanent duty of defending the purity of our mother tongue from any foreign taint. This theory may or may not be valid, but I must confess that I find it fascinating.

HERE is a really important book, full of stimulating ideas, written by one of the most distinguished historians and critics of contemporary Brazil.

ERICO VERISSIMO

Pôrto Alegre, January 1968

CONTENTS

BRAZIL SOUTH

Its Conquest & Settlement

Introduction

WHEN the Fifth Eucharistic Congress convened in the capital of Rio Grande do Sul in 1948, one estimable lady from Bahia, interviewed by a local paper, remarked that she was pleasantly surprised. In some embarrassment she confessed to feeling relieved, because (in her own words) she had come to Rio Grande with misgivings, expecting to find an alien people with alien customs. Instead, on arriving in Pôrto Alegre she had found herself among her own kind, people with essentially the same way of life and feeling as the rest of the Brazilians. Her great desire to attend the Congress had been stronger than her misgivings, but she had come as one reconnoitering the terrain of a world not her own,

3

and only after her first contacts with our city and state had she been able to banish her intangible fears.

That is but one illustration of the prejudices and misunderstandings with which many of our fellow countrymen regard us. Often it is we Rio-Grandenses[1] who must admit being responsible, directly or indirectly, for other Brazilians' unfavorable reactions to the historical and social reality of Rio Grande do Sul.

Consider, for example, Alfredo Varela's major book.* In his zeal to prove the supposed relationship of the War of the Farrapos[2] to the long chain of cisplatine[3] revolutions, Varela dusted off the most recherché arguments to support his sterile theory in some three thousand pages. And not content with that effort to denationalize a movement so Brazilian in its nature, its motives, and its ties, Varela permeated his six volumes

[1] For convenient reference to people of the State of Rio Grande do Sul, the term is adopted from the Portuguese *rio-grandense*. (Translators.)

[2] War of the Farrapos ("rags, tatters"), the revolution of 1835-45 in Rio Grande do Sul. Those who held republican ideals rebelled against the federal government, which had oppressed the state and in its centralism had transgressed states' rights, as the Rio-Grandenses saw the situation. The revolutionists organized the Republic of Piratini, breaking with the Brazilian Empire, but were defeated by the general who later became the Duque de Caxias. Thus the secession was short-lived, and Rio Grande was reinstated in 1845 as part of Brazil. (Translators.)

[3] Cisplatine: "On this, that is, usually, the Brazilian, side of the Plata" (*Webster's New International Dictionary*, 2nd edn. unabridged). The word is used throughout this book in that sense. In many references it includes what is now Uruguay, that area having long been a part of the Portuguese dominions. (Translators.)

4

with an aggressive exaltation of regional values together with deep-seated prejudices against everything Brazilian. Imagine the tidal wave of ill will that his work can raise among readers without better sources of information, and without realization that his anti-Brazilian sentiments are purely subjective and personal! Not all readers can bring an open mind to the task of interpreting historical facts. Therefore, as in the case of the fortuitous separatism of republicans and federalists in 1835, they are not in a position to grasp the strength of the sentiment for complete integration into the Brazilian Empire that impelled the republicans of Rio Grande do Sul to take up arms and go to the extreme step of breaking with it. Considering the pronouncements of the Instituto Histórico e Geográfico do Rio Grande do Sul and the conclusive studies by so many experts in Rio Grande's past, the separatist theory ought to have been put aside long ago.* Not even Varela would dare mention any particle of irredentism among the factors influencing that grave political and institutional crisis. The breaking of ties with the Crown was nothing more than an expedient, serious but circumstantial, forced on the revolutionists by the Regency's own mistakes.[4] But the situation is not

---

[4] Brazil was governed by a Regency during 1831–40. Dom Pedro I of Brazil abdicated in favor of his five-year-old son on April 7, 1831. Four stages of regency followed in those nine years, ending with the young Prince Pedro being declared of age on July 23, 1840, and crowned as Dom Pedro II. This was one of the most turbulent periods in Brazilian history, largely because of the repressive federal-

as bad as it might be, for Varela is all but unreadable. His prolix, cumbersome style rises like a barrier against the reader, who, having once encountered it, rarely returns to the attack. He does so only—if at all—out of professional duty.

But there are other sources and motives for error and misapprehension. Even the two famous writers from the Northeast, Gilberto Freyre and José Lins do Rêgo, on their first visit to our state, set out to find a *gaúcho* who would fit their image of the type, the image so widely current.[5] After many days of searching, they caught sight of one, indubitably (they thought) an old *gaúcho* in all his traditional nonchalant elegance. Exultant, they went to inspect their find at closer range, only to learn that he came from Freyre's own home state!

It is a truism that mistakes proliferate, sometimes in the most disconcerting ways. How frequently Rio

---

ist policies of the joint regents in the first two stages. The Regency's mistakes included poor choices of provincial presidents, and an excessively centralized administration, both resented by a frontier province jealous of its political privileges. Revolutions broke out in Pará, Maranhão, and Rio Grande do Sul; the first two were put down without undue prolongation of the war, but the last was by far the most serious, not to be ended until 1845. (Translators.)

[5] The *gaúcho* is the Brazilian, especially the Rio-Grandense, version of the Gaucho, a subject treated in the next to the last essay in this book. The type being more closely associated with Rio Grande do Sul than with any other part of Brazil, the people of that state are popularly called *gaúchos*, much as we might call inhabitants of Indiana "Hoosiers." Both meanings, that of the sociological type of the cowboy and that of the native of Rio Grande do Sul, occur in this book. (Translators.)

Grande has been regarded as more or less, or totally, foreign to the Luso-Brazilian complex! In books and newspapers, or through chance encounters with compatriots from other regions, we have been struck innumerable times by curious misstatements, ingenuous or spiteful or prejudice-free, all of them expressing the same notion, namely, that Rio Grande do Sul is not really Brazilian.

It is beyond doubt that this preconception has been considerably reinforced by the eccentricity of the Castilhos decree of July 14, 1891,[6] and the divisive, separatist postulates of its philosophy. It is also certain that the unease caused in Rio Grande by that decree, which was to be adapted to the general standard only in consequence of the Revolution of 1923, contaminated other aspects of our life. A document singularly expressive of that error of judgment is the record of José Veríssimo's impressions of Rio Grande do Sul after a short stay here in 1912. With the harshness natural to

[6] The Castilhos decree ran counter to the Federal Constitution adopted February 24, 1891, as may be inferred from José Veríssimo's accusations in the next paragraph, outlining the contents of the decree. Júlio Prates de Castilhos (1859–1903) was prominent in his native Rio Grande do Sul before the proclamation of the Republic (1889), and then became member of Congress (1890), resigning when elected president of his native state in 1891. Deposed by revolution shortly after issuing his *Carta* of July 14, he regained power in 1892, but resigned to re-enter Congress. He took power in Rio Grande do Sul once more in 1893, combatting the rebelling federalists. Finally handing over the government in 1898 to Dr. Borges de Medeiros, he remained head of his political party. (Translators.)

him, the eminent critic bluntly stated his opinions. The official newspaper of the state's reigning political power immediately took up the cudgels. Stunned, José Veríssimo promptly retorted with an intemperate, almost ferocious, rebuttal. He began by saying that the situation created by "the monstrous act of Castilhos" was simply confirmation of the fact that Rio Grande was nothing more than "a foreign body in the Brazilian federation." "I am one of those who think," he declaimed, "and thousands of us Brazilians think likewise, that a State where all other powers have been sacrificed to the executive; where the jury, chosen in utter inconformity with their and our juridical tradition, is selected by public ballot; where municipalities can be suppressed, divided, or annexed to others at the whim of the governor; where the organ of public justice is merely an agent of his, appointed, removed, or discharged at his pleasure; where no official proof of ability is required for any public position, even a technical one, or for the practice of any profession, thus raising incompetence to the level of a virtue; where the legislative power has only financial functions and where the holder of the executive power passes it on to whom he wishes—a State so organized is virtually outside the Brazilian union, because it is practically outside the Constitution of the Republic."* What José Veríssimo could not see was that Rio Grande's reality, its history, its habits of life and ways of thinking, were not confined within the rigid molds of the institutions he was so virulently attacking.

Among the commonplaces of Brazilian sociology is the notion that our country, in its continental vastness, is not and cannot be a homogeneous entity. Each region necessarily has its own characteristics or accents without thereby jeopardizing the attainment of a common destiny. Those who rave about a centralized, uniform Brazil, with artificially standardized cultural values, forget that the very safeguard of our territorial unity, in Paulo Prado's sage admonition, in great part lies in dependence upon the "legitimate expansion of regionalisms, the living, plastic part in which the variety and originality of the national complex are preserved and developed."*

The origins of Rio-Grandense life are to be found in natural and cultural factors in action. The people of the Rio Grande do Sul are of the same blood, the same heritage, the same roots as those of the other parts of Brazil. But unlike the rest of Brazil, they have been influenced by wars and frontier conflicts, by having to maintain constant vigilance over the national border at a supremely critical point.

As subjects of Portugal and as plain Brazilians after Independence, we faced up to the vicissitudes of a prolonged, bloody frontier drama. The need to defend the national community, threatened most along its borders with the Spanish territory south of the Plata, sharpened and lent an urgent military meaning to our consciousness of being Brazilians. "This captaincy," Saint-Hilaire declared back in 1820, "will in some degree be a school

9

for the others . . . endowed as it is with activity and energy, with military spirit, and with a sense of nationality that is born only of war."*

If the effect of the repeated wars was to activate and strengthen the sense of belonging to a great land, that feeling was to be maintained as a living legacy even after the cycle of frontier disputes was ended. Sharing boundaries with other nations along two thirds of its human frontiers, it was natural that the Brazilian of the extreme South, faithful to his warrior heritage, should be hardened in an attitude of vigilant patriotic affirmation, without prejudice to the sentiments of close cordiality which nowadays animate our neighborly relations with Uruguayans and Argentines. Nevertheless, some persons have interpreted these characteristics as symptoms of detachment from national solidarity. Many look on us as a culturally undefined unity fluctuating between the Luso-Brazilian and the Hispanic-American worlds.

Here, too, part of the blame is ours. Father Balduíno Rambo, S.J., for example, wrote that in the fact that the port of Montevideo became "a magnet for shipping" lies the principal, although not the only, reason why Rio Grande formed a neutral zone between the centrifugal movements from the Portuguese sphere on the north and from the Castilian on the south, a situation reflected throughout the history of its growth.* It is plain from such blunders that the learned Jesuit, impressed disproportionately by economic factors, either ignored or was

when Rio Grande was a province of the Brazilian Empire, those errors were to arise again. In the name of local rights, which had been contemptuously flouted by agents of the Regency, the men of Rio Grande rose up in arms. It was the beginning of the turbulent decade of the Farrapos War. One of the members of Parliament, Ferreira França, on May 16, 1837, came up with a proposal that included, among other things, the expulsion of the rebellious province from the nation!* This unfortunate proposal may have been only an ironic challenge to the Regency's inertia in the face of the serious events developing in the extreme South.[9]

In 1930 history was to repeat itself. Once again under arms, Rio Grande do Sul, side by side with Minas Gerais and Paraíba, led the national revolt against the perverting of republican institutions.[1] Tiradentes Palace,

[9] The Regency of Father Diogo Antônio Feijó was more successful in putting down other insurrections than it was in Rio Grande do Sul, whether the latter failure was due to inertia or not. In fairness it should be added that Feijó had to cope with tremendous opposition throughout his term in office. (Translators.)

[1] If the objectives of the rebellion were distorted and betrayed, as they were, this does not mar the original inspiration of the movement. Its failure resulted from the enormous mistake of having entrusted the destinies of the revolution to a man who did not know what to do with it and who for that reason played a shabby, opportunistic game. It was not possible to cure the vices of the Old Republic with a dictatorship, and that was what Getúlio Vargas imposed on the country with no excuse whatever.

[The revolt began in protest against the endorsement of Júlio Prestes from São Paulo by the President, Washington Luíz, as candidate to succeed the latter, also a Paulista. The apparent perpetuation in office by Paulistas, and the corruption in political affairs,

seat of the Ministry of Foreign Affairs, was shaken and seething. Among the deputies, more agitated and fearful than the rest, was the same Humberto de Campos. To a man so ignorant of our national history it could not mean much to resort to the heroic measure of excommunication in order to rid Brazil once and for all of an eternal source of disorder, one that he regarded as a merely spurious piece of the nation. Hence, as he himself recalls in his *Diário*, his decision to propose afresh the idea of dismemberment by showing Rio Grande the door!

When the Aliança Liberal[2] campaign was about to burst into flames in the Revolution of 1930, the worthy historian Basílio de Magalhães, at the time a member of the national House of Deputies, raised his voice against the men of Rio Grande. As Othelo Rosa states it, Magalhães said that we had "not even the right, bordering on insolence, to intervene in the political solutions of a national entity in which, against its will, the Rio-

---

especially the falsification of elections, aroused the states of Minas Gerais, Paraíba, and Rio Grande do Sul. Popular sentiment mounted in other parts of Brazil against the regime, and many demanded that Vargas and his colleagues reject the outcome of what they considered a corrupt election and take over the government by force. Even so, months passed before any overt act occurred, and when military action began, little was needed for the revolutionaries to assume control of the government. (Translators.)]

[2] The political coalition formed by Getúlio Vargas and his allies, in opposition to the Washington Luíz regime and its candidate. The Aliança had the support of all opposition parties throughout the nation. (Translators.)

Grandenses stand in the uncomfortably awkward position of genuinely marginal people."* The honorable deputy from Minas Gerais was basing his attacks on the people of Rio Grande on the premise, to him indisputable, that we are not Brazilians but rather, in great part, Hispanized in the manner peculiar to the Hispano-Americans of Argentina.

Unfortunately he has not been the only historian to utter such nonsense about Rio Grande do Sul and its people. The occasional forays of Capistrano de Abreu and João Ribeiro[3] have left well-known markers along that road.

Capistrano went so far as to lament that the frontiers of Brazil had been consolidated without having left Rio Grande outside. To his way of thinking the former Continente de São Pedro, by reason of its latent or overt threats to the country, constituted a new Trojan Horse introduced by trickery within the nation's walls.* In a letter to the Baron de Rio Branco[4] dated 1887,* the indefatigable scholar, referring with ill-disguised disdain to what he called "the Southern questions," confessed

[3] João Capistrano de Abreu (1853–1927) was an outstanding historian, an authority especially on the early period of Brazil. João Batista Ribeiro de Andrade Fernandes (1860–1934) was one of the most versatile writers in Brazil's history: poet, short-story writer, philologist, critic, historian, and folklorist. (Translators.)

[4] José Maria da Silva Paranhos, Baron de Rio Branco (1845–1912), politician and diplomat, distinguished himself particularly in negotiations over frontier questions with Argentina, French Guiana, Uruguay, and Peru. (Translators.)

that he had never understood "that business." Several years later, in 1900, the date of his attack on Rio Grande, he was still a stranger to the history of southern Brazil, a more than sufficient reason for a historian of his quality and responsibility to guard against such serious judgments. Not even the most casual glance at our past would have denied the truth to him, as was to be proved soon afterward. Indeed, writing in 1903 about the great Caxias,[5] he had to gain closer acquaintance with the "Southern questions," and then, less ill-informed, he recognized, although superficially, that Rio-Grandenses had "so often shed their blood for their country, and that—he emphasized—ever since the colonial period."*

As for João Ribeiro, he let himself get entangled in a garbled conception of Brazil's development. Apparently believing in the exclusive influence of natural factors on the processes of historic evolution, he disdained all others, including those elements that have been so decisive in the civilizing work of Portugal: the Portuguese genius for unity, and the ease with which they adapted

[5] Luíz Alves de Lima e Silva, Duque de Caxias (1803–80), was a field marshal of Brazil. As a lieutenant in 1821 he fought for Brazil's independence, as captain against the Uruguayan rebellion in 1825, as major against revolts in 1832 and 1839, as colonel against the insurrectionists of Maranhão, São Paulo, Minas Gerais, and Rio Grande do Sul, and succeeded in putting an end to the War of the Farrapos in 1845. He commanded the Brazilian forces against the Argentine dictator Rosas, served as Minister of War, President of the Cabinet, and national Senator. He led the Brazilian forces against Paraguay when that country attacked Brazil (and Argentina and Uruguay), and served once more as Minister of War afterward. (Translators.)

themselves to new environments. Natural factors have never predominated either in the Peninsula or overseas. Furthermore, the eminent historian did not realize that the enterprise of Luso-Brazilian expansion was not carried out blindly, but rather directed over the whole of the vast geographic, economic, and cultural unit which already, before the Discovery, had been the home of the Tupi-Guarani, and which embraced all the area between the Amazon and the Plata.* The spirit of adventure of the *sertanistas*, those hardy explorers of the backlands, not only overcame the natural barriers but drove them on and on, farther into an ever-widening geography. João Ribeiro, on the other hand, theorized that Brazilian unity was due to the Rio São Francisco.* And so he set about slicing up the national territory, a cut here, a slash there, taking it upon himself to amputate the regions outside the network of that great river basin!

Naturally, Rio Grande do Sul, whose incorporation into Brazil flatly contradicted such a false concept, was pitilessly included among the excisions of that infelicitous operation: we were too much of the Plata, as the Amazon was too Indian, to be legitimate links in the chain of nationality. This idea has for two generations been circulating with impunity in schools as national history!

Oliveira Viana himself, closer to us, lapsed into surprising fallacies about Rio Grande do Sul. Let us ignore the deplorable carelessness he displayed in confusing the

Revolutions of 1835 and 1893[6] with the movements
that, according to him, are somehow related to "institutions of banditry."* We have had just refutations by
representatives of two generations, each in his turn:
Othelo Rosa, a master of Rio Grande history, and Sérgio
Costa Franco, the young sociologist well on his way to
maturity, the former in a study presented to the Instituto
Histórico e Geográfico do Rio Grande do Sul,* and the
latter in the pages of the press.*

It may be conceded that Viana, in the second volume
of his *Populações Meridionais do Brasil*,* has sought to
do penance for his earlier carelessness in *Instituições
Políticas*. Although that subsequent volume, subtitled
O Campeador Rio-Grandense, had been composed many
years before *Instituições Políticas*, the fact that he published it later means that the eminent sociologist had not
disavowed what he had written earlier—some of the
most gripping, comprehensive pages on Rio Grande's
historical formation and characterization.

Yet in spite of the great abundance of data and arguments marshaled throughout his book and unmistakably
disposed in behalf of the Luso-Brazilian authenticity
of Rio Grande's formation, an extremely disconcerting preface directly contradicts the text. From the
first chapter to the last, what we see is a Rio Grande

[6] For the Revolution of 1835 see note above on "War of the *Farrapos*." The Revolution of 1893, which lasted three years, fought for
the parliamentary system, as opposed to the presidential system of the
1891 Constitution. (Translators.)

born of the tremendous affirmation of the Luso-Brazilian world in the face of a traditionally adverse one, the Spanish-American world, both of them expanding aggressively over the same geographic area. Then, as if the author had suddenly turned against his own arguments and conclusions, without deigning to give the slightest explanation to his reader, lo and behold in the preface he seems to place Rio Grande in an ambiguous position between two moorings, one representing the forces of Lusitanian culture but dominated by the influence of the Plata, and the other, Spanish culture and its Plata environment.

When Rubens de Barcelos published his essay on the social formation of Rio Grande in 1922, it was Oliveira Viana himself who protested in a letter to Roque Callage: "I have a little disagreement with the author when he declares that the nucleus of our Campanha[7] gravitates toward the Plata, which I do not think absolutely true."* Later came his about-face.

If these misapprehensions about Rio Grande do Sul are found in the highest circles of Brazilian historical thinking, it is not surprising that when compatriots from other regions arrive in our state they are astonished to see that we speak the same language they do, without the sprinkling of Castilian words they expected, and that our

[7] Name of the Rio Grande plains region east of the Uruguay River. It extended south to the Plata before division by national boundaries; so references herein are to the larger or the smaller area depending on contextual date. (Translators.)

racial and political background is the same as theirs, too. They admit that Rio Grande is much like Brazil. Yes, those good people are ignorant of the truth, that Rio Grande has from its infancy been a part of Brazil, of the Brazil that grew of itself.

The Southern Expansion
of Brazil

"IT WOULD BEHOOVE HIS MAJESTY TO COLONIZE RIO GRANDE, in order to prevent the Castilians' onward progress." (*From a petition by the councilmen of the Câmara de São Francisco, Santa Catarina, to the emissary of the Government of Rio de Janeiro and Captaincies of the South, in 1714.*)

ONE DAY EARLY IN 1680 MARCOS ROMÁN, a sailor from Buenos Aires, was tacking among the islands in the Plata in quest of wood when a startling sight sent him scurrying back to his home port. Leaping ashore, he went straight to the authorities with his momentous news: five Portuguese sloops had put in at the other bank of the river, directly opposite the Castilian stronghold.*

Despite his shock, Marcos Román was far from foreseeing that he had just witnessed the prologue of the bloodiest, most long-drawn-out frontier war to be waged in the vast South American dominions of Portugal and Spain.

It was the little squadron of Dom Manuel Lôbo that had dropped anchor, with orders to lay the foundations of a fort, the Colônia do Sacramento, for the purpose of establishing the southern boundary of Brazil.

In the last quarter of the seventeenth century, almost two hundred years after the Discovery, Brazil was still growing, swelling the immensity of its territory. The enormous country was being gradually and painfully populated by scanty contingents from overseas, recruited in the Kingdom from among the leavings spared from the East Indies enterprise, which swallowed up so many of Portugal's resources with meager return. These levies for Brazil had in the course of two centuries been plentifully reinforced by the fruits of miscegenation.

Far from their homeland, the colonists made up for the fatigues of the voyage and for their profound nostalgia by satisfying their appetites in the pursuit of the native women. Pero Vaz de Caminha[1] has not misled

---

[1] As the official scribe of Cabral's fleet, which discovered Brazil in 1500, Caminha wrote a report to King Manuel I, the document thus being the first official notice about Brazil. (Translators.)

us in his famous dispatch: The sturdy Indian women who wandered among them, within reach, so clean of body, and living in, as it were, the aura of sin, lusty females wearing the very shadow of the thick forest in the color of their skin, were undoubtedly the same described by the fleet's clerk to Dom Manuel I so realistically and lustfully. The pioneers procreated lawlessly, unrestrainedly, creating such a population explosion as can have occurred only in the infancy of the world.

Hardly fifty years had passed since the first Mass when Father Manuel da Nóbrega, visiting the Captaincy of Pernambuco, was shocked to see the backlands full of the children of Christians, "great and small, male and female."* It is said of João Ramalho, one of the most remote settlers in the new land of Santa Cruz—later to be known as Brazil—that he peopled the lonely Piratininga with such an abundance of children and descendants that even the official communiqués showed some constraint in estimating the total. In fact, it was in these cautious terms that the first Governor-General reported to Dom João III about Ramalho: "He has so many children and grandchildren, great-grandchildren and descendants, that I dare not tell Your Highness."* Not even the clerics, themselves considered by the Jesuits as "the dregs of the Kingdom," escaped temptation. According to the members of the Company of Jesus, among the secular clergy there were not only those who turned a blind eye to the iniquities of the laymen but even some who stimulated and encouraged them by their own evil example. In the words of the severe Ignatians, such "were by trade more demons than priests."* Criticizing such abuses, Nóbrega could not contain his indignation. "I shall vociferate as loud as I can,"* he declared, overcome by shame.

But if the intemperance of the Christians afflicted the disciples of Saint Ignatius, severely intent upon the cure and salvation of souls, the agents of the King did not regard it with the same repugnance. In the case of João Ramalho, Tomé de Souza, the Governor-General, drew the scandalous matter to the royal attention. He deftly added, as though to excuse his boldness, "He has not a white hair on his head or face, and he can walk nine leagues before dinner." One can sense between the lines of this report that the Governor-General could hardly hide the excitement with which he informed his sovereign of the excessive contribution by the sixteenth-century faun toward populating the land.

As a matter of fact, we are now beginning to entertain a suspicion that João Ramalho was not just one but several individuals answering to the same name.*

In the esteem with which the pioneer of Piratininga was held by the authorities of the Colônia, and which more than once was expressed at public functions,* it is possible to glimpse the foresight which from those earliest times the Portuguese displayed in realizing the necessity of encouraging cross-breeding as the only means of assuring and spreading the conquest.*

The colonizers' incontinence, soon exacerbated by the slave quarters on the plantations, nevertheless did not answer by a long way the insatiable need of population. The people whose numbers swelled gradually around the trading posts of the coast or the hamlets of the interior, and who ventured far into the hinterland, did not suffice for the minimum demands of colonization.

IT IS THEREFORE NOT SURPRISING that as the 1700's approached nothing had been attempted effectively to incorporate the north and south borderlands into the Portuguese dominions. We were an organism in obscure gestation, developing with neither plan nor measure along the littoral and in the virgin recesses of the Continente. The country, as though in an amazing leaven, swelled out on every side, from the edges of the Atlantic to the eastern slopes of the Andes. However, only the trunk and arms of the immense disjointed body grew: the head and the feet of the giant were lost in the fluidity of the wilderness.

The Crown, together with the North and South Divisions[2] of the Colony, and also urged by local peti-

---

[2] Without official decree of any kind the division came about through the dictates of circumstance around 1700. The sheer multiplicity and extent of colonial interests necessitated dividing the vast territory: the Captaincy General of Rio de Janeiro, together with those of Espírito Santo, São Paulo, Minas Gerais, and the southern lands not yet integrated as a political or even geographic entity,

tions, resolved to appropriate the remote lands lying beyond the Amazon and on the Brazilian side of the Plata. Both areas were considered by Lisbon as legitimate Portuguese property, for already the archaic and imprecise line of Tordesillas had been extensively overrun by the *bandeiras*.[3] In consequence of that transcendent decision by the Regent Dom Pedro,[4] new efforts would be undertaken, stretching to the limit the resources still available to the Kingdom after the disastrous liquidation of its enterprise in the Orient. The necessity was imperative: without that double movement of expansion, beyond the Amazon and toward the Plata, the geographic unity of the conquest would not have been consummated.

IF IT WAS POSSIBLE INITIALLY to entrust the enterprise in the North to missionaries, that in the South was to take on very quickly the character of a military operation of

broke away from the central government of Bahia to have their own direct relations with Lisbon. The Captaincies of Maranhão and Pará, in the extreme North, had had their own regime from the start.

[3] Armed groups of adventurers, called *bandeirantes*, seeking gold or other quickly won wealth in Brazil's hinterlands in the 1600's and 1700's. (Translators.)

[4] The decree ordering the founding of the Colônia do Sacramento is dated November 12, 1678,* and the order to occupy "the other bank of the Rio das Amazonas" bears the date of April 1, 1680.* [Dom Pedro governed Portugal from 1668 as Regent for his inept brother Afonso VI, and was himself crowned as Pedro II of Portugal on Afonso's death in 1683. (Translators.)]

high importance. Its objectives, aimed at the mouth of the Río de la Plata, could not fail to be taken as a direct threat to one of the most opulent dominions of the Spanish Crown, jealously closed to foreign commerce under the laws then governing the colonies of Spain.

IT WAS THERE at the back of the estuary into which the Paraná and the Uruguay rivers spill their waters that our most intense and long-drawn-out frontier drama had its origin.

The geographic expansion of Brazil, almost always aided by the complicity of the wilderness and carried out in great part during the interregnum when Portugal and her colonies lay under Spanish domination (1580–1640), usually took place without organized opposition* or major repercussions abroad. After 1640, however, Portugal being once more independent and the two Iberian powers back at their eternal bickering, the Plata and its adjacent land became the central point of the overseas controversies between Spaniards and Portuguese.

To aspire to a joint domain of the great estuary did not signify merely a territorial violation, in the Spanish Monarchs' point of view: it amounted to a direct menace to the monopoly of access roads to the prodigious Viceroyalty of Peru. And that the wondrous region of Potosí lay within range of the first stages of conquest by Luso-Brazilian explorers is attested not only by documents of the period,[5] but by the itinerary of the *bandeiras* in their chosen westward course.

Therefore every precaution was taken against the impudence of the Portuguese. It was inevitable that the Spaniards would react most energetically and determinedly to the dispute over the north bank of the Plata by their long-standing rivals. Thus the Conselho Ultramarino in Lisbon counseled extreme caution in executing the undertaking: let a fortress be planted there, but "with so many men and with such secrecy that when [the Spaniards] learn of it, it will be ready for its own defense."* So that everything should contribute to the success of the operation, it was entrusted to Dom Manuel Lôbo, the experienced commander in chief already seasoned in Peninsular campaigns.

All these careful measures, nevertheless, were to end in total loss. Hardly had the first stones been piled, so to speak, for the construction of the presidio, when Buenos Aires, alerted from the first, launched a heavy attack on the Portuguese. With the crushing, decisive aid of an army of 3,000 Guarani Indians mobilized and provided

[5] In 1695 the Conselho Ultramarino singled out, among the reasons justifying the Portuguese expansion southward, the fact that with the Indians of the Jesuit mission towns subject to Portugal, "we can easily extend our settlements until we make common boundary with the Kingdom of Peru; and if there is war between the two crowns, with the same Indians captained by the said Paulistas we can invade and sack the border strongholds of Peru, because their defenses are open to attack."*

by the Spanish Jesuits, the bastion was captured and destroyed. The few survivors of the resistance, their commanding officer among them, were taken prisoner and hauled off to Chile.

The victory, which the attackers had confidently anticipated, being more than ten to one, was so utterly complete and devastating that it may have convinced the Castilians and their allies, the Jesuits, that their adversary's plan had been nipped in the bud. But events were to evolve after their own fashion: hostilities having begun, it was only after a hundred and fifty years that the struggle finally ceased with the birth of a new nation—the República Oriental del Uruguay.[6] And indeed it was only the War of Paraguay (1865–70) that marked the end of the cisplatine wrangles.

The bloody controversy, which kept the cabinets of both kingdoms in turmoil for a whole century, forcing European diplomacy into action with their clamoring,*

[6] The precedent set by the Portuguese occupation of the north bank of the Plata must have acted strongly as one of the political factors in the annexation of the cisplatine [later Uruguay] to the territory of Brazil, then still a part of the Lusitanian Empire. That operation was inopportune, to be sure, but without it Uruguay would never have been freed from the catalytic power of Buenos Aires. "The earliest reason for this independence (of Uruguay)," Father Leite adds, "we believe must be sought in that first urban nucleus of Uruguay, the Colônia do Sacramento, which led to the founding of Montevideo and gave Uruguay a mixed formation, half Spanish and half Portuguese, which in the evolution of history, with other new factors, was to burgeon into a buffer state between the two great Republics of Brazil and Argentina."* [The independence of Uruguay was recognized in 1828. (Translators.)]

was not to be resolved without entailing consequences particularly decisive for the boundaries and the historical destiny of what is today the state of Rio Grande do Sul. The conflict, breaking out to the north of the Río de la Plata, was to fall back upon the soil of Rio Grande, where at last the line of resistance would be extended to guard the vast southern portions of the Luso-Brazilian dominions, including the area from the Paranapanema River to the Plata.

THE REPERCUSSION of these events had a deeper significance for the founders of Rio Grande and their descendants than appears in the records. The underlying memory of those struggles still survives in fragmentary expressions of *gaúcho* folklore. Even today in out-of-the-way places far distant from the old Spanish border one may catch a stray echo of the hatreds and resentments of former times, and, if the ear is attentive, hear the past and its ghosts return:

> "Long live the King of Portugal!
> Death to damnable Spain!"

Such verses still crop up in obscure litanies mumbled by the common folk in ceremonies that are touching in their sheer ingenuousness.[7]

[7] According to the Rio-Grandense writer Alfredo Jacques some time back when he, a subordinate officer in the state's Military Brigade, was assigned to police duty in the interior of the Municipality of Lagoa Vermelha, near Santa Catarina, he had occasion to witness a

. . .

BEFORE MATTERS DEGENERATED into the stubborn chain of conflicts provoked by the establishment of the Colônia do Sacramento, Brazil's expansion toward the Plata had come up against the heavy forests covering the east basin of the Paraná and the two steep banks of the upper Uruguay. Save for sporadic incursions by slave traders hunting Indians, and by São Vicente traders, whose caravels had been crossing the Rio Grande bar and sailing up to the Jacuí and Taquari rivers to "liberate" Indians since the middle of the sixteenth century,* it was a silent and all but unknown world unfolding beyond the outermost limits of Luso-Brazil, on the São Paulo coast, as far as the solitary wilderness of the cisplatine area. Hundreds of leagues lay between the last Portuguese lines and the support and protection afforded by natural barriers.

From 1605 to 1637 the Portuguese Jesuits, coming down the coastal strip, more than once attempted to establish themselves in the old district of Rio Grande* at points not far from the Guaíba[8] with the aim of convert-

---

strange ritual attended by quite a number of the faithful. Before a small wooden packing box that served as an improvised altar, an old black woman officiated. The congregation, of various racial colorings, listened respectfully as she intoned something analogous to a litany. It was a confused doggerel interlarded with religious invocations and interrupted at intervals by the congregation, chorusing the refrain quoted above, but without knowing what it meant.

[8] The Guaíba, more an estuary than a river, flows by the present city of Pôrto Alegre, carrying waters from the Jacuí and tributaries into the Lagoa dos Patos.

ing the heathen dwelling there. Adverse factors, however, particularly the hostility of the Indian-white half-breeds and the insurmountable distance from possible sources of help, were to lead to the complete undoing of the work of the missionaries.

Around 1628 the Spanish Jesuits, after the havoc wreaked in Guaíra by the Paulistas[9]—and with the connivance of the Paraguayan authorities*—infiltrated the western part of what is now Rio Grande do Sul for the first time. They came in the names of God and the Monarchs of Castile, though it seems unquestionable that they came also in the name of the temporal interests of the Company of Jesus. As a result of this infiltration Portuguese Brazil was exposed to increasing clashes between the *bandeirantes* and the Jesuits of the Province of Paraguay.

Once across the Uruguay, the Spanish priests penetrated as far as the basin of the Jacuí, halfway to the coast for which they were aiming. They were seeking an outlet to the sea, perhaps because they intended to evade subjection to the customs authority of Buenos Aires.

The courageous undertaking was slowing down amid hardships, alarms, and mortal danger which came to render their position untenable. That peril, which later resulted in disaster for the Jesuit strongholds, was the irruption of the *bandeirantes*, old hands in the

[9] Guaíra at that time was a Spanish province lying between the Paranapanema, Paraná, and Iguazú rivers. The Paulista assaults on Guaíra began in 1628 and ended in 1631 with the destruction of the last Jesuit town. (Translators.)

region vaguely known at that time as "País dos Paulistas" (Paulista Country) or "Adjacências do Paraguay" (Lands Adjacent to Paraguay), names which by their mutual antagonism foretold the disputes that were to come. As in Guaíra, the formidable explorers of the backlands suddenly appeared out of the thick forest at the head of their Tupi allies and burst upon the "doctrines"[1] like a plague from hell.

The ordeals faced by the earliest inhabitants of São Paulo before they could settle down on the plateau, the torments of hunger and inclemencies of weather no less dire than the aggressiveness of the heathen—all this made them fiercely ready for the struggle for survival. And in addition they had to contend with the open opposition of the local Jesuits.

These experiences armed the tough, hardened pioneers of Piratininga with the will to tackle first the backlands in the last half of the sixteenth century, then move against the native breeding places of Guaíra in 1628–31, and finally attack the reductions[2] that were beginning to flourish in the Tape.[3]

---

[1] The word *doutrina*, besides its usual meaning, commonly denoted an Indian town not yet a full-fledged parish with priest, and by extension came to mean any mission town of baptized Indians. It is therefore often a synonym for "reduction," defined below. (Translators.)

[2] In Portuguese (and Spanish) America the word stands for mission towns under Jesuit rule. "To reduce" also means "to convert" in those languages, hence "reduction" for a community of converted Indians. (Translators.)

[3] Tape (two syllables): The Guarani Indians called the Santo Tomé reduction "ta-pe" (Guarani for "city"); the word came to be applied

For several years the forays of the *bandeirantes* were repeated against these inviting targets until defeat overtook them at M'Bororé in 1641. By that time, however, the Spanish Regular Clerics[4] had been thrown out of the lands occupied by them on the Brazilian side of the river. They would return only after nearly fifty years, when the predatory cycle of the *bandeirantes* was nearing its end.

This time[5] the soldiers of Saint Ignatius would be better supplied: besides the Gospel, they brought along enough war matériel to defend the dual undertaking—religious and political. This time, as Oliveira Martins said, the divine cavalry sought to gain the world for God not only with the arms of heaven but with the arms of earth.

THE MEN FROM São Paulo, whose feelers toward the South long antedated the first expansionist movements of the Jesuits of Paraguay, from early days began plunging

---

by the Europeans to the Guaranis of the missions in the Paraná and Uruguay river lands, and by further extension it refers to that region. (Translators.)

[4] The ordained Jesuits, for many of the Society were not ordained priests. In 1750 about half of the Jesuits in Brazil were priests.* (Translators.)

[5] The Jesuits, after half a century of containment west of the Uruguay, returned to the east bank in 1687 and between that date and 1709 founded seven reductions, the "Seven Towns of the Missions" conquered by Brazil in 1801. (Translators.)

into the backlands wilderness. In the seventeenth century the *bandeirante* eruption would reach its climax, at times luring away nearly the whole able-bodied population of the plateau.* When the monsoon came, the *sertanistas*[6] slipped on their fighting clothes or bundled themselves in leather and dived into the unknown, guided by the Indians' prodigious topographic sense. Their journeys lasted months and months, even years on end.[7]

They were motivated primarily by hunting Indians for slaves, either to keep or to sell for service to others. Their principal market was the sugar plantations of the Northeast Captaincies before the Negro slave trade became great. In the late seventeenth century when gold was discovered, these wilderness experts were infected by the new fever and migrated in great numbers to the Continente.

---

[6] The term derives from *sertão*, the "bush" or hinterland wilderness of the remote interior: *sertanista*, then, is one intimately acquainted with the *sertão*, as the *bandeirantes* were, and the word is often used as a synonym of *bandeirante*. (Translators.)

[7] Antônio Raposo Tavares (1598–1658), for example, native of Portugal, emigrated to São Paulo in his youth. After experience in warfare and in the *sertão* he organized a *bandeira* and drove the Spaniards west of the Paraná River. He razed Guaíra and captured 10,000 Indians (ca. 1630). After fighting the Dutch in the North, he made a long, adventurous trip westward, up the Paraguay and tributary rivers to the Amazon, and sailed up that river. Some say he went as far as Quito, others claim he reached the Pacific. In 1651 he arrived in Pará, and finally returned home after three years, so changed by the effects of battle and hardship that his own people failed to recognize him. His feats added thousands upon thousands of square miles to Brazil's territory. (Translators.)

The *bandeiras* set out under the command of white *sertanistas* or Indian half-breeds. Enslaved Indians had the job of guiding and of cutting paths, and moreover formed the bulk of the forces when enemies attacked. Black slaves were used mainly in the harvesting of back-woods plantations and in guarding the corrals set up at suitable spots in the interminable wanderings.* For the cure of these burdened souls the *bandeiras* were not always provided with chaplains, even when they were preparing to contend with the Spanish Jesuits for the already converted Indians.[8]

In their forays southward the *bandeiras* descended as far as the reductions of the Tape country, demolishing them after successive attacks (ending in 1641) and forc-ing the priests to retreat to the right bank of the Uruguay. This exploit, apparently an isolated event, nevertheless had its consequences in the subsequent his-tory of these regions. If the Jesuits of Paraguay had not been ejected at that moment, it might not have been possible to recover the broad lands that they eventually took over in 1687, when they again attempted to carry their politico-religious conquests across the area that was to form Rio Grande do Sul and on to the Atlantic. By then the Luso-Brazilians had established themselves on

[8] The Jesuits harshly censured the incorporation of priests into the *bandeiras*. "These priests," they said, "went to the extravagant lengths of accompanying expeditions hunting Indians. Of several it was known that they had set out more than once with *bandeiras*. A Carmelite served as chaplain on the raids with Manuel Prêto."*

the Plata and created a powerful argument for the future claims of Brazil to the territory.

WHILE BUENOS AIRES WAS CLAIMING that its jurisdiction should extend up to the limits of São Paulo and Rio de Janeiro,* Lisbon took the view that, despite the stipulations of the Treaty of Tordesillas, the territory today comprising the state of Rio Grande do Sul, as well as the cisplatine countryside, was properly contained within the Portuguese boundaries. Before the Spanish Jesuits' infiltrations, however, those broad, fertile lands had not been permanently occupied by anyone.

Among the causes of this neglect we may single out the political unification of the Iberian peninsula, imposed by Spanish arms in 1580. The combination of the two crowns under Philip II caught the South American conquests by the two peoples in full spate, but thereafter sixty years of relative quiet were to pass. The expansionist attacks from both sides were to slow to a vegetative tempo until the separation of the two sovereignties in 1640, when Lisbon began to think seriously about the effective possession of its dominions.

IN 1678 THE ORDER TO FOUND the Colônia do Sacramento was issued. After some ill-fated attempts the Portuguese had finally succeeded in recruiting men in Brazil for the operations on the upper bank of the Plata. Dom Manuel Lôbo brought with him two hundred men—soldiers, officers, and officials of war, justice, and treasury; priests, stonemasons, carpenters, several dozen slaves, and everything else necessary for the construction of a fort and the founding of a city.

The meticulous orders issued to the experienced old officer contained very wise and cautious instructions, among them that of trading and communicating with neighbors, letting them know immediately that the Portuguese came only to secure what was already theirs.*

Naturally, Buenos Aires was not fooled. What about the Treaty of Tordesillas? Didn't the territory where the little Portuguese squadron was anchoring lie within the Castilian borders?

It has been said over and over that the diplomatic history of America was inaugurated with the precarious agreement signed in 1494 at Tordesillas by Spain and Portugal under the powerful aegis of Pope Alexander VI. In reality, however, the old papal treaty was of no avail against the living forces of history. How to contain the portentous achievement of the Paulista *bandeiras* or the nominally illegal advance of the Castilian Empire in other areas of conquest? As a compromise it was impracticable because of its lack of precision and the "moral impossibility" of its being respected.*

It is not known what Dom Manuel Lôbo thought

about these problems, but when Don José de Garro, the irascible governor of Buenos Aires, tried to bar his passage, alleging the terms of Tordesillas (already violated by both parties), Dom Manuel promptly evaded a showdown by pointing out that the matter was of too great importance to be argued over in that out-of-the-way spot, and that it would be wiser to submit it to the highest tribunal of the courts.

INDEED, DIPLOMATIC INCIDENTS caused by the question of sovereignty over the Plata began with the earliest days of the conquest. When Solís discovered the Río de la Plata for Spain in 1516 he was merely following in the wake of the Portuguese caravels, which at least twice before him had ventured well inside the great estuary. Such antecedents, aggravated later by Martim Afonso de Souza's 1532 expedition, were shrewdly invoked by Lisbon whenever circumstances permitted, causing bitter controversies between the two powers. And the Castilians could hardly have forgotten the humiliation suffered when the Emperor Charles V, urged by his father-in-law, Dom Manuel of Portugal, found himself constrained to punish those involved in Solís's exploit, which amounted to a violation of territory recognized at that time as an integral part of the Portuguese possessions.*

In the records of that period are stories of other events that fanned the enmity between the two peoples, events that tended to strengthen Portugal's claims. There is the tale, transmitted by a Spanish Jesuit, of the awe-inspiring feat of an almost legendary Portuguese, Aleixo Garcia. Not a quarter of a century had passed after the Discovery when that adventurer, setting out from Cananéia with three companions, all outcasts like himself, headed for the "lands beyond Paraguay," leading an army of two thousand Indians recruited along the way. He was already on his way back from Peru with precious treasures when the men from Castile, commanded by the Genoese Caboto, were making their way for the first time up the course of the Paraná and the Paraguay!* Although that journey belonged to an already distant past, it naturally continued to have repercussions in Buenos Aires, all the more because it had been repeated in more recent times and with the same adventurous spirit by another Portuguese, one, if anything, even more intrepid than Aleixo Garcia, the *bandeirante* Raposo Tavares.

Now if the Portuguese were the first Europeans to glimpse the treasures of Peru, one can assume that Portugal was simply hoping to share in the spoliation of the Inca Empire. And what surer means of opening a path to it than to fix a base on the Plata, which was then the natural route of access to Peru?

And Buenos Aires was further concerned by the suspicion that the Portuguese actually outnumbered the Spanish in Buenos Aires.* Indeed we might even regard Buenos Aires at that time as a real Luso-Spanish city.*

Moreover, the presence of secret emissaries on missions that might prove dangerous to the Spanish had just been discovered. And finally, there were plenty of recent and pressing warnings from various sources, but principally from the Superior of the Jesuits, who was on the alert and ready to second the governor in the immediate and relentless repulse of the Portuguese. To the Buenos Aires authorities the 1680 landing by Dom Manuel Lôbo thus merely confirmed deeply rooted suspicions.

Although the instructions given to the old *mestre-de-campo* stressed the need to keep relations amicable, his settlement was taken as a challenge. Nor could it be otherwise: the whole system of a closed economy[9] was going to be split wide open, the very unity of the Spanish Empire was threatening to fall apart. Buenos Aires saw the scope of the peril and, before consulting with Madrid, decided on its own initiative to attack the fort in the first year of its existence and eliminate it.

From the military point of view the clash was painfully unequal. With no possibility of immediate aid, with

[9] As did other countries, Spain held a monopoly on all trade by her colonies. Two officially dispatched fleets sailed annually from Spain for America. Dividing in the Caribbean, ships went to Cartagena (Colombia), Portobelo (Panama), and Vera Cruz (Mexico). From Vera Cruz goods were carried to Acapulco to be shipped to the Philippines; from Portobelo merchandise was hauled overland and transshipped to Lima, to be transported overland again to Buenos Aires (and Montevideo when that was under Spanish rule). En route from Spain the fleet touched at Havana. This closed economy was maintained until 1778, when more ports on both sides of the Atlantic were opened to trade and ships were allowed to sail without escort by men-of-war. The natural outgrowth of such a system was wide-scale smuggling and piracy. (Translators.)

land communications speedily intercepted by parties of Indians under the command of the Jesuits, the Colônia do Sacramento thus planted in the desert was left to its own fate. Even though founded a hundred years earlier,[1] Buenos Aires was still nothing but an obscure outpost without autonomous life. Nevertheless, it could count on support from Santa Fe, Corrientes, and Tucumán, and especially on the considerable military aid of the Jesuits, who had at their disposal a bellicose, well-equipped native army. For the Spanish priests the holy hour of revenge had come at last. The total crushing of the Portuguese fort, thanks almost exclusively to the missionary soldiers, was their retort to the series of devastations wreaked by the *bandeirantes* on the Guaíra and the Tape reductions half a century before, in 1628–41.

Under such disadvantageous conditions it was simply not possible for Portugal to offer resistance beyond the sacrifice of the Luso-Brazilian garrison. The episode has been commemorated in a vigorous monograph by the Uruguayan historian, Luis Enrique Azarola Gil.*

Attacked and taken in the first days of its existence, when the mortar of its walls had not yet dried, the remote Portuguese military colony was to enjoy few

[1] Buenos Aires was first founded in 1536, but was immediately destroyed by Indians. It was resettled in 1580 (the date referred to above), made a Captaincy-General in 1617, and Viceroyalty in 1776. The founding of the Colônia and its destruction both took place in 1680. (Translators.)

periods of truce. Choked off by enemy-held territory, besieged five times, thrice conquered and razed, it was to be reborn from its own ruins under the impulse of factors other than political.

Indeed, from the first the Colônia do Sacramento had become a potent economic center. There the cattle trade and its attendant occupations had been born and developed, there the basis had been laid for intensive and extensive smuggling with the Spanish dominions, a business that attained the annual figure—enormous for those times—of 300,000 pounds sterling!* Handelmann goes so far as to say that from 1700 all the clandestine trading in South America was concentrated there.* One can therefore understand the ferocity of the fighting that blazed up around the Portuguese stronghold. But not even this caused Portugal to neglect sending over civilian colonists and agriculturists. When a little relative quiet was attained about 1717, the regular cultivation of wheat and other cereals, and of grapes, was begun.*

ONE USUALLY READS that the bloody dispute between Portugal and Spain in the Plata delta was simply the manifestation in still another part of the world of immemorial rivalries. But regardless of that heritage, the Colônia do Sacramento, in view of its obvious strategic and economic importance, constituted in itself motive enough for dissension, all the more because in its shadow

professional merchants and unscrupulous Spanish officials carried on clandestine deals.*

No matter how strongly Madrid and Lisbon emphasized its strategic and economic importance, their South
American agents felt it even more deeply. And the
Jesuits did not neglect to fan the live coals that were ever
ready to flare up in the Castilian camp. Indeed, the
political fate of the north bank of the Plata would have
been different had it not been for the military cooperation, impassioned and decisive, lent to Spain by the
Company of Jesus. So strong was the Jesuits' power that
the governors, if we are to believe Alexandre de Gusmão's accusations, found themselves constrained to act in
accordance with their will.*

What is certain is that the signal for the outbreak of
hostilities did not always come from Madrid, but only
the pretext. The rest was up to Buenos Aires, always on
the verge of explosion. Madrid, on the other hand, actually temporized, adopting a policy of appeasement and
compromise in the Plata question. But its agents invariably acted differently. The most insignificant incidents
sometimes had irrelevant and disproportionate repercussions, quickly taking on the weight of a *casus belli*. For
example, the servants of the Portuguese ambassador in
Madrid were arrested on February 22, 1735. On March
13 the Portuguese Secretary of State informed the diplomatic corps in Lisbon that His Majesty was obliged to
arrest the Spanish ambassador's servants in reprisal for
the "shocking insult."* The consequence of this little

comedy: no outbreak in the Peninsula, but a fresh attack on the Colônia do Sacramento, and two more long years of war (1735–37)!

The Portuguese bulwark burned like a red-hot iron on the flank of the Spanish conquests that were directly or indirectly tributary to the Río de la Plata. Because of all this, and the extreme disparity of the conflicting forces, the maintenance of the fort in the hands of its founders for nearly a century can be explained less as a military miracle than as the result of diligent and skillful Portuguese diplomacy. It would not be fair, however, to ignore the fact that the blood shed by the brave frontiersmen who had been charged with the defense of the Colônia do Sacramento lent epic color to the history of the beleaguered outpost which Dom Manuel Lôbo had so boldly planted across the Plata from Buenos Aires.

EVEN IF THE SEVERAL AGREEMENTS between Spain and Portugal on the Colônia do Sacramento initially contained indecisive clauses regarding the authenticity of the Portuguese claims, they ended by admitting the latter in explicit language. Not until Portugal's impoverishment culminated in the capitulation of San Ildefonso in 1777 did the Lusitanian fort pass permanently into Spanish hands.

Robert Southey wrote quite accurately that "Never has so important an objective been more weakly undertaken." And yet no point on the widespread frontiers of

Brazil deserved more support from Lisbon than this advance post in the extreme south. Around it, in Azarola Gil's just judgment, was fought the first of South America's struggles.* If the enterprise was unsuccessful it was because by the time Portugal led her first card, the game had already slipped from her hands. Her vital reserves deeply drained by her adventures in the seven corners of the world, the little country had tried to achieve through diplomatic expedients what arms could no longer give her.

The causes of the defeat speak for themselves. It is easy to deduce them without having to resort to the imputation that the defense of the Colônia had been neglected through failure to understand its enormous political and economic importance. Such an accusation is plainly denied by the facts.* If indeed the drama of the Lusitanian bulwark offers one constant throughout its vicissitudes, that constant is the perfect awareness, in Portugal as well as in her South American possession, of the necessity to maintain at any price the position won on the Plata. It was the integration of Brazil within her natural boundaries and her economy that cried aloud for the safeguarding of that post.

NOT ALL HAD BEEN IN VAIN, however. The failure of the attempt to establish a base at Montevideo, undertaken with the aim of supporting the Colônia do Sacramento, led the Portuguese in 1737, under the command of Silva

Pais, to settle some sixty leagues to the north, at the mouth of the Lagoa dos Patos and on the right bank of the natural canal that two centuries earlier Pero Lopes de Souza, of the expedition under Martim Afonso, had mistaken for a river and given the name of Rio Grande de São Pedro. There the fort of Jesus-Maria-José was erected. It marked the official addition of the new territory to the Luso-Brazilian colonial complex under the name of the Captaincy of El-Rei.

The critical situation of the Colônia fort made it imperative to speed up the occupation and settlement of the territory. The authorities entertained the illusion that such a step might yet guarantee the stability of the Portuguese in the Plata basin.

But this was no longer possible. A few years later, in 1750, the Treaty of Madrid stipulated that the Colônia do Sacramento was to be yielded up to Spain in exchange for the Seven Towns of the Missions, which were deep in Rio-Grandense territory. The famous pact, inspired by one of the great minds of the eighteenth century, Alexandre de Gusmão, proposed to assure peace between the South American possessions of the two Iberian nations. The causes that had so disturbed the quiet of their dominions would be exorcised once and for all. The peace established would be formally safeguarded against future crises: even in the event of war between the two mother countries the peace of their colonies in this part of the world would be guaranteed.

Unhappily, events betrayed these generous arrangements, as nearly always happens in relations between nations. The eternal rivals were soon at war again. And then Rio Grande was forced to bear the brunt of the enemy's hostility. The new conflict was sealed in 1777 by the Treaty of San Ildefonso, which imposed the harshest conditions on the King of Portugal: besides the surrender of the Colônia do Sacramento already stipulated in the Treaty of Madrid, it included the restoration of the Jesuit overlordship, which had spread over the rear guard of the cisplatine strip already occupied by the Luso-Brazilians. With this defeat of Portugal everything was lost, including possession of the herds of cattle in the Vacarias do Mar, which represented a serious threat to the system of economy linked with the exploitation of gold and the very stability of populations in the interior of central Brazil, that is, São Paulo, Minas Gerais, Goiás, and Mato Grosso.*

What the pact of San Ildefonso authorized was no less than the humiliating restoration of conditions that existed prior to the founding of the Colônia do Sacramento. Almost a hundred years of bloody conflict had gone for naught.

As IT HAPPENED, however, the people in Rio Grande de São Pedro were already on the point of taking up arms to defend their land. Soldiers and herders, sons and grandsons of the pioneers, descendants of *bandeirantes* and of those who had come from other captaincies, men from Portugal, refugees from the Colônia, islanders from the Azores and their sons—all had awakened to an urgent duty: to contain by fire and sword the enemy invasion.

The political and economic situation of Portugal hardly permitted her to encourage from afar the resistance by her distant and undaunted subjects. Even the little encouragement she could offer had to be made with great caution lest the slightest imprudence unleash repercussions disastrous for problems in the homeland. That is why, when Rio Grande was invaded and partly conquered in the second half of the eighteenth century, its defense and reconquest assumed, as Calógeras has pointed out, the character of a national undertaking.*

The Spanish were already aware that the men standing guard over the Continente de São Pedro were ready to defend themselves. For thirteen years (1763–76), the former had taken and held a vital part of the Captaincy, including both sides of the Rio Grande natural canal, but in the end they were overcome and dislodged by the decisive action of three Portuguese regiments under the command of Lieutenant General José Henrique Böhm. The cooperation of local elements also had proved effective as the frontiersmen of Rio Grande came to realize they could defend themselves. It was the Brazilian desire for self-determination that was once more arising, this time with redoubled vigor, and that would later on achieve the country's independence.

Faced with the enemy and harassed in its most vulnerable part, southern Brazil could no longer count on even the impetus of *bandeirism* for its existence. The *sertanistas* had become politically conscious. The chapter of pure geographic expansion had closed. All energies would now be directed toward the safeguarding of the southern limits of the Empire.

Hardly had the news reached the Continente do Rio Grande in 1801 that Portugal and Spain were engaged in another conflict—even though the details were vague—when the Captaincy mobilized on its own initiative. The moment had come to settle old scores with the enemy. "There are no words," a witness of the episode informed the Prince Regent,[2] "with which to express adequately the joy of the people in all parts of the Captaincy over the declaration of war, because they have always thought that the Spaniards ought to keep themselves beyond the Río de la Plata." And shortly afterwards the

[2] The witness was Sergeant-Major Domingos José Marques Fernandes, whose *Descrição Corográfica, Política, Civil e Militar da Capitania do Rio Grande de São Pedro* has recently been published by the Instituto Anchietano de Pesquisas in Pôrto Alegre. The *Description*, dated 1804, is dedicated to the "Serene Highness, Senhor Dom João, Prince of Brazil and Regent of Portugal." [Dom João became Regent when his mother, Maria I, went insane after her eldest son's death in 1788. She died in 1816, and Dom João became King João VI. (Translators.)]

same witness says: "The people again grew exhilarated with the certainty of war, and, unable to restrain themselves, several influential men of the Captaincy came in person to the Governor and to the aforesaid leaders, and some of lesser holdings came banded in a group, all asking leave to raise companies of armed cavalry against the Castilians. They all received permission, and it is incredible how much came in to contribute to the army of innumerable men, all resplendent, valiant, constant, and strong, with authorization, also requested and obtained, to march forth and make war on the enemy." Rio Grande armed itself out of its own resources; clad its soldiers at its own expense, for they were all but naked, many without pay; organized itself into militias, and attacked the Spanish on all fronts. First, the assault on the Missions; then, fording the disputed rivers, the attack on the South; and having beaten the enemy, who had let himself be taken by surprise, our forces did everything but sweep him back beyond the Plata. They stopped thus short as the Captaincy Command forbade going any farther. It was by virtue of that collective uprising of 1801, in which even women took an active part, that the Continente grew by force of arms to its present limits, thus reversing the Treaty of San Ildefonso, which had been signed without its knowledge or consent. The Província de São Pedro resulted.

According to Gilberto Freyre, the early colonizer of Brazil converted purity of faith into a source of political unity. But in the extreme South, where the struggle was not against unbelievers but against enemies belonging to the same confession, the sense of unity derived from a . different inspiration, in which the political considerations predominated.

The Colônia do Sacramento episode, autonomous as it was, constituted a constant problem for European diplomacy at the time. But the defense of Rio-Grandense soil, so intimately bound to the political destiny and the territorial integration of southern Brazil, was far more conditioned by "the internal causes of national development."*

One of the factors that bound the political destiny of the Continente de São Pedro to the demands of the "national development" of the Viceroyalty of Brazil was indubitably that pointed out by Jaime Cortesão: "Rio Grande was the economic complement of Brazil's mining."* Indeed, the gold-mining industry in Minas Gerais, and immediately thereafter in Goiás and Mato Grosso, was to continue depending strictly on the meat and mules thenceforth transported in abundance to those markets. Hence the capital importance attributed by modern historians to the opening of the road from Rio Grande to São Paulo at the beginning of the eighteenth century. Alfredo Élis Júnior says that "without it there would have been no cycle of gold, nor that of coffee, nor would national unification have been effected."*

In her zeal to define the southern frontiers of Brazil,

Portugal had taken the offensive, but when the winds changed, the defense of the imperiled territory fell to the lot of the builders of the Continente de São Pedro—the heritage of the last expansionist adventure of the colonial cycle.

To further the political, geographic, and economic consolidation of the Viceroyalty of Brazil, a new territorial entity under military government was formed by royal charter of September 9, 1760, separate from the Captaincy-General of Rio de Janeiro. Rio Grande was thus born amid the alarms of war, and the wars, each following hard on the heels of the last, were to stretch over more than a hundred years with rare interludes of quiet. Its first settlers had hardly begun to cultivate the land and raise cattle when they had to fight. Thus it was during the whole cycle of the Colônia's formation. With the loss of natural boundaries, it became necessary to extend a new line of resistance. Such was the mission imposed upon the builders of Rio Grande by the political and economic demands of Brazil's development.

We are not, then, a territorial appendix clinging to the enormous body of the Fatherland through fortuitous caprices of history. The conquest and populating of Rio Grande were necessary from the start to the pioneers of São Paulo and Santa Catarina, and its defense was so important to the interests of Brazil that when it was invaded by the Spanish in the 1760's it precipitated the transfer of the Viceroyalty capital* south from Bahia to

Rio de Janeiro.[3] And when the Marquês de Lavradio, Viceroy of Brazil, 1769–79, released his own honor guard and dispatched it to the South to reinforce Böhm's army in 1776,* he demonstrated the extreme importance of the Rio-Grandense frontier.

No mere excrescence, Rio Grande is, by reason of its origins, development, and destiny, a living part of Brazil, vitally bound to the organic process of her growth and integration.

[3] The transfer was ordered by the Marquis of Pombal, the greatest statesman of his generation in Portugal and minister of Dom José I from 1750 to 1777. Manoel Cardozo says: "He gave Portuguese America the political unity that it was destined thenceforth to maintain. Through purchase or confiscation he abolished the eleven remaining private captaincies, created two new Crown captaincies in the north, moved the capital from Baía to Rio de Janeiro in 1763, . . ."*

The Jesuits

THE VIGOROUS DETERMINATION with which the Company of Jesus sought to convert the heathen for the Kingdom of God at the same time that it was vying for its share of the Kingdom of Caesar is one of the most fascinating aspects of the history of the New World. The struggle to attain both objectives lasted for two centuries, from the sixteenth to the eighteenth; and the contradiction implicit in that duality explains in great part the controversies unleashed by the stalwart apostles of Saint Ignatius deep in the shadow of the American forests.

News of their undertaking, brought to the Old World in annual reports and private correspondence,

spread over Europe and became the topic of conversa-
tion and speculation everywhere. Imaginations were excited by the prodigious religio-sociological experiment in
the spacious midland territory girdled by the rivers that
feed the Plata delta. The savages that formerly wandered
aimlessly through the backlands of the Paraná basin,
eating each other, now displayed to the world the true
face of "happy Christianity" in the perfect communion
of the reductions. The spectacle, as Lodovico Antonio
Muratori commented about the middle of the eighteenth
century, was "worthy of the eyes of Paradise."* "From
a barbarous race without customs and without religion,"
Bougainville wrote, "was made a gentle, educated people
who scrupulously observed Christian ceremonies. These
Indians, enchanted by the persuasive eloquence of their
apostles, obeyed with pleasure the men whom they saw
sacrificing themselves for the sake of [their protégés']
happiness."*

Even so, a still vaster dream had been exciting the
missionaries' imagination ever since their initial thrust
into the wilderness. In that dream the empire begun in
the early seventeenth century (the first reduction was
established in 1609) would push its borders far and wide,
descend as far as the Atlantic to the east, and expand
northward through the heart of the continent and on
through Brazil until it reached the Caribbean!*

But what had already been achieved of that rash plan
had been enough to catch the attention of the political

and intellectual circles of Europe. Philosophers, with Voltaire leading the way, speculated about the reports by the Province of Paraguay concerning the astounding results of their catechization. From that distance everything indicated that the spiritual conquest of the Guaranis under Castilian auspices was proceeding with amazing speed.

The truth of the matter, however, was that the enterprise was difficult and its results less than certain. Despite all the praise and the high hopes lavished upon it, the undertaking was encountering obstacles. Bougainville, observing at close range the results of the work done by the Jesuits, was constrained to rectify what he had described as a bit of Paradise.*

HISTORIANS, FROM THE FIRST to the most recent, have been forced to take note of the controversy stirred up by the operations of the Company of Jesus in colonial Brazil. The Jesuits came into the Land of the Holy Cross, as Brazil was first called, in the dawn of the settlement of the territory; their influence continually grew and spread until they were expelled after two centuries of bold activity in both spiritual and secular areas.

In *The Masters and the Slaves* Gilberto Freyre describes with acute objectivity the social effects of the Jesuit operation in the first centuries of Brazilian development. His conclusions run counter to those who, like Joaquim Nabuco and Eduardo Prado, could see only the positive side of the Jesuits' enterprise. Other modern essayists like Caio Prado Júnior* and Júlio de Mesquita Filho,* notably the latter, are even more severe than Freyre in criticizing the work of the Jesuits.

It is not possible, however, to ignore the tremendous struggle waged by the Ignatians on behalf of the Indians and against the growing laxity of customs among the Christians. Jaime Cortesão emphasizes this: "We are not unacquainted with the great services for culture performed by the Jesuits everywhere, and especially by the Portuguese Jesuits in Brazil, where in earliest time they carried out a highly moralizing mission."* If instincts went unchecked, the members of the Company of Jesus outdid themselves to restrain and discipline them and to rekindle the old fear of God in the hearts of the colonists. The tough, aggressive action of the missionaries, however, was to occasion serious conflicts, even collective revolts, as in São Paulo, Maranhão, and Pará, sometimes fostered if not directed by civil authorities. Even so, there was no disregarding the effects of the Jesuits' "vociferating as loud as they could," in Father Nóbrega's words,* against the immoderate urges of the flesh. These effects made themselves powerfully felt also in the education of children and in the native villages and left an indelible imprint on our formation.

One question immediately suggests itself: Were the Lusitanian Jesuits content with the spread of the faith and the spiritual conquest of the heathen, or did they, like the Castilian Ignatians, pursue objectives of a less transcendent nature at the same time? There is some basis for suspecting that they were governed by the general policy of the organization, since that policy, independent of race or nationality, was supposed to be the same for all members of the Company of Jesus, subject as they were to common discipline and obedience.

What was that policy?

All the evidence leads us to believe that the Jesuits tenaciously held to the purpose of constructing an empire of their own in the heart of the New World. An enclave between the nominal dominions of the two Iberian crowns, that singular state would grow under the aegis of the Catholic Monarchs, but inevitably evolving toward emancipation because it held not only spiritual but civil and criminal jurisdiction, and was free to organize its own militia. The Catholic Monarchs, to defend the faith threatened by the Reformation, were capable of sacrificing a part of their dominions to enable the Company of Jesus to create a source of income badly needed for their crusade in Europe.

This perilous utopia, so out of step with the time, did not completely disappear even with the dismantling of the Province of Paraguay, with its so-called Seven Towns of the Missions.[1] As late as Miranda's scheme for

---

[1] The Seven Towns, lying to the east of the Uruguay River in what is now the State of Rio Grande do Sul, were (to use their Portuguese names) São Miguel, São Nicolau, São Luiz Gonzaga, São Borja, São Lourenço, São João Velho, and Santo Ângelo.

the liberation of the Spanish colonies in South America, two Jesuits conspired with him in hope of restoring the ancient, shattered Inca Empire under the sign of Saint Ignatius.*

IN BRAZIL THE POLICY of social and economic segregation of the Indian, doggedly practiced by the Jesuits, would have led our destiny along different paths, perhaps even to splitting us into different nations, had it not been for the determined opposition of the colonists.* But this is a problem that may never be satisfactorily cleared up, riddled as it is with contradictions.

To what extent did the nationalistic sentiment of the Portuguese Jesuit in Brazil lead him to rebel against the general policy of the Company? What effects can the sense of Lusitanism, which so strongly manifested itself in the opposition of the Jesuits of the Assistancy of Portugal to the Hispanizing tendencies of the nobility and the high secular clergy, have had on the attitude and conduct of the missionaries sent to Brazil? Although such tendencies were to result in the foundering of Portuguese sovereignty in 1580, following the battle of Alcazarquivir and the death of King Sebastian, the stubborn resistance of the Portuguese Regular Clerics to capitulation must not be forgotten. They openly rebelled against the instructions dictated by Rome in favor of Philip II's claims to the Portuguese crown. Not even the powerful intervention, direct and personal, of the General of the Company, who went to Lisbon expressly to summon them to obedience, succeeded in putting them down.*

The Jesuits of Brazil could hardly be strangers to such a tradition of national loyalty. This must account for the border clashes between them and the Spanish Jesuits. Such incidents Father Leite justifies with exemplary frankness, saying that the strict obligation of each group was none other than to defend the flag of its country.* That is what happened in the fighting around the Colônia do Sacramento. There the Spanish and Portuguese priests confronted each other not as brothers of the cloth but as adversaries.

As for the patriotism of the Lusitanian Jesuits, it seems beyond question that the rulers of Portugal felt easy on that score. This can be inferred from several testimonies, including a letter in which Father Antônio Vieira calls for the dispatch of more missionaries to Brazil, noting that the number of Portuguese should be much larger, because, he explains, "not even the princes permitted anything else."* That is, Portuguese policy did not trust the Indians' education to foreign priests. Even so, the motherland sought to safeguard her interests with wise precautions: although initially she consented to the priests' gaining spiritual and temporal authority over the Indians in the villages, she later arrogated to her direct agents the exclusive civil administration of the natives. Lisbon simply concluded, perhaps less from her own than from others' experience, that it was only sensible to trust the matter of sovereignty to no other agents than those under her own authority.

The Monarchs of Castile apparently did not sin on the side of excess caution. If they had used greater foresight, they would not have left the immense Guarani vivarium, scattered over nearly half a continent, to the discretion of the military power of the Missions for a hundred and fifty years.[2] This want of foresight explains the alarmingly pre-eminent position of the Jesuits in the Province of Paraguay.

FOR A LONG TIME it has been held as unquestionable that the Spanish Regular Clerics were the first members of the Company of Jesus to enter the lands that were later to become part of the Província de São Pedro. It is equally unquestionable that those lands were frequented long before the Jesuits by traders and Indian-hunters who came down from São Vicente, the first permanent settlement in Brazil (1532), and went deep into the heart of the Tape country. But between these sporadic incursions, which seem to have started about the middle of the sixteenth century,* and the establishment of the first Spanish reductions on the left bank of the Uruguay

---

[2] Jaime Cortesão alludes to the frequency with which Spain abdicated her functions of political sovereignty to the religious institutions.*

River half a century later, a Portuguese Jesuit penetration must be recorded.

Thanks to the publication of the De Angelis Collection,* full of documents previously unavailable, we now know that the Fathers of the Assistancy of Portugal anticipated those of the Assistancy of Spain in the first efforts at catechization in Rio-Grandense territory. In fact, from 1605 to 1637 the Portuguese Regular Clerics, going down the coast, sought to establish themselves in the vicinity of Pôrto Alegre.*

The precedence of the Lusitanian Jesuits in the region suggests extremely interesting questions.

Father Serafim Leite says that the failure of those first attempts at evangelization delayed the work of colonizing Rio Grande do Sul for a century, and he severely casts the responsibility for such delay on the shoulders of the *bandeirantes*. But, accepting this theory, what sort of civilization would have resulted here had it not been for the action of the trouble-making half-breeds? With the Indians segregated into the bonds of catechization, it is obvious that the ethnic composition of our population would be different. And one must consider the probable reaction of a more or less stabilized indigenous people when confronted with the Luso-Brazilians flowing into Rio Grande de São Pedro from the first quarter of the eighteenth century. Conflict would have been inevitable. Two cultural echelons separated by millenniums do not collide harmlessly. And the millenniums of backwardness of our heathen could not be overcome by mass baptism or by sermons or corporal discipline. The Jesuits were convinced that such expedients were enough to open the gates of heaven to the infidels.[3] But they were not enough to lead them to civilization. Catechization no doubt worked miracles, even including abandonment of cannibalism, but the long-term result could only be "an Indio-cretinous Brazil," as Oliveira Martins diagnosed.*

And what would have been the political fate of Rio Grande do Sul if the Portuguese Jesuits had carried their mission to a successful conclusion, at the same time that their brothers of the Assistancy of Spain, reaching out from the Province of Paraguay, penetrated deeply into the area?

It was about 1626 that the Spanish missionaries established themselves in the Tape region. Since those lands had long been frequented by adventurers from São Paulo, and the Jesuit enterprise of Guaíra had come to naught, it was essential for the Spanish to move quickly to take possession. Only the fearless militia of Saint Ignatius was in a position to do so in the interests of Castile. The Spanish soldiers were untrained in backlands fighting and nothing could be expected of them. As

[3] "And so this is the greatest crown of those tireless laborers in the Vineyard of the Lord, which the hatred of their enemies could not and never can snatch from them: finding themselves today in heaven surrounded by half a million souls and maybe more, saved by their zeal and labors."*

Father Antonio Roiz de Montoya remarked to the King: "They are very good marksmen, but quite useless on the paths: they are good horsemen, but afoot they cannot take a step."* Thus the Governor of Buenos Aires, wishing to take the east bank of the Uruguay River, entered into an agreement with the Jesuits of Paraguay to give Father Roque González of Santa Cruz the task of converting the tribes living there.[4] It was the first step in the spread of conquest in that direction, but the Spanish Jesuits proceeded tenaciously, hurriedly covering the area partially limited by the curve of the Uruguay as it turns southward from its westward course. Eventually they reached the basin of the Jacuí.

REGARDING THE COINCIDENCE of the simultaneous attempts at permanent establishment by the Jesuits of both Portugal and Spain in the Rio Grande area, one tempting question is whether there was any understanding, even though not expressly stated, between the two groups—one skirting the sea, the other going from the interior toward the coast.

The question is not easily answered, for the information on the subject is quite imprecise. But did not their

[4] Once the initial reconnaissance was made and the first "doctrines" planted, the ill-fated missionary was ruthlessly murdered by his neophytes, thus taking his place among the martyrs of the diocese of Buenos Aires. Other martyrs of the same diocese were Fathers Alonso Rodríguez, Juan del Castillo, and Cristóbal Mendoza.*

activities tend toward the same objective? What were they after if not the wholesale conversion of the heathen and their entire spiritual and economic absorption? The consequence of this would necessarily have been the stifling of the European colonist and the impossibility of his living and developing on the Spanish American continent.[5] Thus the obstacles to the dream-glimpsed theocratic empire would be swept away.[6]

The temporal plans of the Spanish Jesuits became aggressive and were soon discovered, alarming the Court of Madrid itself. But in the case of the Portuguese Regular Clerics things were different. The old settlers of Brazil, with the covert backing of the authorities, re-acted from the first against the missionaries' attempts to monopolize the Indians. But one proposal of Father Antônio Vieira does reveal the constancy of the temporal plans of the Company, in spite of the fact that he was going to the extreme of defying one of the cardinal rules of Saint Ignatius's *Exercises,* namely, the instruc-

[5] "There can be no doubt," Francisco Xavier Mendonça Furtado, Governor of Maranhão, said in 1751, "that it is the Religious that have the greatest interest in the administration and service of the Indians, and that the latter are kept in their present state, or in a still tighter grip, so that the administration by the Religious will be yet freer and more powerful, the Indians more tyrannized, and the people completely ruined."*

[6] Inácio José Veríssimo states that the invasion of Rio de Janeiro in 1555–67 by the French "prevented the Ignatians from forming in Brazil, with seat in São Paulo, the indigenous empire that they sought to found in the likeness of the one in Paraguay, since it forced them to use means and leaders in support of Mem de Sá."*

tion to members of the Order to rise above national ties.*
What Father Vieira suggested was that whoever owned
the Indian would become master of Brazil.* Portugal,
however, was on the alert, for the civil administration of
the natives was the exclusive problem of secular authority.

The hypothesis regarding a possible combination of
the Portuguese and the Spanish missionaries in the lands
of Rio Grande is not in contradiction to the political
conduct of the former. Not only was this remote district
still an unnamed area at that time, but also, when the
encounter probably took place—at the beginning of the
seventeenth century—the crowns of Portugal and Spain
were under the same scepter. Even though this did not
bring about the fusion of the two nations or of their
South American possessions,[7] it seems unquestionable
that from the point of view of the Company the joining
of the Spanish and the Portuguese Jesuits would have
been of decisive importance. The hypothesis is strengthened further by the argument that both groups of missionaries had a common enemy opposing them: the *bandeirante.* But in the event of conflicts of jurisdiction
between the two parties, the dispute would inevitably
have been resolved in favor of the Regular Clerics of

[7] "Far from forming with Spain a single nation, Portugal, by the
letter patent of Nov. 12, 1582, a truly constitutional charter signed by
Philip II, retained all its rights, freedoms, privileges, uses, and
customs, forming a kingdom and crown apart, both in the homeland
and in the overseas provinces."*

Castile, who were inspired by a more spirited determination to conquer ample geographic support for the Company.

But we are in the realm of conjecture. What matters, finally, is that their joining never took place. Both Jesuit lines of expansion were stopped, each in its turn, by the action of the Indian-hunters.

Despite the failure of their first effort to settle on the east bank of the Uruguay, the work of the Spanish Fathers was less transitory than that of the Portuguese. There were tribes that violently rebelled against religious indoctrination, some Fathers even paying the price of their apostleship with martyrdom. These brutal reactions were attributed to the intervention of witch doctors, who in the missionaries' eyes were simply repulsive agents of the devil. The Indians, however, in the end surrendered to the preaching of the Jesuits and adapted themselves to the shadow of the Cross.

The nascent missions maintained close official contact with the agents of Castile, so that each "doctrine" planted by the Fathers was quickly honored by eager official acknowledgment dispatched from Buenos Aires. Thus the Jesuit expansion, in addition to its apostolic stamp, took on an openly political character. Because of the missionaries alone Castilian rule was to grow. But after continual conflict between 1628 and 1641, the *bandeirantes* evicted the Jesuits, driving them back to the west bank of the Uruguay: Indian slave labor was no less vital for the Paulistas than for the economy of the reductions.

The notion has long been current that the early Jesuit settlements surrendered to the *bandeirantes* because they were defenseless and there was no possibility of resistance. Today, however, we know that there was armed resistance[8] by the neophytes under the Fathers' inspiriting command. We know, further, that the attackers suffered some reverses, although in the end the settlements were broken up and masses of Indians taken away to São Paulo to be used or sold as slaves, according to the harsh customs of the time and circumstances.

The Paulistas' attacks, if we discount small subsequent forays, were brought to a close in 1641 with the

[8] "A certain passage of the annual report, which has been scratched out but can be read for all that, is particularly explanatory on the point: 'Your Reverence's order that there be noise of arms in the reductions has been in accord with the need and desire of all. And so it has been done with very good effect, because the people of this reduction and that of La Encarnación have taken very good booty among the Tupis, capturing them and depriving them of the plunder that they were carrying out and of the spoils such as wedges, machetes, bucklers and other weapons with which they were plentifully supplied, and desiring more surprise attacks for the sake of the spoils. The action was carried out modestly: I mean, they have killed no one, administering first aid afterwards. The captives we sent to Villa Rica to help Father Pablo, but the Lieutenant, who is our friend and interpreter, has enticed some away from him and put them in his service, of which, if I remember to do so later, I shall then speak, deferring to what Father Pablo will write to Your Reverence and Father Joseph.' Or, in other and clearer terms, the Jesuits, besides taking Indians prisoner, enslaved them, forcing them to work in Villa Rica with Father Pablo and permitting the municipal authorities to choose some for their own use."*

battle of M'Bororé, in which they were defeated and driven out of the area of Jesuit expansion. In the final combat the *bandeirantes* were repulsed with heavy casualties, but the first advance outposts of Castile on those lands were destroyed. Nevertheless, having pursued the Indians in retreat from Guaíra, the *bandeirantes*, as an illustrious contemporary Jesuit of Rio Grande observed, "became acquainted with the topography of the interior of Southern Brazil, and, although thrown back from the shores of the Uruguay, they never forgot the lands of the South."*

IF AT THAT MOMENT the Spanish Jesuits had not been pushed back to the west bank of the Uruguay, it might not have been possible later on to conquer the broad region which they came to encompass on the left bank after their second incursion, carried out half a century later, beginning in 1687. By the time they again moved eastward into what was to become Rio Grande, the Luso-Brazilians had already established themselves on the Plata (1680), thereby creating a powerful argument for subsequent claims.

This time, with the Colônia do Sacramento founded, the Conselho Ultramarino in Lisbon deemed that it had grounds for accusing the Jesuits as invaders.* And the town of Laguna, its communications with the Lusitanian stronghold threatened, could protest the violation of a domain that the Luso-Brazilians no longer doubted belonged to the crown of Portugal.*

Moreover, the return of the Province of Paraguay to the Tape cannot fail to be considered as a retort to the founding of the Colônia do Sacramento. The position on the Plata won by the Portuguese seriously endangered the countless herds there, descendants of the tiny handful of cattle introduced by Father Mendoza fifty years before. Hence the fury with which the missionary army hurled itself so many times against the enemy.

THE *bandeirantes* HAVE BEEN VITUPERATED unthinkingly and immoderately. Robert Southey's *History of Brazil* reflects the influence which such libels have exerted upon Christian-trained minds. The English poet and historian accepted as pure truth the testimony left by the Jesuits.

As in all expansionist movements, even those of a religious or ideological nature, deeds of impulsive violence dotted the itineraries of the *bandeirantes*. Nobody could or would dare deny it. But in spite of the brutality and the toughness and fearlessness of their onslaughts, to them was reserved the integration of Portuguese America in nearly the whole of its extent.

If the *bandeirantes* devoted themselves to the pursuit of private objectives, they, at the same time, were fulfilling a political mandate. It was not without reason that some of them, like Raposo Tavares, held public office, and others, like Lourenço Castanho Taques, were distinguished by the King's direct summons to mop up the *sertão* with only the aid of "their own resources and force of arms."* Hence the action they undertook was not simply the hunting or "liberating" of Indians, or the relatively uncertain taming of virgin lands, or the search for El Dorados. Their work, executed with the cooperation of the Tupis, evolved by instinct and political inspiration within the area already delineated by the Tupi-Guarani Indians before the Discovery—[9] this geographic area was coveted by the homeland from the first.

There is no way to measure the debt of Brazil to *bandeirism*. Beyond the discovery of the mines, beyond the spread of cultivated farms and of cattle ranches in the most remote confines, beyond the cities whose seeds the *bandeirantes* scattered along the routes of their wild journeys—what we owe to those crude *bandeirantes* is the expansion of the bounds of an empire. Artur Labriola observes that the great movement that determined the supremacy of the white race originated in Portugal and Spain. He adds: "It would nevertheless fall to the lot of the Luso-Brazilian of the Piratininga tableland to project, outside the bounds of Europe, the bases for the

[9] "The indigenous culture and the *língua geral* [an uninflected language with Tupi base, widely used in Brazil], products of a geographic, economic, and human unity, represented a powerful force of political aggregation. As the sixteenth century began, the Tupi-Guarani were already prefiguring over the territory, even though in a wavering fashion, the colonial foundation of the Portuguese in South America."*

first construction of a society cast in the molds of Western economy."*

Before entering the second phase of the history of the Jesuits in Rio Grande do Sul (1687–1767), it is well to pause over the matter of the relations between the Regular Clerics and the colonists, especially the founders of Piratininga.

We know that Brazil was neither the result of chance nor the product of spontaneous engendering. She grew out of the pertinacity and courage with which the pioneers confronted the terrible vicissitudes of the new environment. The territorial empire which we have inherited was largely the result of *bandeirism*. And one of the most resistant and aggressive obstacles that the early settlers had to overcome was the temporal action of the Jesuits.[1]

When the Paulistas attacked and destroyed the Spanish reductions of Guaíra in the 1630's their dealings with the Jesuits had for a long time been marked by the gravest incidents. The first contacts of the Piratininga people with the Ignatians, from the time of João

[1] "Whatever was saved of the native, Amerindian culture of Brazil was saved in spite of the Jesuit influence; for if the padres had had their way, only vague and formless phases of that culture would have remained following the Portuguese conquest, and these would have been cleverly adapted by them to Roman theology and European morals. . . . With the segregation of the natives into large settlements, the Jesuits fostered in the bosom of the aboriginal populations one of the most deadly and deep-going influences. It was the entire rhythm of social life that was thus altered for the Indians; for peoples accustomed to a scattered and roaming life are always degraded when concentrated into large communities and forced to adopt an absolutely settled mode of existence."*

7 3

Ramalho, had been stormy. It was natural that the pioneers—Portuguese or sons of Portuguese—with all checks and impediments slackened, should seek in the versatile, submissive love of the native women a compensation for the hardships of isolation. Because of that the conflict with the missionaries' never-questioned severity of habits was inevitable, and the colonists' resistance frequently took the form of open contempt of authority. A son of João Ramalho, that prolific patriarch of Santo André da Borda do Campo, was once threatened by Anchieta with the wrath of the Holy Inquisition. The half-breed, far from being intimidated, promptly defied him: "Ah, I'll shoot the Inquisition full of arrows!"* That defiance continued and the fighting became more and more bitter, until in 1640 it exploded in the local expulsion of the Jesuits. Piratininga was left to its excesses.

THE ASSAULTS ON THE BACKLANDS and the wilderness by the *bandeirantes* at times actually swept along with it nearly the whole population of Piratininga. São Paulo turned into a nomad city, a "city on the march," as Jaime Cortesão has put it. "There were times," he adds, "when São Paulo had the Atlantic and the Andes for its suburbs, and the Plata and the Amazon for its avenues."* The dearth of local resources before the discovery of the mines and of the herds in the South, the lack of everything in those beginnings of colonial life,* would either explode in violent *sertanista* expeditions[2] or bring the nascent community to utter ruin. If the early dwellers of the Planalto vacillated for some time in taking positive action against the Indians' constant attacks, in which so many of them were mercilessly killed and eaten, they finally yielded to the lure of adventure. Determined to survive, to sell their lives dear, the irascible Paulistas of Serra Acima resolved to go any distance deep into the Continente in search of what they lacked: security and workhands.

Here they again encountered the pertinacious action of the Jesuits ahead of them. This time it was not just the outrages of the flesh that turned the missionaries against them. The Jesuits did all they could to prevent the enslavement of the Indian, although later they themselves became powerful masters of slaves, not excluding Indians. But in the beginning of colonization things were different. The struggle initially manifested in Piratininga was afterwards extended to the rest of Brazil and ended only in 1759 with the proscription of the Company of Jesus.

[2] "From the documents Alcântara Machado draws a *bandeirante* poor, illiterate, with gross manners and scanty possessions, living in near-indigence, hard on himself and on his fellows, austere, primitive, permanently struggling with difficulties of every kind, a terror-filled addict to the *sertão*—and for all these natural, sensate, logical reasons a man capable of the amazing expeditions that did not strike him as opportunities for glory but as inexorably urgent solutions [of his problems]."*

Yet the founders of São Paulo were only acting as other conquistadors had before them. There never had been an empire not constructed upon the servitude and the sacrifice of the conquered. The colonists were merely obeying a law of life in capturing and enslaving Indians. The Spanish Jesuits themselves many and many a time placed their duly militarized Indians at the disposition of the authorities of Buenos Aires and of Asunción against the menacing hostility of revolting tribes. One can count by dozens the missionary expeditions sent out on these war maneuvers, which had as their natural result the capture and enslavement of the rebels. In the name of the elementary principle of survival many cruelties were committed under the aegis of the Company of Jesus. There is no lack of examples. In the vicinity of the São Borja reduction lived a tribe which the Fathers had tried in vain to bring into the fold, the Guenoas. The Indians were also committing the sin of negotiating with the Portuguese of the Colônia do Sacramento. As a result the followers of Saint Ignatius organized a punitive expedition, fell upon the Guenoas, and simply decimated them on February 14, 1708. The victorious force was commanded by Father Jerónimo Herrán.* Another indication of Jesuit violence is provided by Father Roiz de Montoya's imploring the Catholic Monarchs to authorize the razing of São Paulo for the purpose of stamping out *bandeirism* in its own nest.*

. . .

TODAY THE INSTITUTION of slavery is revolting to us, but in those first centuries of colonial life no one argued against its legitimacy. Not even the Jesuits.[3]

It is in the ordinary, routine peacetime activities of the Jesuit missions that we find the most active conformity with the institution of slavery. Despite their explicit condemnations and their spirited campaigns addressed to the Court and its agents on behalf of the freedom of the Indian, the Jesuits, yielding to the pressure of their own needs, finally capitulated. Like everyone they came unquestioningly to accept slave labor. "The multitude of slaves that the Company has in this Province," one of them, recently arrived from Europe, wrote, "is a thing that I can in no wise swallow, all the more because I cannot conceive that they were legitimately acquired." In 1583, Father Miguel Garcia was shocked to find seventy black slaves in the Jesuit school in Bahia. "And those of the land," he added in deep affront, "between certain and doubtful, the number is so great . . . that it angers me; and with these things and seeing the dangers of conscience *in multis*, it has sometimes passed through my mind in this land that I should

[3] The letters of Father Manuel da Nóbrega, the precursor of the Jesuits in Brazil, from the first insistently demand that he be given slaves. In one letter he says: "We all confess that one cannot live without some to fetch firewood and water, and to prepare each day what is to be eaten, and other services that it is not possible for the Brothers to do, especially they being so few that it would be necessary to abandon confession and everything else."*

more surely serve God and be saved *in saeculo* than in a Province where I see the things I see here." Another Jesuit, equally scandalized, unburdened himself: "Those who go to Brazil may well be persuaded that they are not going to save souls but to damn their own." And to flee eternal damnation, he, who had come inspired by the ideal of an immaculate apostleship, found it more prudent to turn back . . . "the victim of inadaptability," as Father Leite explains, unable to reconcile "his conscience with the economic realities that conditioned the existence of the colonizers of Brazil."* The Company of Jesus, compelled by the same necessities as the laymen, thus yielded to economic exigencies and went so far as to obtain exemption from import duties on as many as three Negro slave ships per year, to be loaded on the coast of Africa.*

Confronted with the blatant contradiction of the Jesuits' actions, nothing was more natural than rebellion by our spirited ancestors. Hence the agitations and revolts, in which the people of the Colônia united against the Regular Clerics. Father Antônio Vieira said: "We have the people against us, the religious, the proprietors of grants from the captaincy governors, and likewise all those who in this Kingdom and this State are profiting from the blood and sweat of the Indians. . . . We are incurring the hate and persecution of all."*

Certainly they all knew that without the "blood and sweat" of the Indians, and especially that of the Negroes, they would all be crushed by invincible force of "economic realities." For that very reason the Jesuits' plea on behalf of the Indians' freedom rang false. Many people saw or divined in the Company's humanitarian preaching only an expedient to reduce the colonist to impotence and failure.

Considering the respect imposed by the Jesuit Fathers, the impersonality of their interests, the fascination exerted by the liturgical ceremonial upon the timorous, impressionable minds of the neophytes, the situation of the Indians in the Fathers' service is more tolerable, less inhuman than that imposed on them by lay masters; but for all that it was still based upon the total suppression of freedom. In either case the sorry social condition of the Indian was the same, differing only in degree.

As the sentiment against the Jesuits was one of the constants in early Brazil, the boldness with which the Paulistas attacked the Guaíra reductions in the early seventeenth century is no surprise. The *bandeirantes* regarded the Paraná backlands, inexhaustible hives of Indians, as belonging to Portuguese jurisdiction, and they had been plundering them for a long time. Thus the presence of the Province of Paraguay Fathers in the very heart of those lands could only be taken by the men of Piratininga as a challenge. When Raposo Tavares assaulted the incipient "doctrines" of Guaíra, he did so shouting that he intended to expel the Spanish Jesuits because those lands belonged to the Portuguese "and not to the King of Spain."*

Both the *sertanista* expansion and the catechizing operations of the Spanish missionaries[4] had political motives. The Jesuits repeatedly emphasized to the authorities the strategic importance of their expansion and also its warranty for the security of the treasures of Peru, exposed as they were to the Portuguese hunger for gold and conquest. Nevertheless, it is evident that the clash between *bandeirantes* and Jesuits had other causes besides greed. Although Brazil at the time was a colony of Spain (1580–1640), the territorial rivalries between Portuguese and Spaniards in America never found a lasting solution.

To RECAPITULATE: The Guaíra reductions having been destroyed, the Jesuits herded their Indians who had escaped capture southward to the left bank of the Uruguay. From there they were forcibly evicted by the *bandeirantes*. Falling back to the other side of the river, they left the vast region of the Tape again unoccupied for nearly half a century. Then the Luso-Brazilians, in a veritable somersault, attempted to gain possession of the upper bank of the Plata by founding the Colônia do

[4] "The establishment of the Guarani reductions from 1626 . . . certainly strengthened the sphere of Spanish domination in the whole western part of the State. . . . Moreover, the Castilian occupation of Rio Grande do Sul in the time of the Jesuits was not achieved by Spanish arms but solely by the missionaries."*

Sacramento in 1680. Some hundreds of soldiers at the disposal of the Spanish, reinforced by an army of three thousand Indians recruited and trained by the Fathers, fell upon the still insecure Lusitanian fort and razed it. After it had been rebuilt and returned to the Portuguese crown the following year, the Jesuits tried again to recover the east bank of the Uruguay, installing new reductions there and building them into real military barracks. From then on, constantly threatened by enemy-held territory all about, the Colônia do Sacramento was never left in peace.

Its fate would have been different, no doubt, and different, too, the southern boundaries of Brazil today, if the powerful missionary army had not always been on the alert against the Portuguese garrison.[5] At the slightest beckoning from Buenos Aires the Jesuits immediately hastened forward—coming from a hundred, two hundred, three hundred leagues' distance—and placed the troops requested of them at the governor's disposal with no burden on the royal exchequer.

THE RETURN OF THE FATHERS to the lands on the east shore of the Uruguay dates from 1687, nearly fifty years after the last assault by the Paulistas. They were now free of danger from the *bandeirantes*, although more and

[5] Father Burgés proclaimed that without the aid of the Guaranis the five hundred or six hundred soldiers recruited in Buenos Aires, Tucumán, and other cities could not have dislodged the Portuguese from Sacramento.*

more wary of the Portuguese. The area that they eventually covered, which would subsequently be included in Rio Grande do Sul, included the Seven Towns and their unmarked Vacarias, or herdlands—the Vacarias do Mar, which spread as far as the cisplatine shore, and the Vacaria do Pinhal, hidden in the countryside of Cima da Serra. That broad domain nominally belonged to the colonial complex of Spain under the immediate jurisdiction of Buenos Aires, and was grimly patrolled by parties of missionary Indians who were rotated constantly under the vigilance of the priests. Outside the precincts of the Spanish Jesuits, there was nothing but the barren, inhospitable littoral, crossed and recrossed by the first Luso-Brazilian cowboys driving their herds from the Colônia do Sacramento to the Sorocaba markets far to the north. This narrow corridor of the herdsmen, compressed between the sea and the Spanish territory of the Missions, was the origin of Rio Grande de São Pedro. From there the Continente was gradually widened into the interior toward the present borders, won against two enemy fronts—the Castilians of Buenos Aires and the Guaranis of the Missions. The advance of the pioneers would end only with the integration of the territory at the beginning of the nineteenth century.

ALTHOUGH PART OF THE AREA in which the Spanish Jesuit experiment was begun and developed belongs today to Rio Grande do Sul, at the time it was a Spanish possession. The Jesuits never left room for confusion on the matter. A definite sense of ownership is revealed in the missionaries' references, through their spokesman Father Antônio Sepp, to the Tape region—it was all "our Paraguay," "my Paraguayan colony."* The Seven Towns, first under the Fathers, then under military command, before 1801 were only a parcel of the Spanish dominions, for the Treaty of Madrid was not effectively executed. For this reason their history cannot constitute an integral chapter of Rio Grande's history.

The Guaranis whom the Jesuits organized and supervised in the Seven Towns had their political status perfectly defined: they were vassals and taxpayers of the Catholic Monarchs in their condition of "Paraguayan colonists," as the founder of the San Juan Bautista reduction, Father Sepp, called them in his correspondence.* Whether embryo of a theocratic empire or simply a part of the Castilian dominions, the Misiones Orientales, all of them being subject to the immediate jurisdiction of Buenos Aires, could offer Brazil only hostile relations. The missionary organization consisted of a powerful system of enemy posts strategically placed in territory within the scope of the Luso-Brazilian expansion, for the natural keys to Portuguese America were the Amazon and the Plata.

It was therefore in an atmosphere of wariness that the Seven Towns developed. The missions became centers of military preparation, always at the service of the offensive or defensive needs of Buenos Aires and Asunción. In their constant protests of political fealty the Jesuits boasted of having given to Spain an uninterrupted, decisive cooperation throughout the history of the missions. They went so far as to list, one by one, fifty services rendered during more than a hundred years of cooperating with the Spanish in war expeditions or in strategic works.*

The Guaranis, besides toiling with the cattle and cultivating the fields, were subjected to intensive military exercises under the direction of former European officers admitted into the Order. Parallel with the religious ceremonies, which were celebrated with great liturgical splendor, and artistic and economic activities,* the priests took care to keep their numerous and bellicose army always ready. According to one of Father Sepp's letters, the Province of Paraguay could promptly mobilize no less than thirty thousand Indians, "all mounted, knowing very well how to fight with muskets and wield the sword, . . . form squadrons, fight on the offensive and the defensive as well as any European . . ., exclusively trained by the Fathers."* The fact is confirmed by a modern Jesuit, Father Pablo Hernández: "The Guaranis, skilfully worked on by the Jesuits and obeying the orders of the governors of these provinces, did not confine themselves to keeping watch over the perpetually menaced frontiers, permitting no enemies to penetrate the territory, but set guards at the most advanced points, such as the Pinares, and on several occasions sallied out to destroy the forts which the Portuguese raised on the land of Spain, and sent their detachments at a certain time every year to reconnoiter the suspect places to forestall surprise."*

The efficiency in men and arms, the capacity for mobilization on which the missionaries so prided themselves, made the Jesuit Province of Paraguay a great military power, without a doubt the greatest in the Plata dependencies if not in South America. Such a power eventually awakened disquiet in Spain herself. It became evident that the Spanish possessions tributary to the Plata were, militarily speaking, living at the expense of the Company. How long would the Province of Paraguay, with its thirty armed, bellicose towns, consent to remain faithful to the Catholic Monarchs?

These doubts and fears explain the warlike apparatus with which Portugal and Spain prepared to carry out the Treaty of Madrid, especially as regards the southern frontiers. Events were to prove them right. During the demarcation operations everything went badly for the interests of the Company of Jesus, and the Indians, explicitly forbidden by the priests to rebel, found no native chief competent to lead them. But the military preparations by Gomes Freire and Andonaegue were not needless, because the Guaranis did revolt eventually. Were the royal commissaries of Portugal and Spain expected to stand by, letting their men be slain by Indian arrows? The massacre of Caiboaté[6] was forced upon them by the stupidity of the Indians themselves.

THE SUCCESS OF THE MISSIONARY ENTERPRISE was not as assured as the annual reports, composed to impress the Old World favorably, tried to make it seem.* The truth is that the great experiment suffered from inherent evils that profoundly endangered the viability of the Jesuit dream. What could result from the way of life imposed on the aborigine? His cultural tradition, his modes of living, his nomadism were all abruptly cut short. Bound to the soil, the neophytes had to submit under fear of punishment to new types of labor and mode of living. Their timorous respect for the witch doctor, the priest and medicine man of the tribe, was crushed by violence.[7] Such radical measures, even though for the best

[6] The battle took place on February 10, 1756. Three days earlier, in a preliminary skirmish, the Missionary Indian hero Sepé Tiaraju was killed. He had led the rebellion for more than a year. (Translators.)
[7] According to Father Nicolau del Techo, regarded as the most accurate and trustworthy chronicler of the Company: "Filled with rage, Father Cataldino ordered the bystanders to seize the witch doctor and give him a good lashing. The shaman soon shrieked his admission that he was not God but only a poor wretch whose breath could do nothing. Notwithstanding his retractions, the most robust neophytes continued to beat him until they had given him a hundred lashes, this to the great glee of the children. For two days he was castigated in the same way so that he might solemnly abjure his errors. . . . Some time thereafter the medicine man was converted to our faith, in which act Providence showed its inexhaustible mercy."*

of purposes,[8] could not lead to good results. The human material in the experiment, being of the lowest grade, was all but unusable as a factor of civilization. Jesuits themselves were convinced of this, although they were often impelled to say the contrary in documents intended for publication. It is known that the intelligence of the Indians progressed satisfactorily under the Fathers' teaching up to the age of twelve. There it stopped, or began to regress. Two centuries earlier Father Manuel da Nóbrega had reached the discouraging conclusion that our aborigines were "the sorriest and basest heathen in the whole world."* Father Cardiel was even more radical in his testimony. In his opinion the least stupid Indians merely had lucid intervals.*

It was easier for the Jesuit to utilize the Indian for war than for work. According to the natives' cultural tradition, agriculture, a domestic, sedentary occupation, was for women only. The men reserved for themselves activities that they considered more noble and virile: warfare, hunting, and fishing. When sent to the fields they showed stubborn if mute resistance, sometimes behaving in a way most upsetting to the economy of the missions: they broke plows, built fires with the pieces, and then roasted and ate the oxen lent them by the priests for the cultivation of the fields. In war, on the other hand, they saw themselves returning to the laws

[8] Father Lozano said: "Our Lord being pleased that castigation exists, we shall undoubtedly make a very good Christendom here."*

and ways of the tribe. Their aversion to labor, their dull irresponsibility, their instability of character, their inclination to vices all represented a constant challenge to the Fathers' patience and hope. The *Regulamento Geral das Doutrinas* differentiated among the penalties, prescribed the number of lashes for the correction of specific faults and sins, stressing the failure to attend punctiliously to religious practices.

Incomparable overseers, the Jesuits unconsciously and gradually allowed the spiritual objectives preached by Loyola to give way to the Company's rash temporal designs. The point was reached when it was no longer certain whether it was a religious enterprise or a vast economic organization exempt from taxes.

It was natural, therefore, that the missionary enclave should strive to safeguard by military means a project that was costing it so much hardship, but the profit from which might someday provide it with full political emancipation.

NEVERTHELESS, in spite of the considerable material progress attained through utilization of indigenous labor, the Spanish Jesuits' enterprise as a social and economic organization carried within it the germ of its own destruction. "They sought to make a perfect Catholic construction," De Gothe, of the University of Breslau, declared, "but only achieved a dazzling, artificial fabric that lacked internal support."*

The Indians were outstanding in mechanical arts because of their singular capacity for imitation, and had an aptitude for music, although incapable of adding a single note to the ones they learned.* They were also good warriors, although entirely unsuited for command. Except for these abilities the Indians, according to the Fathers themselves, were so innately inferior that more than a hundred and fifty years of intensive catechizing could not overcome it. Hoping to save the indigenous remnants, to preserve them from contagion with the civilized world, the Company resorted to the extreme recourse of segregation. The Spanish Fathers thought as did Father Antônio Vieira, that "the farther we stay away from the 'old Christians' the better fruit will result."* Convinced of this half-truth, the missionaries of the Province of Paraguay sought to keep their wards from all contact with the outside world. For a century and a half the Guaranis were guarded from contamination by even the Spanish language. They were allowed no more than to spell out the letters; the meaning of the words was zealously denied them. In the end, even the reductions would become mutually incommunicable, for the Indians had been forbidden access to any other "town" than their own.*

This system of cloistering could in time only lead to collapse and ruin. According to Lévy Bruhl's theory of primitive societies: "They are organisms capable of living well enough as long as the external environment varies little, but if new elements break in they degenerate rapidly and die."* In the case of the Jesuit missions, besides the mortal danger of the irruption which the Fathers did everything in their power to prevent, there was another, more serious, gnawing from within, threatening the reductions.

No witness testifies more bluntly to that effect than a report in the De Angelis Collection,* in which several Jesuits, high in the administration of the missions, lay bare, in 1735, the alarming conditions from which the vast Ignatian organism was suffering. The report consists of depositions by Fathers Antonio de Villagarcía, Apostolic Notary of the Company of Jesus; Francisco Ribera, parish priest of San Miguel; the parish priests of San Lorenzo and Santa María Mayor; Fathers Antonio and Miguel Ximénez, Diego Ignacio Altamirano, and others, all toughened by missionary experience.

The depositions, given under oath to the Superior of the Missions, Father Bernardo Nusdorffer, disclosed an appalling state of things. The population of the "doctrines," instead of growing, was diminishing. There were many causes for this, beginning with the frequent military expeditions in the service of the governors of Buenos Aires and Asunción, in which always "the best men in the towns" were sacrificed. Other causes cited by the priests were the constant escapes, disappearances, hunger, and pestilences. From 1732 to 1735, the number of Indians in the Missions dropped from 139,244 to 107,549. Military conscription was followed by abandonment of houses and cultivated fields. Mothers and children, left without support, died of destitution and disease. Beyond the Fathers' vigilance the orphans turned wicked and sly, and finally vanished. Add to all this the inconstancy, the incapacity, the laziness, the depravation, the incurable stupidity of the natives. Father Joseph de Texedes was fully justified in predicting that with such a situation "these Missions will irremediably be lost." Such was the current devastation, in fact, that according to the pathetic report of one of the Fathers, "Many are the corpses of both sexes and all ages to be found dead everywhere; to such an extent that it seems we are already nearing the end of the world."[9]

At this period the royal treasury was experiencing an increasing drop in receipts from the capitation tax levied on the Indians. As a result the Fathers must have felt it necessary to dispel any and all suspicions of dishonest concealment of taxes. Hence the recourse to the inquiry and its shocking conclusions. Nevertheless, the distressing statements which so many respectable Jesuits laid before the eyes of their superiors were solemnly sworn to *"in verbo sacerdotis, tacto pectoris."*

The missionary organization was unquestionably suffering from grave symptoms of disintegration. No symptom must have caused deeper unrest than the demo-

[9] The annual report of 1735 fully confirms the depositions collected by Father Nusdorffer. It states that in 1734 alone 8,022 Indians disappeared, not counting the dead.*

graphic state of the "doctrines." It actually seemed that the Indians were neglecting the old commandment, "Be fruitful and multiply." The priests resolved to intervene in the private lives of their charges, but with great discretion. Every morning, an hour before the summons to work, the bell would ring out a new call, though with a different intention, that of leading the married couples to concentrate on increasing the birth rate after the restorative night's sleep.*

UPON SO RUINOUS A HUMAN BASE one cannot build a civilization. Such was the opinion delivered by Saint-Hilaire as he passed the ruins of the missionary structure in 1821. The learned traveler recorded this painful observation in his diary: "Civilization was not created for Indians, since it is founded entirely upon the concept of the future, which is absolutely foreign to them."* Our Indian, who had never attained even the stage of fetishism, was millenniums away from civilization, and could not stand contact with it. Thus it is not surprising that he adopted the most repugnant demonstrations of humility with no great reluctance. The poor Guaranis reached the point of taking physical punishment without the shadow of rebellion. And after the prescribed flogging they would drag themselves along the ground in gratitude to kiss the hand of the priest who had ordered them punished. According to Fathers Antonio Sepp and

Pedro Lozano, both Jesuits, when the Indians went some
time without being seized for whipping, they interpreted
this as a lack of love for them on the part of the priest,
and would go whining to him to offer their backs for the
lash. Father Lozano recorded in detail the cunning
stratagem by which the neophytes came to accept castigation not merely passively but with a certain pleasure.[1]

[1] "As it is impossible that there be so well ordered a republic in
which human frailty is long preserved from committing some outrage
against the sanctity of laws, and as the curb of servile fear is necessary to restrain those who do not do it out of love, much thought was
taken up to that time about how to introduce gently a punishment
that would not exasperate the delicate mind of the neophytes. At last
a stratagem was found that seemed surely inspired by heaven.

"The Fathers had in their company a Spanish boy who assisted at
Mass, and they reached an agreement with him whereby, mingling
with the young Indians of his age in some innocent mischievousness,
he would let himself be beaten in punishment, to enable [the priests]
to do the same on other occasions to the Indian boys, thus testing
how the fathers of those boys would take it and seeing whether [the
priests] could go further and try the same punishment with those of
more advanced age.

"To carry out the plan agreed upon, the young Spaniard—and it
was no small victory for him to rise above the fear that generally a
boy of his age has of corporal punishment—started a brawl with the
others at play, and they ordered him given several lashes, which he
endured humbly and patiently, and afterwards knelt down and kissed
Father Roque's hand, thanking him for the correction he had admin-
istered for the boy's own good.

"The aforementioned Father took advantage of this occasion to
address the persons who chanced to be present, telling them that this
was the means by which the Spaniards brought up their children,
corrected their faults, emended their wicked inclinations, and set
them straight while they were young so that they would grow up
without vices. [Those present] found this good, and not only their
reason but the example of the master nation disposed them to consent
that the same punishment be meted out to their children. The latter

Out of this came also the morbid voluptuosity with which they gave themselves up to corporal disciplines. During the Holy Week celebrations the streets and squares of the reductions were stained with blood from the voluntary self-tortures. Even the children "practiced on their bodies the penance that would defend them from their spiritual enemies and give them mastery over themselves."* More than a hundred years after the expulsion of the Jesuits the deplorable revival of such customs could still be seen in the old Missions: Indians would offer themselves with disgusting humility for flagellation, saying that they wanted to expiate in this way their own guilt and that of their racial brothers.*

IN SPITE OF THE DEGENERATIVE FACTORS which were quietly undermining them, the Seven Towns had at-

---

after having received it began to practice the same ceremony of humbling themselves reverently before the missionary who ordered them corrected.

"This practice having been approved by all for the correction of the youngest, a step further was taken, applying it to the young of greater age; and the old councilmen being consulted, who deemed themselves exempt from such castigation and who could see the profit they derived from keeping the young well-behaved, made no difficulties in consenting that the same punishment be used also with young men. Happily, the first culprit deserving exemplary penalty happened to be a young man, son of a major cacique who held it as a point of pride that the young delinquent should be castigated as he deserved without distinction of person.

"Thus the inferiors showed less repugnance to submitting, and it was gradually carried to the point where adult men are flogged if they commit wrongs, and serve as examples to the others to restrain themselves and not sin."*

tained a degree of development which, although illusory, did honor to the Jesuits' amazing capacity for organization and administration. But to check the evils that were threatening the stability of the system it became necessary to relegate the spiritual conquest of the heathen to a secondary plane. Even a sincere apologist for the work of the Jesuits, Aurélio Pôrto, recognized that the religious objectives of the "doctrines" were gradually being subordinated to the economic interests of the organization.[2] Aurélio Pôrto reveals that the Provincial, insistent on the defense of the herds, did not hesitate to prohibit distribution of meat to the Indians even when they were sick or dying of hunger.* The reductions, units with autonomous interests, sank to fighting among themselves over the cattle and the maté-growing areas,* reproducing in the Tape country one more episode of the incurable Spanish sectionalism.

IT WAS THE HERDS, after all, that contributed to the downfall of the Jesuit edifice. The Colônia do Sacramento suddenly became the focus of heavy smuggling of hides and other sub-products of the cattle of the Va-

[2] The same thing happened in Brazil. According to Gilberto Freyre: "When the period that Pires de Almeida regards as the heroic age of Jesuit activity in Brazil had passed, a number of the missions became little more than export warehouses, dealing in sugar and drugs, but chiefly in maté in the South and cacao in the North. This to the prejudice of the moral and even the religious culture of the natives, who were now reduced to a mere instrument for commercial exploitation."*

carias do Mar. Around the new activity the Gaucho type, composed of Portuguese and Spanish adventurers, half-breeds, and Indians, began to develop. Among these were the Guaranis who succeeded in eluding the vigilance of the priests. Before long the raiders from the right bank of the Uruguay, authorized or not by the Buenos Aires government, came in to fight for a share in the wild herds.

The devastation wrought by the depredators threatened utter ruin to the cattle that had multiplied freely for more than fifty years. The Jesuits managed to drive eighty thousand head to the highland plateau, thus establishing what they called the Vacaría del Pinar. As it happened, though, at that time the Luso-Brazilians came down the Rio-Grandense littoral and set themselves up in the countryside of Viamão and vicinity. They soon gained the plateau and stole cattle which the Fathers thought inaccessible.* The immense area dominated by the Seven Towns, thus attacked on all sides, began diminishing in extent and wealth. Thenceforth the internal disintegration that was gradually sapping the Jesuits' powerful enterprise would be stimulated by external agents.

In the middle of the eighteenth century, when Rio Grande was being born and the Luso-Brazilians were beginning their efforts toward the integration of the territory that is now southern Brazil, it was not possible to reconcile the political scheme of the Spanish Jesuits with the natural evolution of events. Times were different. Monarchic absolutism, then the established system, did not tolerate partitions. It was inevitable that the missionary enterprise would crumble.* Despite the great services rendered to Spain by the Jesuit organization, the power of the Company of Jesus, far superior to that of the lay provinces, finally awakened real misgivings in the homeland. The result was Clause XVI of the Treaty of Madrid which ordered the withdrawal of the missionaries with their Indians and all movable goods from the Seven Towns, and the relocation of the multitude in Spanish territory.

That provision has always merited the world's abhorrence. Why the expulsion of the Indians en masse? What was the real reason for such unnecessary violence? Spain could not willingly hand over to the Portuguese crown the most warlike portion of the Guarani army, which until then had been the outer rampart of the Spanish conquest against the Luso-Brazilian expansion. Once sovereign over these Indians so accustomed to war, who could tell how far Portugal would push the frontiers of her South American possession?*

The opposition by the Company of Jesus to the Treaty, with the subsequent insurrection of the Guaranis, was natural and human. But the agreement as a whole can be considered one of the wisest diplomatic instruments ever put together. It was never executed officially, but because it expressed the reality of the expansion of two empires it made itself efficacious and valid per se. The Jesuits, fallen from favor, were expelled by Spain herself. The missions were secularized and turned over to military administration, which precipitated their decadence and total annihilation.[3]

THE REGION OF THE MISIONES ORIENTALES, a fragment of the Thirty Towns composing the Jesuit Province of Paraguay, a few decades after the expulsion of the Jesuits was incorporated, through military capitulation, into Rio-Grandense territory. Previously the area, although long baited by the Luso-Portuguese, belonged wholly to the Spanish. The events associated with the Jesuit missions thus occurred on the other side of our historical and political frontier, and are therefore alien to our tradition. The bold experiment of the Company of Jesus was carried out in open hostility to the Luso-Brazilian world.[4] It transmitted nothing, no cultural legacy, to Rio Grande do Sul.

[3] "The Indians did not understand a word of Castilian. The towns were deserted because their inhabitants had fled. The herds had been lost. The Indians who were left in the towns were in great part given over to license and drunkenness. As for the authorities in charge of them, many were the prohibited traffickings, oppressions and examples of dissolute living. The frontiers of Portugal were seriously threatened. The former Guarani militia forces had been reduced to nothing."*
[4] The Lusitanian Jesuit historian, Father Serafim Leite, unequivocally recognizes the "anti-Brazilian" character of the Paraguayan cycle of the Missions.*

When Brazil annexed the former Seven Towns in 1801 there was no longer anything there to assimilate. There was not a living being in any condition to receive or to transmit any sort of influence. Of the splendor of liturgical festivals that once lent life and color to the missionary cloister, not a human vestige remained. Little was left except rubble, stories of underground passages, hidden treasures, and vague superstitions. More than thirty years after the expulsion of the Jesuits, when Borges do Canto and Santos Pedroso hurled back the Castilian commands in 1801, it was plain that the over-praised peak of the Misiones Orientales had passed and that the warlike neophytes of bygone days were but the disillusioned remnants of a frustrated experiment in civilization.

Some time later the exploits of Andresito Artigas[5] attracted and sacrificed many of the remaining Indians. Then Fructuoso Rivera[6] was to strike in surprise attacks in 1827 and haul away nearly all that were left. The Jesuit tradition was utterly extinguished. "Rivera's invasion," Aurélio Pôrto concludes, "the exodus of the leftovers of the indigenous populations who followed the caudillo in his departure, and the complete depopula-

[5] An Indian, born 1776 in the Misiones Orientales, he was adopted by General José Gervasio de Artigas, the Uruguayan hero. Andresito led abortive uprisings by the Mission Indians, was captured 1819 by the Portuguese, and died in Rio de Janeiro prison. (Translators.)
[6] 1778-1854. He served under General Artigas (1811-20), was prominent in Uruguayan struggle for independence, and became president of Uruguay in 1830. (Translators.)

tion of the Seven Towns, undeniably mark the end of the missionary regime."* Alcides Lima could thus state in 1882: "The missions in no way influenced the character of the Rio-Grandense formation."* The past wiped out, another experiment began there in the form of Rio Grande do Sul. It was not a matter of simple grafting; it was a new plant thrusting down new roots. A different civilization under another flag was born and took shape.

Only one thing has been left to us from the dead past: alien ruins, which have been sold for so much per cubic meter, used in the construction of pigpens,* served as feed trough for mules, etc.* The rubble of the Seven Towns has meant nothing in particular to us.

But the Company of Jesus was restored at the beginning of the past century after fifty years' recess, and it was not to be long before the Jesuits returned to Rio Grande do Sul. The new Ignatians came from Argentina, where they had suffered greatly under Rosas. From the Old World soon afterwards came other illustrious and pious members of the Order. They were no longer impelled by the temporal designs of old. Despite the anticlericalism of Masonry, the Jesuits were welcomed. They were to write a new chapter in the lands of São Pedro, this one in full cooperation with our people and our affairs. Moved by purely educational and spiritual purposes, the Jesuits today are prominent in the intellectual, moral, and social progress of Rio Grande do Sul.

III

The Misiones Orientales
& Rio Grande do Sul

THE GEOGRAPHIC AREA OF BRAZIL is completed in the
extreme south by a natural quadrilateral, almost a
rhombus, precisely balanced on its lowest angle. That
neatly outlined figure, almost completely girdled by
water, is the State of Rio Grande do Sul. To the east is
the Atlantic, which in these latitudes was at one period
called the "Sea of Paraguay." To the north, the west,
and the south are the rivers and lakes that separate Rio
Grande do Sul from the adjoining State of Santa Catarina, the Republic of Argentina, and the República Oriental del Uruguay. The short dry boundary lines to the
north and south are prolongations of the dividing lines
of the rivers. They are there to confirm the lines laid

out by nature. In short, it is all so arranged and composed that it is not difficult to accept a poet's image of his province:

> Your map is throbbing in my breast
> because you have the shape of my heart.*

There is indeed something anatomical in the shape of this piece of Brazil.

To this province belongs a historical personality and a distinctly individual social and economic life, although this individuality must be considered only in terms of Rio Grande's role in the national complex. Rio Grande's peculiarities are the result of natural and ecological factors native to the region, and political conditions created by the frontier. The first settlers in the Continente de São Pedro were also its first soldiers. They came, knowing what they were coming to, from other regions of the Luso-Brazilian world, largely from the Azores and Portugal, all of them bearers of the same political tradition. For generations upon generations those pioneers and their descendants would never cease to be admonished that the most urgent of their duties was to spread the conquest and guard the frontiers. Rio Grande do Sul thus developed out of the geographic expansion and integration of Brazil. It was first the Lusitanian, then the Luso-Brazilian, and finally the Brazilian that gave direction to Rio-Grandense development. Responsible for the conquest and defense of Brazilian territory along its most vulnerable frontiers, our elders constructed the Província de São Pedro on the broad, solitary plains of the Capitania d'El-Rei.

Often ventures not only foreign but demonstrably adverse to us, such as the operations in the name of Castile by the missions, are considered legitimate elements of our tradition. But because such ventures were executed outside of the Luso-Brazilian jurisdiction and in opposition to Portuguese rule, it is evident that they cannot be considered a part of our formative process. We shall not ignore them, however. Rather, it is up to us to identify and define them. If the forces of Spain had prevailed, it is most likely that Rio Grande do Sul today, instead of being a living part of Brazil, would be nothing but a tiny country in the turbulent Hispanic-American world, a semi-Guarani nation, an obscure remnant of the former Misiones Orientales.

AFTER NEARLY TWO CENTURIES OF SUBTERFUGES and feints, Portugal and Spain finally prepared to settle fairly the problem of their confrontation in this distant spot. At the other points where the Brazilian area touched the vast dominions of Spain, the process of expansion was effected without wars and external rumblings. As a rule the wilderness alone had to be conquered. But conditions were different along the Plata. The two litigant crowns, each on its side, wrote the chronicle of the Río de la Plata and its dependencies in blood. They fought savagely for possession of the same territory, beginning with the founding of the Colônia do Sacramento.

There is not the slightest doubt that the Seven Towns, the most important part of the Province of Paraguay, were not simple strongholds of catechization and edification. They were intensely occupied in the military training of the Indians and openly performed a political function. Complete information on this subject is available in the documents of the period, starting with those of the Jesuits; the data are copious and convincing.

CONSIDERING ALL THIS it is not easy to determine what impelled Father Carlos Teschauer, S.J., to write his exhaustive chronicle of the Seven Towns under the disconcerting title of *História do Rio Grande do Sul nos Dois Primeiros Séculos.** The first to censure him was the essayist Augusto Meyer, who observed that the incriminated book "did nothing but suggest the picture of a fictitious Rio Grande that could have been but never was—more or less the 'might have been' of the poet. . . . Thus he scorned any consideration of organic and defined historical process based upon political history in order to adopt a dubious criterion, pliable and mixed, in which the binocular view of events permitted embracing at a single glance the apology of the Misiones Orientales and, on a more distant plane, far in the distance, the vague historical formation of the present Rio Grande do Sul."*

The eminent Jesuit writer goes to the extreme of applying the name of "Rio-Grandenses" to the Indians converted by the Spanish Fathers. The "poor Paraguayans," as Father Antonio Sepp, founder of the San Juan Bautista reduction, called them with greater accuracy, were labeled by a name that was to appear only more than a century later, and even then not in the area of Spanish occupation. But Father Teschauer went even further in his entanglement of facts. Since for him the Indians enticed by the Fathers of the Assistancy of Spain were already "Rio-Grandenses," the *sertanista* exploits resulting in the destruction of the first "doctrines" were called clashes between "Paulistas" and "Rio-Grandenses."

In his critical commentary appended to Volume III, João Ribeiro compounds the error:

"To the painstaking labor and erudition of Father Carlos Teschauer we owe the precious volumes consecrated to the first two centuries and to the moral, economic, ethnographic, and political origins of the great State which today is notable as an unexampled balance of constructive forces of our civilization. The happy land of Rio Grande began with the internal, Indian civilization of the extreme West, with its missions on the Uruguay River, early disturbed by the predatory ambitions of the half-breeds. . . . In spite of its littoral civilization the Rio Grande do Sul of today owes much to the first founders of settlements; and what there is and subsists among some of its primordial riches, its fields of cattle, its wheat or its vineyards, or its yerba maté: all this had started in the missionary culture of the West before the conquest of the littoral. Father Teschauer's book, intended to commemorate the first centenary of our independence, has the appreciable significance on the current occasion that we shall not be indifferent to the glorious date. . . . As in a bivalve shell, we see the progressive contact between the Indian civilization which began in the interior and the littoral civilization which established itself only later, about the middle of the eighteenth century, on the beaches. . . . Rio Grande retains differential and distinctive traits, an almost patriarchal direction in its politics, derived from pastoral customs. Its people's soul is revealed in the poetry and legends belonging to it: the *gaúcho* type, entirely different from the *caipira* (hillbilly, backwoods yokel) or the *sertanejo* (hinterlander), is related to that of an enormous Hispanic region, and from that all but common region the picturesque language with which we are acquainted."

The missionary territory, in which the Jesuits' protégés lived and operated, fell wholly within the Spanish jurisdiction. The toponym "Rio Grande" was but the name of a remote, out-of-the-way natural canal on the coast. The real Rio-Grandenses, of pure Luso-Brazilian stock, appeared in the Tape country only after 1801, when the missionary area was incorporated into the

Captaincy of São Pedro. This occurred more than forty years after the expulsion of the Jesuits by the owners of the land, who at that time were the Spaniards themselves.

Before the episode of Borges Canto and Santos Pedroso (1801) it was not the legitimate Rio-Grandenses that made history on that fertile, desirable shore of the Uruguay, but the Spanish Jesuits with their Indians, with their martyrs, with their herds and their cultivated fields, with their arduous and valiant collectivist experiment, with their vigilant military action, with their war parties, with their heroes.

That picture is entirely foreign to Rio Grande's history. It was all conceived and put into effect under the strict jurisdiction of Buenos Aires and in open opposition to the Luso-Brazilian world. The Jesuits having been expelled, they were replaced by military commanders; the process of devastation of the Misiones Orientales began at that moment. Only after more than four decades of violence and internal spoliation was the missionary area conquered and annexed to Rio Grande. The men, then, who forged our history there were the heroes of that incorporation. They were Borges do Canto and Santos Pedroso, the Baron de Cêrro Largo and Chagas Santos; they were the numerous donees of great land grants, called *sesmarias*, and their overseers and peons; they were, finally, the immigrants and their descendants, with their prosperous farms and industries.

The Seven Towns, which composed the richest part

of the Province of Paraguay, itself a part of the Assistancy of Spain, must figure among the factors mobilized against the development of southern Brazil and Rio Grande. Their history is a frustrated chapter of Spanish expansion in this section of America and interests us only as an element of contrast and antagonism. No one on the Spanish side of our frontier has yet considered it otherwise. Father Pablo Hernández, for example, himself a Jesuit and one of the most authoritative Spanish historians of the Jesuit enterprise in Paraguay, gives as his considered opinion that Robert Southey, in writing his *History of Brazil*, was excused from dealing with the Missions, for—he declares—that history is not included among the achievements of Lusitanian colonization.*

The march of Rio-Grandense civilization was homogeneous. And because it obeyed one single command, one perfectly determined policy, the course that it followed could not have been other than from east to west, from the littoral into the interior, and finally north to south. It is therefore easy to single out the factors that actively contributed to shaping Rio Grande do Sul.

It was among the last areas of Portuguese America to be occupied, even though ever since the first Lusitanian maps it had been included in Portugal's dominions, for it lay between the natural gateways to Brazil, the Amazon and the Plata. When the pioneers, furnished by the men of Laguna, started coming down the Atlantic strip, the 1720's had begun. And it was in 1737 that the fort of

Jesus-Maria-José was built on the dangerous bar which two centuries before had received the name of Rio Grande de São Pedro.

Around Viamão and at the foot of the modest military establishment erected by Silva Pais was developed the first stable settlement in the Continent de São Pedro. Thence, in successively greater and greater movements, the conquest of the interior would radiate outward in defiance of the plans and ambitions of Spain, whose dominion, entrusted to the exclusive religious and civil administration of the Jesuits, comprised nearly the whole of the territory from the east bank of the Uruguay to the Vacarias do Mar on the plains and to the Vacaria do Pinhal on the flats of Cima da Serra. Planted at strategic points in those immense natural pasture lands were the posts of missionary Indians, always closely attended by priests, and, crossing the countryside in all directions, their patrols.

It was in the early years of the seventeenth century that the missionaries, duly accredited by the government of Buenos Aires, overstepped the borders onto the left bank of the Uruguay. In that first penetration the Regular Clerics of the Company of Jesus were not successful, for the initial group of converted Indians were to be entirely routed by the *bandeirantes*. Only subsequently, after the decline of the Paulista thrust, would they return to occupy the same region and its surrounding country, spreading out with their maté plantations and cattle ranges through nearly all the territory that is Rio Grande do Sul today.

Well equipped now for war, the missionary Indians under the military command of the Fathers would guarantee to the crown of Spain the possession of the new dominion, and would remain a constant threat to the rearguard of the Portuguese who, in 1680, had established themselves on the left bank of the Plata. It is Father Teschauer himself who declares that at that time "the fame of the valorous Guarani army had crossed the ocean, so high was the esteem won by the bravery and discipline of the Indians of the reductions."*

Together with the desire for land, what most kindled the cupidity of Portuguese and Spaniards was a new wealth: the innumerable herds that filled the grazing lands of Rio Grande and the cisplatine shore. The cattle that had multiplied in those smooth flatlands were the descendants of the animals introduced there by Hernando Arias de Saavedra in the south, and by the Jesuits to the west, across the Uruguay. The plateau of Cima da Serra had also been turned into an immense reservation for wild cattle. This was the Vacaria do Pinhal, where the Fathers sought to conceal part of their herds from the hide-hunters. Out of these cattle-raidings was born the adventurer-Gaucho of the Uruguayan plains, a mixture of Spaniard, Portuguese, and Indian in unequal proportions.

At the end of the seventeenth and the beginning of

the eighteenth centuries, Rio Grande was merely a string of land along the seaboard, infrequently crossed by primitive drovers. Flanking the Spanish region of the Missions, the pioneers drove their herds across litigious territory, sandy wastes, and backlands, from one stop-over spot to another, improvising corrals along their route. They would go as far as the Sorocaba market fairs, and farther.

THE SEMI-BARBAROUS CATTLE INDUSTRY, which at the time attracted adventurers of varied origins, also engrossed the first settlers. But they were soon installed on broad tracts of land—the *sesmarias*—or else placed in service to them as overseers or peons and were simultaneously enlisted in the line corps or in the militia. The strategic situation of those disputed lands required that every subject of Portugal who settled there should maintain a constant vigil.

The construction of the presidio of Rio Grande was a step that failed, because of its tardiness, to achieve its objectives as regards the Plata. The Colônia do Sacramento was isolated by territory completely in the hands of the enemy and had no other communications than by sea. The Treaty of Madrid (1750) provided for the exchange of the Colônia do Sacramento for the Seven Towns, but with the rebellion of the missionary Indians everything reverted in 1761 to the previous situation.

The ruinous Treaty of San Ildefonso (1777) annulled the cession of the Seven Towns, then under the military administration of the Spanish, and the bridgehead over the Plata was lost.

In the Continente de São Pedro, however, things went less badly. The Spaniards, who in 1763 had taken possession of the Vila de Rio Grande, capital of the Captaincy, and the upper bank of the channel, causing the government to move to Viamão, were expelled from those bases in 1776. And two sensational assaults on Rio Pardo in 1767, where the Corps of Dragoons of Rio Grande had been transferred, also failed, with the Spaniards forced into a disastrous retreat.

IN SPITE OF THE HAZARDS INVOLVED, the settlement of the interior continued at an ever increasing rate, particularly in the valley of the Jacuí after the treaty of 1750. With irresistible magnetism the ownerless or government-owned lands and the herds attracted large numbers of people competing for their share. Besides the spontaneous mobilization of the inhabitants of the Captaincy, other men hastened there from all parts, principally from São Paulo. Cities and towns of the plateau of Curitiba, formerly prosperous, were now dwindling away: their able-bodied men, catching the same fever, gave up everything to head for the southern plains.*

From the sparse, unobtrusive initial penetrations

(about 1725 or perhaps before) to the first frontier clashes, the builders of Rio Grande do Sul, all of them Portuguese, came to play an important role: Brito Peixoto; his native son-in-law João de Magalhães; the brave, celebrated Silva Pais, to whom the official installation of the Captaincy had been entrusted; his successor André Ribeiro Coutinho; Cristóvão Pereira de Abreu; Gomes Freire de Andrade, High Commissioner of the demarcation stipulated by the Treaty of Madrid; Governor José Marcelino de Figueiredo; Francisco and Rafael Pinto Bandeira, father and son; and many others.

IN THE PRESENCE OF AN ENEMY prepared to fight for the disputed lands, Brazil could no longer count on more than the momentum of the *sertanistas*. Nevertheless, it was thanks to the impetus of those *bandeirantes* that the frontiers of the country had widened. The tremendous raider of hinterland and wilderness had now disappeared, to give way to the soldier and cowboy, both merged into one. The frontiersman of Rio Grande and the *bandeirante* were generated by the same impulse; only the time and place were different.

When the eighteenth century came to a close, little more than sixty years after the installation of the Captaincy, this new administrative unit of the Viceroyalty of Brazil contained more or less half of its present area. The Uruguay, with its tributaries, was a Spanish river, except its upper course, and Rio Pardo was nothing but a frontier garrison. All of the Campanha, including lands adjacent to it, was still under Spain's rule, although without a trace of civil occupation. It was all wilderness and desert occupied by cattle, insecurely watched over by transient military patrols. The Luso-Rio-Grandense territory was no more than that watered by the tributaries of the seaward slopes. The Spanish forces that guarded the Jaguarão to the south were thrown back to the right bank only in consequence of the outbreak of hostilities in 1801. As for the area of the Seven Towns, it was so alien to the Rio-Grandense world that until about 1825, after it had been annexed for a quarter of a century, it continued to be popularly known as the Province of the Missions. Saint-Hilaire knew the region by no other name.

But Rio Grande de São Pedro was now aware that it would attain its destiny only after it had incorporated the lands within its natural boundaries to the west and to the south. And a scant few months after the close of the eighteenth century, tensions in Europe furnished the pretext for attacks against the Misiones Orientales and the broad strip north of the Jaguarão and Quaraí, the rivers that divide today's Rio Grande do Sul from Uruguay.

Thus Rio Grande grew bit by bit. The advance of her boundary lines against the enemy frontier was slow and laborious. Prior to the beginning of the nineteenth century, the region was cut into two enormous slices, set obliquely, each with a different owner. The lower and the western parts contained the elements hostile to the Rio-Grandense tradition: the bastion of Santa Tecla, the Spanish armies under Salcedo and Ceballos, and in particular the Misiones Orientales. There since the end of the seventeenth century, the missions became advanced outposts of the Spanish dominion. The mass of converted Indians, on constant military vigil, became the most feared and efficient defense against Luso-Brazilian expansion.

In light of this, we cannot imagine how the venerable Father Carlos Teschauer was led to confuse the birth, life, and death of the Spanish missions on the left bank of the Uruguay with the early chapters of the history of Rio Grande. The experiment carried out there, in an area alien and hostile to the Luso-Brazilian tradition, was in complete opposition to Rio-Grandense development. Unhappily the author of *História do Rio Grande do Sul nos Dois Primeiros Séculos* has not been alone in his mistake. The seeds sown by him contiue to germinate.

There is no reason to consider the deeds of the Mission heroes, among them the Indian, Sepé,[1] as part of the Rio-Grandense tradition. Nevertheless there has

---

[1] Sepé Tiaraju, chief magistrate (*corregidor*) of San Miguel, led the Mission Indians' revolt in 1754 against the Portuguese in consequence of the Treaty of Madrid, by which Spain traded the Seven Towns for the Colônia. Sepé's military talents prolonged the conflict until he was killed in battle in 1756.

been a movement to erect a statue in bronze or marble to the missionary tribal chieftain, to set him up as a proper object of Rio Grande homage. Often, it seems, we prefer sentiment to truth. Hence our readiness to be seduced, as demonstrated in the case of Sepé. But really there can be no spot for him in the gallery of our legitimate heroes. He not only belonged to a historical tradition other than ours, he performed his feats in the enemy camp. It has been said wittily and correctly that Sepé Tiaraju is a phantom in Rio-Grandense history.*

The hard, laborious growth of Rio Grande included the area of the Misiones Orientales only after the total disintegration of the experiment attempted there by the Jesuits of the Province of Paraguay. Yet there are writers who assert that "Rio-Grandense civilization" marched from west to east, originating in the Seven Towns. They forget that our tradition, forged in conquest, has cultural bonds only with the Luso-Brazilian cause.

OUR INSTITUTO HISTÓRICO E GEOGRÁFICO, in an attempt to end the current misunderstandings about the Misiones Orientales, has, with exemplary objectivity, taken a stand on the subject of Sepé.* It has stated that our civic pantheon cannot entertain "a native who had a sense of patriotism and stood firm against the Portuguese." The Spanish chieftain acted, in fact, in the service of an enterprise stimulated largely by militant hatred of the people who ultimately conquered Rio Grande for the Luso-Brazilian world.

Nobody denies the gallantry of the Guarani warrior, already exalted with literary brilliance by Manoelito de Ornellas.* But imagine the disaster if Sepé's cause had won out against our pioneers. Rio Grande do Sul today would be a disjointed territory without political consistency, perhaps split between two or more sovereignties.

JUST WHAT DO WE KNOW of Sepé Tiaraju? To begin with, no one knows certainly on which side of the Uruguay he was born. But born on the left bank or on the right, the fact is that when the Jesuits enlisted him in their service all that territory was still Castilian, although the region east of the river lay within the area of Luso-Brazilian expansion. The Seven Towns portion of Paraguay was to be incorporated into Brazil only after nearly half a century following the death of Sepé Tiaraju.[1]

The chief magistrate and military leader of San Miguel came into the world, then, under the Castilian

[1] General Assis Brasil says: "When Tiaraju was closely pursued, riding pell-mell, his horse stumbled in an armadillo (or agouara) hole and fell, rolling over on him and injuring him in such a way that he could not get up in time to avoid being speared by the lance of a Portuguese dragoon and immediately killed by a pistol shot (almost a mercy shot) fired by the governor of Montevideo himself."*

flag and, as was natural, his weapons were always turned against the scouts of the Continente de São Pedro. Born and brought up in the Ignatian enclosure, he was to leave it, like the other council members, only when the governors of Buenos Aires took formal office in that high post. On such occasions the Indian officials went down to the port city to give the usual welcome to the agent of the Spanish monarch and pledge obedience to him.* Another reason for leaving the reductions, always under the watchful eye of the priests, was the constant military expeditions to put down outbursts of rebellion or to carry on operations against the Luso-Brazilian enemy. It is needless to emphasize that the hostility of the Guaranis toward our ancestors was instigated by the Regular Clerics of the Company of Jesus, who thus revenged themselves for the damages they suffered from the *bandeirantes.*

WE DO NOT THINK IT RIGHT to consider Sepé Tiaraju's case an unimportant matter. And yet, even though today we are, more than good neighbors, friends of the peoples surrounding us, we must not tolerate the falsification of history to the point of confusing our real heroes with those who warred against us. Can it be that someone is seeking to convert Rio-Grande into a kind of neutral, indiscriminate land devoid of national character? What concealed design lies therein?

Whether as vassal and taxpayer to Castile, or as instrument of the temporal dreams of the Company of Jesus, the Guarani chieftain escaped being entirely foreign to Rio Grande's past only because he figures among the elements actively opposed to it. When the men of Gomes Freire, among them Cristóvão Pereira de Abreu and Francisco Pinto Bandeira, father of the greatest warrior of these regions, found themselves at the stockade of Rio Pardo, who was on the enemy side to dispute the possession of the land? Sepé Tiaraju.

What would the builders of Rio Grande de São Pedro say, from the depths of their tombs, if they knew of the attempt to aggrandize those who most stubbornly opposed the advance of our civilization? There is no more effective way to adulterate the meaning of a tradition, to corrupt it at its very sources, than to jumble the values that the forces of history have set in conflict. And yet we are sure that not all are deliberately applying themselves to that objective. But be that as it may, to forget the "naturalized citizenship" of the spirited military leader of San Miguel is an absurdity. If the missionary hero is really deserving of a monument, let it be put up outside of our jurisdiction.

Furthermore, the figure of Sepé bulks larger in mythology than in history. Here let us again consult our Instituto: "From the historical point of view the characterization of the figure of Sepé Tiaraju is difficult. Over him there is a mythic vision, dominant and generalized, which alters and distorts in its essential lines the real, the only personality seen and comprehended by the exegesis of history. It is simple to prove the statement: hardly does this valiant, astute Indian emerge in the events unfolding in the war of the Missions, when his legend imposes itself, enveloping him in an aura of fantasy and mystery that is to lead him in a short time to popular canonization."

That mythic halo we must not take away from him. There, under his birthmark,[2] he is almost a saint, rising above even the mean death reserved for him. But we do not really know whether the feats of the chief magistrate of San Miguel ought to be inscribed in the overseas chronicles of Castile or in the history of the Company of Jesus. But this problem is not up to us to solve.

THERE ARE THOSE WHO ALLEGE on behalf of the post-humous naturalization of Sepé that he is, first of all, an obscure force of nature, the expression of elemental powers in blind protest against the greedy European invader. The argument goes on from there, following the course of an intemperate dialectic that would lead us

[2] His popular (never official) canonization was facilitated by the fact that his forehead bore the shape of a cross, which according to legend glowed in the dark. It was naturally taken by the Mission Indians as a sign of divine inspiration and support. Hence the popular term "São (Saint) Sepé." One little village of Rio Grande do Sul even bears the name, São Sepé. (Translators.)

backward to one of the least felicitous stages of literary romanticism, that of the "good savage." But when the "caudillo" of the Spanish Jesuits began to play his part in the drama of the Misiones Orientales, he had already risen above the status of simple savage. He has been considered by some as "the first Gaucho writer," because he must have scribbled at least fourteen letters, although none of them of course in Portuguese, which was not his language. The man responsible for this discovery is Professor José Hansel,* for whom the "great Rio-Grandense officer," "an Indian of relative culture," was, "like other illustrious chieftains," "an acme of Jesuit culture."

In addition he must have distinguished himself from his poor racial brothers to be elevated as he was to functions of responsibility in the administration and defense of the Jesuit organization, such as that of chief magistrate and military commander.

IT DOES SEEM THAT EVERYTHING would be easier to understand if we went on to look squarely at the case of the Jesuit missions as it was in reality: not merely alien but hostile to the formation of Rio Grande do Sul. Regardless of how much we respect the utopian ideas which led the Ignatians to attempt their experiment in a geographic area disputed by two colonial powers, there is one fact that stands above any ethical or sentimental

reactions: the relationship of the Luso-Brazilian world
with the Jesuits of the Province of Paraguay was one of
open hostility. And in the collision of those two forces
Sepé had his place among the adversaries of the builders
of Rio Grande.

Cristóvão Pereira

IN THE THIRD DECADE of the eighteenth century, Rio Grande de São Pedro was merely a flat coastal belt stretched between the sea and the series of lagoons that succeeded each other from end to end—more than a hundred leagues of pure whitish sand, piled in dunes ceaselessly made and destroyed by the heavy winds from the sea. Along the sands, inland, were the rustic grazing lands which fed the herds in transit and where the first corrals and winter pasture stations were set up. And well into the interior, in the middle valley of the Uruguay, were the scattering of Spanish reductions. Bands of missionary Indians patrolled the extensive Jesuit cattle stations in all directions, guarding the herds and protecting them against raids, all under the vigilance of the Fathers, with an ever attentive ear to anything that sounded to them like "noise from the Portuguese." Skirting the sea, the pioneers were just beginning to come down from Laguna with the intention of making their home in those vacant lands, which they said were "the best in all America for settling."* It was the stock business, especially in horses and mules, that led to their interest in the appropriation of the coast, the natural route of the drovers who went from the southern plains to the Sorocaba markets, thence spreading out to Minas Gerais, Rio de Janeiro, Goiás, and Mato Grosso. The Colônia do Sacramento, on the River Plata, was the point of departure for those hard journeys.

It was in that dawning of Rio-Grandense life, when the old Captaincy of El-Rei was barely awakening to the history of the Luso-Brazilian world, that a figure of imposing stature began to take shape within the region. The name of that figure was Cristóvão Pereira de Abreu.

MORE THAN TWENTY YEARS AGO the German author Wolfgang Hoffman Harnisch published a book about Rio Grande do Sul,* after living here for some time, absorbing our cultural landscape and our past. In his wanderings and researches many aspects and peculiarities of Rio-Grandense life attracted his attention, but of the personalities linked to the conquest and defense of this part of Brazil one of those who impressed him most was Cristóvão Pereira. The writer marveled at the fact that in these regions, barely touched by the first incursions of the men from Laguna, this extraordinary backlands expert and drover crossed and recrossed the territory with his men, traversing wild prairies, sandy wastes, and hinterlands, all of it immense and deserted, from the cisplatine pampa to the central markets of the country, prodding on their slow herds of cattle, horses, and mules. But he was even more amazed at this pioneer's letters at a time when "not even all the French, Prussian, and Russian generals could sign their names."* This first drover of Rio Grande could also draw maps with the skill of a master topographer and compose what he called his "practical news," that is, reports of his experiences, as one at home in the language, demonstrating at the same time that he was not unaware of the political significance of his wide-ranging peregrinations.

The writer-traveler might not have been so astounded if he had known of Aurélio Pôrto's researches on the real identity of Cristóvão Pereira, and had been acquainted with their enlightening results.* Contrary to what Borges Fortes assumed,* he was not a native of São Paulo. Portuguese by birth, he sprang from the oldest Lusitanian stock, almost certainly with the noble blood of Nuno Álvares Pereira,[1] the Holy Constable, cours-

---

[1] After fighting against Spain's claims to the Portuguese throne following the death of King Fernando in 1383, John of Aviz was

ing through his veins. He was a knight of the Order of Christ and closely related to the strain of the Távoras, possessing escutcheon and coat of arms. Thus, a well-born man, he had been favored with an education above the common level.

CRISTÓVÃO PEREIRA WAS BORN in the same year (1680) in which the Portuguese bastion Colônia do Sacramento was constructed opposite Buenos Aires. Barely twenty-one, he appeared first in the Colônia do Sacramento as a contractor of hides. The enormous importance of the traffic in hides and other cattle products in the Lusitanian market indicates the elevated social class to which the young contractor belonged. Only a person favored by birth could petition for and obtain so advantageous a concession, especially one who was little more than an adolescent. But proof that he was equal to the favor with which he was distinguished is the fact that the commerce

---

proclaimed king, and Nuno Álvares Pereira, who had fought beside him, was made Constable (commander in chief). The latter persuaded King John I to give battle to the Castilians, despite the odds against the Portuguese, at Aljubarrota (about sixty miles north of Lisbon) on August 14, 1385. It was a decisive victory for Portugal, and made a national hero of Nuno Álvares Pereira. [Camões celebrates his prowess in the epic Os Lusíadas, Book IV, stanzas 14–45. As for the Constable's nickname (he was not canonized), Leonard Bacon notes: "Nuno Álvares Pereira, often called, perhaps because of his habit of praying at inconvenient moments, 'the Holy Constable.' "* (Translators.)]

in green hides and other cattle derivatives was to take a spurt upward under his leadership.*

As a hide contractor Cristóvão Pereira would have his first experience of fighting. The traffic in hides was profitable, but it also presented all the risks natural to the raiding of herds grazing over territory occupied by the Spanish, except for the fort and its immediate vicinity. Cristóvão Pereira, directly involved in forays and guerrilla fighting, can be singled out for his contribution to the *gaúcho* type, so closely related, as Cortesão observes, to the economic function performed by the Colônia do Sacramento.*

Wherever Cristóvão Pereira went, his personality asserted itself immediately, dominating those about him. In 1711, in one of the Castilian intervals of the presidio, he was among the prominent men in Rio de Janeiro. Indeed, when the French under the command of Duguay-Trouin attacked and pillaged the city, his name figured among the signatories to the terms of ransom demanded by the pirates. But in 1722 Cristóvão Pereira was once more in the Colônia do Sacramento, back at his rough adventures as a dealer in hides and hunter of cattle. In that capacity the services that he rendered to the Lusitanian possession were enormous.

BUT IT IS IN THE INAUGURAL CHAPTER of Rio-Grandense life that his figure acquired true historical stature. When he came to take his place among the builders of Rio Grande, the Captaincy was no more than a remote portion of the Portuguese crown. The navigators of the 1500's and 1600's passed by the barren coast on the assumption that a desolate, inhospitable strip lacking protective irregularities had nothing to offer. In 1532 Martim Afonso de Souza, on his way back from erecting the Lusitanian standard on both sides of the Río de la Plata, left only a baptismal name to that obscure land: Rio Grande de São Pedro. From the *Diário de Navegação* of Pero Lopes the old toponym was transferred to the map of Gaspar Viegas (1534). With time it was extended to the whole territory, finally absorbing the indiscriminate references of "País dos Paulistas," "Adjacências do Paraguay," or "Província das Missões." The interior lands lying behind the sandy stretches, lagoons, and mountain spurs remained closed to the expansionist action of the Luso-Brazilians for two hundred years and more. Beginning with the eighteenth century, however, news of the riches concealed by the seaboard wastelands excited the cupidity of the pioneers. The gold mining flourishing in Minas Gerais urgently demanded the continual shipment of cattle and mounts as an indispensable complement to the continued development of the mines. The establishment and survival of the communities in the interior of the country, isolated and completely dependent upon burro transport, was another powerful incentive to the traffic in animals with the South.* And the southern cattle stations, with their wild herds and abundance of horses and mules, constituted an open invitation to the predatory action of the cattle-hunters.

AT THIS MOMENT Cristóvão Pereira burst upon the Rio-Grandense scene. A native of Portugal, like Aleixo Garcia and Raposo Tavares, he joined, as a younger brother, the "race of giants" whose fabulous journeys and exploits so amazed the learned Saint-Hilaire. In his work as drover and cattle-hunter he set out from the Colônia do Sacramento, cut through the cisplatine countryside infested with Castilians and missionary Indians, overcame the desolation of the Rio-Grandense littoral, gained the plateau at the Morro dos Conventos in Santa Catarina, and drove his animals toward the markets of the Centro, of which the fairs of Sorocaba were the focus. Along the route he built corrals wherever it was necessary, and one of them, on the shore of the Lagoa dos Patos, still holds the memory of his name. After all that, he returned along the same trail, and so on and so on, back and forth, until called to other destinies.

In the course of those astounding travels Cristóvão Pereira made friends with the Minuanos and became most intimately acquainted with the region. The authorities of São Paulo, whose jurisdiction embraced the districts of the south as far as the Plata, came to see in the cultured, fearless, indefatigable drover the best equipped man to call on every time the services of the King required it.

Since 1720 men had entertained the idea of linking the natural paths of the coast with the Curitiba highland plateau. Its first proponent had been the *sertanista* Bartolomeu Pais de Abreu, who addressed the Court directly, underscoring the urgency and the advantages of the new access road. It was indeed necessary to shorten the distance between the consumer markets and the teeming plains of the south. Lisbon immediately saw the economic and political possibilities of the project and the king himself recommended it with special emphasis to the governor of São Paulo, adding that it was a "matter that must not be neglected."*

Only some years later, however, was it possible to undertake the work, which was entrusted to the sergeant-major Francisco de Souza Faria in 1727. With this old fears were defied: fears that the Jesuits of the Missions, relentless enemies of the Portuguese, would rise up at any moment to dispute the possession of dominions until then belonging to the Luso-Brazilians.

That state of mind was self-interestedly encouraged by the "principals" of Laguna. Threatened with being excluded from the new route, they did not want to lose their position as intermediaries in the trade with the South. There was likewise the probable opposition from outlaw elements who, with the opening of the road, would be placed in reach of legal repression, thus losing the immunity in which they lived "without obedience to or any terror whatever of the law."

Confronted with all these difficulties, the authorities appealed to Cristóvão Pereira to soothe the Laguna people and banish their fears. The great drover proceeded to make the road traced by Souza Faria practicable. Throwing three hundred bridges and countless footbridges across rivers and swamps, he corrected the errors in the original mapping and, after several months, was able to say: "Pedestrians without baggage could traverse in less than a month all that I spent thirteen months covering."* Access to the plateau was considerably shortened and facilitated. What this meant economically and politically to Brazil has been told with great breadth of vision by Paulista historian Alfredo Élis Júnior: "It may be that the road from Rio Grande to São Paulo has been the route of greatest importance in the history of Brazil, for without it there would have been no cycle of gold, no cycle of coffee, and not even the unification of the nation would have been carried out."* Thus the ties between Rio Grande and the rest of the country were decisive and were created very early, even before the official installation of the Captaincy in 1760.

THE CONSTRUCTION OF THE HIGHWAY COMPLETED, Cristóvão Pereira was burdened with debts. As a result the governor of São Paulo issued special instructions for priority to be given his cattle in the passage over the new road, specifying further that "he be not molested by his creditors until he returns to São Paulo."* These orders being respected, the tireless drover-merchant managed to sell the eight hundred head of cattle and three thousand horses and mules that he was driving, pay off his commitments, collect 10,000 *cruzados* in duties for the royal treasury, and return to his wanderings with a lightened spirit.

In these activities Cristóvão Pereira did not let himself be completely absorbed by the material interests of the dealer in cattle. His letters reveal little touches of sensibility. Of the landscapes of the South he wrote: "And turning to Rio Grande I do not say that it is one of the most eye-filling things that Nature has created, so as not to seem to overpraise, nor fall into censure for being ignorant, but by only mentioning its greatness I shall leave the eulogy to the careful consideration of Your Reverence."* These humble, pleasant words are from one of the *Notícias práticas* addressed to Father Diogo Soares, to whom Cristóvão Pereira furnished reports of great service to that worthy prelate and man of science. Among the Lusitanians the extraordinary *sertanista* was perhaps the first to fall in love with the land that he trod. "While in those lands," he wrote, "several times in the day I saw fires strike up, and the first worried me somewhat, and my whole troop, because we thought it must be the heathen, but on sending to examine the place no sign whatever of them could be found, and we finally saw that it came from the great number of crystals throughout those fields and gullies, not only of varied colors but cut and polished, and so fine that with the force of the sun they strike fire, or else [they are] in lumps of different sizes shaped by nature, [consisting] on the outside of a fine flint and inside of a cluster of crystals already polished, which as they burst with the sun makes the same effect."*

Cristóvão Pereira was without doubt an amazing figure. Action, action alone, did not exhaust the resources of his exuberant nature. Proof of this is his correspondence, so rich in many ways, including his forecasts for the future of the new conquest.

EVERY ABLE-BODIED MAN in the Colônia was, above all, at the service of the king and his dominions. Cristóvão Pereira, however, was more than an able-bodied man. His broad, daring experience, because of all that he had "seen and touched," and his efficiency as tamer of the southern trails, had won him singular prestige among the authorities. For that reason, when Buenos Aires was preparing in 1734 for a fresh assault on the Colônia do Sacramento, the governor of the fort, Antônio Pedro de Vasconcelos, requested the government of Brazil to send Cristóvão Pereira to organize a body of cavalry with his friends the Minuano Indians to harass the rear of the besiegers and thus relieve the pressure of the siege. The governor of São Paulo, at that time the Conde de Sarzedas, in a letter to the king thus justified the choice of the famous drover for that important operation: "I am persuaded that Your Majesty will deem the expenditure advisable for the choice of Cristóvão Pereira de Abreu which the governor (of the Colônia do Sacramento) requested, knowing his alertness and usefulness with his great knowledge of the country and the heathen, all of which is not likely to be found in any of the paid officers of this garrison. . . ."* There, saved by the archives, is the official certification of Cristóvão Pereira's repute in connection with southern Brazil.

To assure the execution of the mission entrusted to him, Cristóvão Pereira was appointed colonel and so commanded a regiment of militia. Borges Fortes, whose researches as well as those by Aurélio Pôrto and Jaime Cortesão have been used in this study of Cristóvão Pereira, informs us that the brave drover, pressed by the need to hasten to the besieged fort, straightened once more the route traced by Souza Faria, which curved over the Santa Catarina littoral to pass full into the region of Vacaria. He not only shortened distances but subdued or incorporated into his regiment the Indians he encountered. Thus the road was cleared for the Paulista contingents hurrying to the defense of the southern border on the occasion of the Spanish invasion of 1763.

Shortly thereafter, in 1737, Silva Pais, unsuccessful at

Montevideo, came up the coast to the natural canal of the Lagoa dos Patos, erected a fort, and formalized the official taking of the territory. He found stationed there, aiding him in every way, brave and prompt as ever, the former hide contractor. Events proved that Gomes Freire had not been mistaken in his recommendation to the Conde das Gálveas dated July 24, 1736: "Cristóvão Pereira is a man of great mind, and although a civilian, I find in him admirable qualities [that justify] entrusting the government of the Fortress of Rio Grande to him, not only because of his energy but for his tact and close friendship with the Minuano heathen."*

THE DAYS WHEN HE USED to ford the natural canal with his cattle bound for the gold and diamond works were long past. Now war was everywhere, and he was there with his men to aid the Brigadier, Silva Pais, in the preparations for the occupation and defense.

The first Rio-Grandense fort, named Jesus-Maria-José for the Holy Family, was planted upon the sand, as if it were supposed to yield to the slightest attack. Nevertheless, even though the natural conditions of the place were adverse, it did not fail to perform its important social, political, and military mission. The cement of its foundation was strongly reinforced by the determination of the founders and builders of Rio Grande de São Pedro.

An urgently strategic measure, the construction of the fort of São Miguel, hastily built farther to the south in territory today Uruguayan, had the immediate assistance of Cristóvão Pereira. Moreover, it was he who furnished the initial contingent of the Regiment of Dragoons of Rio Grande, which, first in Silva Pais's town of that name and then in Rio Pardo, was to enrich our military history. A contemporary chronicler, Simão Pereira de Sá, remarked that all the dispositions made by Cristóvão Pereira* had been approved by the Brigadier, which stamped the colonel as a master of the art of war.

BUT NOT ALL DEMANDS had yet been made upon the old drover and worthy vassal of the king. Boundary lines were still shifting as the result of onslaughts of one side or the other, or in consequence of the diplomatic mandates drawn up so many times counter to the situations overseas. Gomes Freire de Andrade, High Commissioner of Portugal, enlisted Cristóvão Pereira's cooperation in marking the boundary set by the Treaty of Madrid. He publicly proclaimed that every man who wished to serve in the boundary expedition should enroll in the "bandeira" that he was organizing. Let us consult Borges Fortes on this point: "Gomes Freire's party was at India Muerta when Cristóvão Pereira arrived there, having left his *sertanistas* at Guarda do Chuí. These were two hundred men who came to do the rough, heavy work of demarcation, to serve as vanguard for the astronomers, to blaze trails, to open roads, to explore the terrain, to ford streams."* Such tasks, in fact, could be done only by the men familiar with those wildernesses, empty of humans except for missionary Indians and occasional cattle hunters. In 1754 the missionary Indians, incited by some Jesuits who were not resigned to the loss of the Missions, rose up against the demarcation operations, and under the leadership of Sepé Tiaraju attacked the Luso-Brazilian forces at Rio Pardo. Cristóvão Pereira and his men were involved in the battle with Francisco Pinto Bandeira (father of the legendary Rafael, who was to be the hero of São Martinho and Santa Tecla) and other frontiersmen, all under the command of Gomes Freire. Cristóvão Pereira was seventy-four at the time.

CRISTÓVÃO PEREIRA ENDED HIS LONG LIFE in the same town he had helped Silva Pais to found and build, Rio Grande. He had owned two *sesmarias*, one in the valley of the Rio das Antas and the other on the seaboard, but at the close of his days he was reduced to only one vassal, poverty-stricken and under a heavy load of debts. Of the whereabouts of his remains nothing is known.

V

Rio Grande & the Plata:

Contrasts

To consider the Rio-Grandense *gaúcho* type can hardly be of purely academic interest. Quite the reverse. The current confusion about the origin and historical character of the Brazilian of the extreme South gives rise to inaccuracies that touch vital aspects of Rio-Grandense tradition and the very position of Rio Grande do Sul in relation to the national community.

How did the Platine Gaucho emerge? What was his origin? What were the historical, psychological, racial, and economic factors that contributed to the fashioning of the type; and in what measure did those factors affect his behavior?

In the first half of the sixteenth century when the subjects of Castile planted encampments on the lower bank of the Plata, they looked out on an immense flat territory, thus far barely touched by the seafaring explorers. On the prairies stretching into the interior wandered barbaric tribes determined to give no quarter to the strange intruders.

The first attempt to found Buenos Aires in 1535 had been crushed by the natives, the initial act in a drama that was to drag on well into the nineteenth century. Under the tyranny of Rosas[1] the old conflict began to die down at the price of the defeat and humiliation of Buenos Aires and the demolition of all the standards of civilization of the country. The struggle, however, sometimes latent, sometimes alive and implacable, convulsed nearly all the steps in Argentina's formation.

The strife between these two fronts began to be more oppressive when Buenos Aires, its economic activity kindled by the by-products of cattle, ceased to be a modest port of passage,* a simple customs entrepôt for the riches being brought down from Alto Peru, from Paraguay, and from Chile, and rose in importance. Thenceforth Indians and Spaniards, the number of the

[1] Juan Manuel Ortiz de Rosas, born in Buenos Aires 1793, rose in military rank and power, took Buenos Aires from General Lavalle and had himself proclaimed governor (1829-32). He instituted and maintained a bloody dictatorship, finally provoking a coalition of Brazil, Paraguay, and Entre Ríos province (Argentina), which routed his forces in 1852. He later fled to England, where he died in 1877. (Translators.)

former swelled by mestizos and bandits, disputed the possession of the same herds in ever-increasing fury.

The menacing presence of the Colônia do Sacramento on the opposite shore, a Portuguese stronghold keenly interested in the smuggling of hides and other cattle products commercially disregarded until then, had played a decisive part in the impetus acquired by Buenos Aires.* And when the herds began to diminish because of the madness of cattle-hunting, the conflict became characterized by extremes of violence and cruelty. When the cattle were used only for food and were free to all, the struggle had no other meaning than the inevitable clash between Indian and conquistador. But the injection of the economic element gave it a new impulse, a broader and more complex scope. From then on the enemy as a hide-hunter posed a more dangerous threat to the Spaniard than as a native.*

BETWEEN THE ADVANCES of the Castilians and the opposition of the aborigines a frontier of blood was drawn over which the two forces, the Europeans and the natives, took each other's measure with inflexible determination. On one side, the constant assaults and incursions of the Indians. On the other, the resistance or the offensive sorties with which the captains-general and the governors responded to them. In 1828, after the country's emancipation, the hostilities were so threatening that

urgent demands were made for military construction
that would reinforce the defense system of Buenos Aires
against surprise attacks from the wilderness.* Such was
the boldness of the natives of the interior that one risked
his skin or his life if he ventured there.* An operation
prearranged between Rosas and Facundo[2] indicates the
extent of the threat: these two caudillos planned a joint
drive against the savages' incursions in the South, em-
ploying three divisions spread four hundred leagues
across the pampas, from Buenos Aires to Mendoza, to
sweep the area clean.*

The oppression of the countryside was further increased by the turbulent swarm of mestizos who, cast
out of the European centers, took to the wilderness to
live as bandits far from police jurisdiction.

In that atmosphere of threat and aggression the
power of the natives attained such a point that the victorious caudillos, supported by the rural masses, went to
the extreme of making pacts with the tribes and enrolling them in their factions.*

THE MESTIZO ISSUED FORTH as from the grasses. The
Spanish conquistadores, like the first Portuguese of

[2] Juan Facundo Quiroga (1790–1835), country-born, a Gaucho, then
soldier, finally rustic caudillo, was one of the two most feared and
powerful men in Argentina (the other was Rosas). Facundo on the
plains, Rosas in the city, between them they ruled the country until
Facundo was assassinated near Córdoba in 1835. (Translators.)

Brazil, came without women and used the submissive native women and mingled their blood with the indigenous, multiplying without thought of consequences. Thus was engendered the dangerous hybrid population of the country, "the pariahs of the plains,"* which was reinforced by the influx of Negro blood in greater proportion than is commonly supposed,[3] beginning at the end of the sixteenth century or early in the seventeenth.*

From the crossing of the European with the Indian came the raw material from which the Gaucho was to emerge. But the new type attained his peculiar role in history and literature only when, with his horse, he took to the pampa and the wild herds. It was the rustic drudgery, with its risks and adventures, that molded the Gaucho type—not the ethnic ingredients.* Presently other elements were integrated in him, such as African blood and that of the Creoles.[4]

The direct blood ties between Gauchos and natives

[3] In his travel impressions Arsène Isabelle informs us: ". . . the corps of defenders of Buenos Aires, composed of Negroes and mulattoes, incontestably of all militia the best organized, the best disciplined, the most necessary to the safety of the city." He goes on: "The country owes much to Negroes; they have contributed more, perhaps, to give independence to the nation than have the Creoles themselves, especially the Creoles of Buenos Aires, who are more braggart than brave, even in the words of their own compatriots of the interior. The Negroes have shed their blood in abundance, with enthusiasm, for the cause of freedom; . . ."*

[4] "Creoles" refers to the American-born offspring of Europeans. (Translators.)

established between both parties a spontaneous line of cooperation. As the mestizo came to be considered, in the best Spanish style, infamous in law and in blood,* it was natural that he refused to take the side of his white forebear, preferring to reanimate the old hostility of the Indians with his hatred and his resentments.*

It would not have been so had he been permitted to participate, however meanly, in the social and political life of the colony. Instead "in the fiesta of the Spaniards" there was no place for the mestizo. "He was repudiated if a civilian and despised if a soldier."* But the pampa was there, and for the downtrodden the pampa was not merely an escape; it was also a protest. Martín Fierro, harassed by ill treatment, took to the desert full of dreary hopes:

> I know out there the chieftains
> give shelter to the Christians,
> and besides they call them "brothers"
> when they go of their own free will.
>
> .   .   .   .   .
>
> Out there we'll find safety
> since here we can't have it;
> we'll suffer far less hardships
> and there'll be merrymaking
> the day we swing down off
> our horse in some Indian camp.

> [José Hernández, *Martín Fierro*,
> Parte I, Canto XIII, stanzas 9 and 16.]

In the desert there was space enough and to spare for all who felt oppressed. Treated with equal contempt, at times degraded to the shabby category of the natives,* the Creoles too spurned their parentage and identified themselves with the mestizos in the same revolt. "Never will the Gaucho's psychology be fully understood," Martínez Estrada warns, "nor the heart of the anarchic multitudes of Argentina, unless thought is given to the psychology of the humiliated son."* Juan A. de García in his turn emphasizes: "Spaniards and Creoles, fathers and sons, lived amid reciprocal distrust and hatred."* According to the "theorists of violence," "the son of Spaniards in America, through the effect of the climate —sky and temperament, it was said—lost the virtues of the progenitive race."*

The underlying resentment between the two social fronts created situations damaging to the spirit of the Buenos Aires government. Weakened in its authority, it more than once found itself obliged to entrust the command of the militia to native chieftains.* The others, those of "clean blood"—why, as for those fellows, ill-regarded, detested, let them stay where they were.

The retort of the humble did not stop there. Colonial records contain cases of mass desertion from their posts by fortress garrisons, going out to find in the desert, together with the enemy, the protection they could not find among the Castilians.*

It is certain that outside of the satisfying of instincts, which has nothing to do with racial or social prejudices,

the Spaniard allowed no accord with the riff-raff.[5] From
the loftiness of this noble intolerance he considered it
unworthy of any gesture of recognition. A high disdain
ruled his relations with his inferior. And woe to the un-
happy wretch who was inadvertently so imprudent as to
raise his eyes to his master: such wicked insolence was
immediately castigated with a rawhide whip. If the
reader wishes to investigate the domestic roots of Rosas's
crude insensibility, he will encounter the authoritarian
figure of the caudillo's mother imposing on her servants
the demeaning ritual of serving her on their knees.*

Going back to the origins of Spanish arrogance to
find its most remote causes, the Argentine writer Carlos
Octavio Bunge reaches a surprising conclusion, namely,
that this trait of character existed earlier than the very
beginnings of history. Where does it come from, then?
In Bunge's judgment the phenomenon can be interpreted
only as the result of geographic inevitability.* Although
it is doubtful that the telluric influence excluded other
factors in the formation of the Spanish temperament,
Bunge's emphatic assertion has merit as the index of one
of the most constant signs of the Spanish temperament.
Their imperious, highhanded nature perhaps explains in
great part why the fabulous conquistadores from Castile
were such poor colonizers.*

5 Mating did not mitigate the extreme repulsion of the conquistador
for the native people: ". . . the Spaniard regards the Indian as so base
and vile that he would rather marry a bastard, a mulatto, a Negro,
than an Indian."*

The oppressive conduct of the conquistador of the
Plata, prompted by his domineering and cruel habits,[6]
and displayed in his relations with subordinates, is a
relevant argument in the present discussion. The reactions with which social groups respond to external
agents, be they natural or cultural, vary in accord with
the passions borne in their hearts. In his noteworthy
essay on Argentine anarchy, Lucas Ayarragaray dwells
upon the grim peculiarities of the Spanish character
incarnate in the Platine conquistador, analyzing them
with vigorous energy and adducing elements that must
be borne in mind in order to understand the profound
difference between the *gaúcho* of Rio Grande and the
Gaucho of the Plata. José Ingenieros's painstaking critical study of the Ayarragaray book shows that the ob-
jections to it are of an interpretative nature, not affecting
the essence or veracity of the findings.*

IT HAS BEEN CALCULATED that at the close of the
eighteenth century in Castile alone there were more than

[6] "As for cruelty, there is no need to belabor the subject. Spain, and
particularly Castile, has been and is a cruel people with others and
with itself. It has the defects that correspond in reverse to its virtues.
A heroic race on one side, on the other it lacks sensibility. It is the
same in its civil wars of the nineteenth century as in its wars of
conquest in the sixteenth. America was left nearly depopulated;
whole races disappeared. . . . Marvelous cities like Cuzco were destroyed. Of the Indian empires nothing but vestiges remained. It has
been said without great exaggeration that we know more today about
the Assyrians, for example, than about the Indian empires of Mexico
and Peru."*

half a million hidalgos!* Such a startling proliferation of title-bearers makes one imagine that in the period of the conquest and colonization they were so numerous, and so faithful to their "aristocratic impulses," that when they went overseas they felt it incumbent on their position to strut before the common people and forcibly impress them. And if they could not boast legitimate coats of arms, the proud lords of the Plata nourished the atavistic presumption that "they had the king in their bellies," that is, that they were better than anyone else.* Thus, by blood or by imagination, between the hidalgos and their inferiors—the natives, the mestizos, and the Creoles—stretched a cordon of isolation. The rigid social structure of Spain, based on hierarchy and privilege of caste, crossed the ocean with all its prejudices and tried to install itself in America* without giving up a jot of that incurable pride which for Ortega y Gasset assumes the proportions of an ethnic vice.

Pretentious display of that "vice" in conquered lands could only exacerbate the natural spirit of revolt in the minds of the conquered, and in the Plata region it caused profound historical and social consequences. According to Ingenieros, such a state of things resulted in two different civilizations. Their mutual opposition still constitutes a grave problem, a problem with no solution in sight.* The conflict was already in full spate when economic pressures caused it to suffer new tensions. Scattered, thinned out by assaults and cattle raids, the Indians, mestizos, deserters, criminals, and bandits astray in the pampa had at first no economic interests in common,* and so it remained until that formless, aimless mass finally coagulated in adherence to the caudillos.

Prior to that, smuggling was the first plainly economic motive to whet the disputes between the city and its hinterland. Up to that time food was available to anyone: it was only a matter of bringing down the animal with the bolas and butchering it, tossing the meat on the coals and sating one's appetite at his ease. The rest was settled in the same throb of hatred, "hatred of the Goth,"[7] as a manifestation of collective feeling, and it preceded the fighting for possession of the herds.

The despotic practices of the Spaniards had a decisive effect on the composition and historical evolution of the Argentine personality, fixing in irreducible terms the antagonism with which the Hispanic and the indigenous elements look on each other today. Several centuries of living together have not sufficed to reconcile those antagonisms. The dissidence pointed out by Ayarragaray* unleashed and incited the Platine struggle between the city and the rural districts.

Compared with the inhabitants of the city the rural masses appeared as a kind of barbaric institution, a primitive force of the desert, ever ready for attack on civilization. The division was so deep that until a very short

[7] The Spanish American phrase, *odio al godo*, means hatred of any Spaniard. In Spain the word *godo*, Goth, simply means Spanish nobleman. (Translators.)

time ago it could be considered as the origin or the historical background of the Argentine political parties.* The painful events that have been agitating that country since Perón may permit extending the validity of Ingenieros's observation to our own time.

Other effects of the long conflict of races and castes within Argentina are not to be discounted. Hemmed in on his own *terruño*, his little patch of native soil, the mestizo armed himself in his rancor, hating, holding aloof, rejecting everything. Although intrepid and addicted to fighting, he could not be relied on for anything, not even for militia service. The weapons with which he resisted were, in general, desertion and crime, if not sheer apathy. When the country gained its independence through the work of the idealists and the urban bourgeois, the mestizo received the news indifferently and passively; it was no affair of his. Emilio Corbiere poses this terrible question: "What beneficial deed is not darkened by an act of treachery or crime by the natives, or has been consummated without their resistance?"* And the same author, who moreover considers the appellations "Gaucho" and "native" as one and the same, does not stop there. He says that half a century after the political emancipation of the country was consolidated, the Argentine mestizo, that is, the Gaucho, was still ignorant of what *patria* meant.* Besides, Sarmiento had already remarked that the plainsman had not the slightest consciousness of his traditions.* We are obviously confronted with the Gaucho in a raw, unfinished state, the direct descendant of those human parasites whom Hernandarias, governor of Asunción, found in the early seventeenth century wandering over the Santa Fe pampa, "wild, treacherous men who had wrung their sustenance from the countryside."*

But that "*gente perdida*," aimlessly roving, living to themselves, were virtually all the population that was scattered beyond the urban areas, entirely given up to the anarchy and chaos that flamed up, after Independence, in the abominable outburst of *caudillismo*.[8] The authorities found no way to fit them into society, not even in the moments of danger to the colony. When the viceroy attempted to call up all the country's reserves to expel the English, who had taken Buenos Aires by assault in 1806, he could count on no more than a wretched contingent of Creoles and mestizos, nearly all of them indifferent to the outcome of the fighting.*

THE FLAT URUGUAYAN PLAINS, although disputed and in part occupied by the crown of Portugal, were for a long time only an appendage of Buenos Aires. And there was pressure to keep it from becoming anything more, for it did not suit the interests of the port tax collection office to have any other stable center of colonization set up

[8] The politico-military philosophy and phenomena related to the caudillo: a Latin American version of "bossism." The Anglicized form, "caudillism," is used elsewhere in this translation. (Translators.)

within its jurisdiction. With those unpopulated lands given over to cattle-raiding, the cowboys and drovers from south of the border and from the west bank of the Uruguay, in addition to the Portuguese and the Indians, were going to rustle cattle with or without a license, all of them lured by the smuggling, centered around and stimulated by the Colônia do Sacramento.

It was that Lusitanian fort that finally led the Spanish, aided by the manpower supplied by the Jesuits of the Missions, to erect the fortress of Montevideo in 1724 at the mouth of the Plata. (The town was founded two years later.) Buenos Aires did not want customs competition, but strategic considerations made the construction of the new stronghold imperative. Half a century after the founding of the Colônia do Sacramento it was the Castilians' decisive reply to that act.

Between the Spanish and Portuguese fronts the fluid, aleatory mass of men who preyed on the cattle roamed without fixed abode, without a shadow of social discipline. Around and in all directions lay the green pampa, filled with wild herds, a constant incitement to banditry. "All that territory," an Argentine historian says, "was abandoned to itself, entirely barbaric and in such disorder that, instead of a province or a social entity of any kind whatever, it was a mass of bandits in anarchy, unchecked, unruly, who warred on their neighbors."*

Zum Felde remarks that the similarities between the Argentine and the Uruguayan Gaucho are as numerous as the differences.* But if the Uruguayan, as Zum Felde says, is less swaggering than the former, and does not exhibit the same gratuitous outbursts of aggressiveness, the fact remains that they share at least one trait in common—active resentment against civilization—which frequently generated similar reactions, even though diverse in their duration or intensity. Both on the lower and upper prairies of the Plata, and generally in all the Argentine regions, we see a territory in rebellion against the city, the rustic populace clustering obstinately about the caudillo. And from the truculent acts of the fierce José Gervasio Artigas through many later decades it was caudillism and its autochthonous nature that gave tone to the country's political life, actively influencing the origin, the character, and even the mechanism of party organizations. Artigas was the precursor of Rosas, and the latter of Latorre, all of them, like the others, products of the same culture. In Uruguay, Ingenieros observes, "as formerly among us, the capital and part of the littoral strove against the interior."* The social and political climate was really the same in the provinces bathed by the waters of the Plata and in the other parts of the Viceroyalty. On account of its sanguinary short-sightedness caudillism caused the fermentation of hatreds surrounding the city for centuries. The caudillo is the product of the state of anarchy and dispersion of the territory. Without that atmosphere which engendered him and on which he feeds, he loses his authenticity.

AND HOW HAVE MATTERS GONE in Rio Grande de São Pedro? It was the year 1737 when Lisbon decided to assert itself in these undivided lands, and ordered a fort to be erected on the natural canal of the Lagoa dos Patos. It was intended to stimulate the settlement of the area, which had been going on spontaneously along the seaboard since the preceding decade, and at the same time to "lift the shadow," as the saying went, from the harassed Colônia do Sacramento. Brigadier José da Silva Pais was charged with the important mission. He was a celebrated statesman and soldier already tried and proven in the peninsular fighting, and moreover a cultured man familiar with the good literature of the period.*

In contrast to what we have seen on the Argentine and Uruguayan plains, where the native populace, by their numbers and their behavior, constituted a tenacious shackle on the work of the conquistador, the new Portuguese establishment found conditions entirely different. The autochthonous element there at the time of Silva Pais's arrival was numerically very scanty. The tumultuous preying on cattle in the cisplatine lands, carried to violent extremes by the proximity of centers for contraband and trading in hides and dealings in other cattle products, exerted a powerful attraction on the primitive inhabitants of Rio Grande, who came to blend indistinguishably with all sorts of roving idlers and adventurers operating in that region. That magnetism must have been stimulated even more in successive stages by the rural rebelliousness and by the blandishments of caudillo demagoguery.

Leaving aside the indigenous populations segregated in the Missions, then under Spanish rule, the natives who wandered over the Rio-Grandense fields and ravines, adrift from tribes already in dissolution, were to end by almost disappearing from our demographic map. Even the missionary population had been considerably curtailed by the Paulista forays of a hundred years before. When the Jesuits later reverted to the east bank of the Uruguay, the bands of Guaranis which then crossed the river to return to the Tape were merely the harshly treated survivors of a vanquished race. The losses suffered by the neophytes have been variously estimated at two, three, even five hundred thousand, counting dead, missing, and captured in the six years of the *bandeirantes'* incursions against the reductions.* These figures, flagrantly unfounded, can be explained, even in their dizzy disparity, as the result of overheated imaginations. We must not, however, suppose that the casualties suffered by the missionary Indians were not really heavy.

Other factors than these would in different periods diminish the native population still further: constant tribal wars, voluntary dispersion, hunger, frequent epidemics. According to the testimony of the Jesuits' own documents, not even the tamed Indians were proof against these evils, since in their case the military expeditions on which missionary soldiers were used, whether on remote fronts of the Spanish dominions or against Luso-Brazilians or recalcitrant heathen, produced the same effect. Also, the constant cooperation of Guarani labor in great numbers was required for the heavy work, nearly always of strategic nature, carried on by order of the Spanish authorities in the most isolated places. In the construction of the Montevideo fort alone thousands upon thousands of neophytes were employed in great relays for five years. Who knows the number, even approximate, of those who perished there—"the poor Indians, homeless and without shelter"[9]—exposed day and night to the inclemencies of the weather? There is not the slightest doubt that the eagerness with which the Jesuits responded to urgent summons from Buenos Aires and Asunción, particularly when the Spanish objective was to bar the Portuguese expansion, must have cost the reductions many lives.

Next came the swift dismantling of the Seven Towns in consequence of the rebellion provoked by the Treaty of Madrid. Suspected of having instigated the rebellion,

[9] This is the deposition by Father Gaetano Cattaneo, S.J., an extract from one of his long letters dated May 18, 1729: "The two above-mentioned Fathers live in one of the huts made of hides; and the poor homeless, shelterless Indians, exposed after their labors to the rain and the wind, and without a penny of wages but only the discount of the tax they would have to pay."*

the Jesuits were at last expelled from there and from the other domains of Spain and Portugal. The Missions were secularized and placed under military administration. The outrages then committed by the Spanish commandants were to increase the desertions and precipitate the catastrophe.

When the territory of the Missions was turned over to Portuguese jurisdiction in 1801, the Guarani population was already in ruin. Nevertheless, new bloodlettings were in store for it. Indeed, the attempts at reincorporation (1816–19) under the command of the Indian Andresito Artigas and the tremendous mopping-up operations of Chagas Santos which they provoked cost the sacrifice of great numbers of Indians on both sides of the river. And to consummate that implacable work of demolition there was, in 1827, the predatory raid by the Uruguayan caudillo Fructuoso Rivera, who carried off, besides valuables and cattle, nearly all the remaining able-bodied men of the old "doctrines."

The following data attest to the frightful devastation suffered by the Guaranis. In 1801, when Borges do Canto and Santos Pedroso attacked the Missions, they found a population reckoned at barely fourteen thousand souls. A little later, in 1814, that number had dropped to less than half, and in 1827, when Rivera sacked them, the number was no higher than three thousand! Such was the sorry remnant that the caudillo managed to seize and carry off as part of his loot. What was left was empty human ruins: according to one modern historian, not more than one inhabitant per fifty-three square kilometers!*

Efforts by the Portuguese to establish the missionary Indian at different points in the territory, starting with Gomes Freire's measures,[1] failed utterly. Despite the Jesuits' extraordinary undertaking, their experience actually demonstrated that the Guarani, when segregated within the scanty limits of his own race, could never be counted an active factor of civilization.

In their dispersive movements the natives were attracted preferentially by cattle-raiding and by occasional robbery. After that they were widely absorbed by the *montoneras*—mounted guerrilla marauders. Zum Felde records the fact that the expulsion of the Jesuits provoked the exodus of a great mass of Indians to the south, where they turned to cattle thieving and herding.* Around 1835, when the Farroupilha Revolution broke out, a scant 318 Indians were idling among the ruins of the vast missionary empire.* Nothing more was left of the Seven Towns!

Here initially lived tribes of other indigenous nations, but when Rio Grande began to grow as a portion of the Portuguese dominion, the population of those tribes was already thin, and the numbers kept diminishing more and

[1] When Gomes Freire was appointed to superintend the fixing of boundaries according to the Treaty of Madrid, he tried to win over the Missionary Indians by various means, including resettlement in Portuguese territory and enrolling their children in schools.

more to the point of total disappearance of some tribes. When the mountain region was settled, the furtive presence of residues of ancient tribes was noted there. Now and again stray Indians might still attack unwary settlers. But defense was a matter of simple police action or private repression, like those related by Hemetério Veloso da Silveira.*

Decisive in the ethnic and moral formation of the Gaucho of the Plata, the indigenous component, whether because of its blood contribution or because of the pressure of its resentment, at once appears as a strongly differentiating element in the comparison between the people of the Plata and of Rio Grande do Sul. It would be well to consider first the diversity of that factor in each case, in seeking to fix the sociological characterization of both. The Indian not only contributed far less to the anthropological formation of our cowboy,* but showed him no such hatred as that with which he reacted to the contempt and cruelties of the Spaniard in the Platine country.

On the lower bank of the great estuary, vengeful, pugnacious native mobs persisted in savage opposition to the march of the conquistadores, composing a bloody, wavelike line, advancing and falling back in an aggressiveness that, although moderated by time, still keeps the worlds of Spanish ancestry and of native descent, including the mestizo, tacitly divorced. The phenomenon was to be reproduced later on the cisplatine side, although in different ways and for a much shorter time.

In Rio Grande other factors, besides the sparsity of the indigenous population, contributed to reduce the hostility and resistance of the natives to practically negligible terms. The small groups coming from Laguna, the two hundred Paulistas of Cristóvão Pereira, the 254 men from several captaincies who disembarked with Silva Pais, and the officially selected married couples from the Azores, besides the refugees from the Colônia do Sacramento and the mainland Portuguese who also drifted to the Continente de São Pedro—it fell to the lot of these to found, populate, and defend a territory constantly menaced from without by their neighbors. It is certain that the aborigine as an element of opposition never really amounted to a serious problem for these pioneers, whose number increased considerably with the opening of the highway between Rio Grande and São Paulo. And we should not forget the *mozuelas*, the young women called for by the Brigadier[2] to come "seek married status" in the nascent community so lacking in women.

There is no evading the conclusion that the Indian was of very little significance among us. Because they did not entertain the least doubt about this, the men of '35 rejected for their war standard a design in which two Indians brandished the tricolor flag. The idea struck

[2] Silva Pais headed the new province from its founding on February 19, 1737, until the following December, when he left for Rio de Janeiro to replace Gomes Freire, who had to go to Minas Gerais, also in his jurisdiction. André Ribeiro Coutinho succeeded Silva Pais in command for the next three years.

them as so absurd that one overwrought republican immediately tried to find out who was responsible for it, because he wanted to "garrote and smoke-cure him."*

There is not the slightest reference to the hostility of the natives in the well-known letter in which André Ribeiro Coutinho, successor to Silva Pais in command of the Captaincy, detailed the roster of difficulties confronting him here. What he found in "the land of the many," indeed, was "a lot of flies, a lot of mosquitoes, a lot of moths, a lot of fleas, . . . a lot of rain, a lot of wind, a lot of cold, a lot of thunder, . . . a lot of work, a lot of fatigue duty, . . . a lot of want of everything else for life and luxury."* Not a word about Indians: it was as if they did not exist.

They did exist, and in considerable numbers up to that time, but they dwelt in the missionary closed area, nearly all of them, subordinate to the authority of Buenos Aires. They were Guaranis, subjects of Spain, living in the Tape under the severe discipline of the priests. Those Indians, by means of fleeting sorties, kept track of the seaboard occupation by the Luso-Brazilians in the beginning of the eighteenth century, but they offered no organized resistance. The fighting would open later, caused by the ceding of the Seven Towns to Portugal under the Treaty of Madrid (1750), but it assumed a military aspect, having nothing in common with the chronic state of rebellion which disturbed the plains on both sides of the Plata and the other Argentine dependencies.

There were instructions from higher authorities that everything should be done to win the friendship and alliance of the Indians who had dropped out of other native groups—Minuanos, principally—and broken tribes to wander in the neighborhood of the Presidio and in the open countryside. From the beginning of colonization similar instructions were handed down to other parts of Brazil without result, but in the case of Rio Grande, owing to the strategic needs of its occupation and to the peculiarities of tending cattle, they did not become merely a dead letter.

But independent of official admonitions, the settlers of the former Captaincy of El-Rei showed no disposition to the deeds of violence that generated the state of tension and revolt unleashed by the Spaniards in the Plata region. The settlers were the descendants of a people not as self-important and arrogant, although as rich in history, as the Spanish. Nearly all were Luso-Brazilian and were already accustomed to the simplicity and severity of colonial life or else were plain folk from the Islands or Portugal, all of whom were ignorant of escutcheons or privileges of blood. Thus it was not hard for them to make friendly contact with the Minuanos and attract them to their cause. The naturalness and the prudent habits of the pioneers stabilized tradition, became a natural attribute of the land, even eventually imposing itself as a point of regional pride. A hundred years after the installation of Rio Grande a Farroupilha newspaper proclaimed that on the soil of the Continente "never did vestiges of aristocracy appear that they were not promptly overlaid by the irresistible homogeneity of the Rio-Grandenses."* That equalitarian sentiment explains the diligence with which the Farrapos safeguarded, over and beyond the stipulations of Poncho Verde,[3] the freedom of the slaves who had fought side by side with them.

There is an episode that reveals with ironic clarity the extreme diversity of the types of outstanding men involved in our struggles on both sides of the frontier. When the triumphant Don Juan José de Vértiz y Salcedo invaded Rio Grande in 1774 at the head of an army of three thousand men to crush Rio Pardo and then turn against Pôrto Alegre, he was no doubt convinced that at the mere jingle of his bright insignia the modest Luso-Brazilian fort would fall without resistance. Who was this man who deigned to attack the poor bastion but the very noble "Comendador de Puertollano en la Orden de Calatrava, Mariscal de Campo de los Reales Ejércitos y Capitán General de la Provincia de la Plata, Uruguay, Paraná, Rio Grande de San Pedro e Islas Mallorvinas"? Lord of so many and such lofty titles, he attempted to confound with his

---

[3] The treaty of peace ending the Farrapos War (1845). Its stipulations included guarantees of immunity for officers and men of the Farrapos forces (including former Imperial Army officers and men who fought for the rebels), both active and prisoner of war, and other concessions by the Imperial Government. Slaves who fought on the Farrapos side were freed under the fourth stipulation, which preceded those concerning all other individuals except officers.

pomp the timid defenders of the southern frontier of Brazil. But the unforeseen turned up on our side to oppose him: Rafael Pinto Bandeira. He was an un-adorned, rough warrior who had only his sheer prowess on his side. Even so, what else was needed in these remote lands to embroil the arrogant invader and send him and his whole army headlong in defeat? The battle over, it was evident that the dried hides which Bandeira had fastened to the tails of his wild ponies raised more racket than the flashy blazons carried by the Captain General of the Mallorvinas Islands.[4]

The aborigines of these plains, finding treatment by the Portuguese wholly different from what they had always received from the Spanish, immediately showed that they were not insensible of the difference. Around 1721 the officer commanding a detachment from Buenos Aires operating in the cisplatine area complained that out of gratitude to the Portuguese the Indians were forever harassing the Spaniards. "For these Portuguese," he ex-plains, "keep them well bribed with continual presents of coarse woolen cloth, hats, swords, caps, tobacco, and aguardiente, which they are constantly giving them so

---

[4] Pinto Bandeira's harassing of Vértiz on the latter's countermarch included an expedient used in an earlier engagement (and to be used long afterwards by the Farrapos): he had rolls of raw leather tied to the tails of wild ponies, which were stampeded toward the enemy camp. With the infernal things banging at their legs, these untamed and now panicked animals dashed through the camp, terrorizing men and beasts. The Spaniards' mounts scattered wildly, many getting lost in the ravines.

that they will serve as an advance guard in preventing the reconnoitering of our detachments and so they may be able to work unhindered."* The Spanish never learned thus to secure the friendship, much less the alliance, of the Indians. On the contrary, they never tried to deal with them except through the language of intolerance and ill treatment. Were it not so, the attack on the Misiones Orientales in 1801 would not have had so shattering a success. The former protégés of the Regular Clerics of Saint Ignatius could no longer endure the oppression of the Spanish authorities.*

When Rio Grande began to be populated, the abuses and outrages of the first centuries in other parts of the Portuguese conquest were long past. The policy of ingratiation, determined by the home capital from the very beginning of the colonization of Brazil, was to yield good fruit in the lands of São Pedro, where the pressure of politico-military needs would make it imperative to gain the friendship and alliance of the heathen.

If the advance of the pioneers came up against a line of resistance and aggression, that line was represented exclusively by the Spanish forts of Buenos Aires and Montevideo and the Jesuit reductions of the Seven Towns, which were also Spanish. As a result the Rio-Grandense *gaúcho* did not suffer the terrible impact of that internal frontier erected by the Indian and the mestizo against the domination of the "Goths," a frontier which by reason of its long duration was to etch such deep lines in the history and character of our neighbors. The unstable boundary line of Rio Grande, always under menace and more than once violated by the Castilian incursions, was a political frontier militarily disputed by a traditional enemy. The other, the internal frontier, cruel, dangerous, without grandeur, was what may be called a frontier of race and caste, created by the arrogance of the Spaniards and by the profound hatred with which the "pariahs of the plain" responded to them.

That line of scission and hostility was to generate another phenomenon entirely unknown in Rio-Grande: the opposition between country and city, between barbarism and civilization. The vigorous antithesis proposed by Sarmiento,[5] whatever one's mental reservations today,* is still substantially valid. The over-schematic presentation of the facts thus contrasted may be open to argument. The facts themselves, no. Not even Zorrilla de San Martín contests them: he will say merely that if the city is civilization, it is not life, meaning that the vital element of the clash is incarnate in the rural sections.*

When the rigid system of authority of the colonial institutions was abolished upon the winning of Independence, the two forces so long antagonistic intensified their struggle against each other in a ceaseless ferocity.

[5] Sarmiento's famous book, *Facundo*, is subtitled *Civilización y barbarie*. (Translators.)

The city represented the principles and interests of a civilization that had not sunk roots into the soil or imposed its authority on the inland wilderness. The country represented the diffuse elements of a territory in a constant state of ferment and rebellion—Indians, mestizos, bandits—harshly relegated to the sidelines in the process of national unification. But with the bonds with the homeland broken, the former system of repression banished, the country people did not take long to congregate around the caudillos, finally installing themselves in the centers of civilization and casting over them for a long time the despicable shadow of their crimes.

THE DEVELOPMENT OF RIO GRANDE was simply unacquainted with such antagonism, because the conditions that generated it were quite alien to us. Between the populations of the country and of the urban centers, there was not a shadow of barrier or break. Commerce being small and industry nonexistent, it was on the pastoral activities that the economic stability of the cities rested. The cities, especially those located in the Campanha, could even be considered condensations of the rural country itself. The influential men, nearly all of rural extraction, were ranchers, and they were in the habit of staying part of the year in their city residences. The sentiments of the people of the country and of the urban populations, nourished by ties of blood and friendship, were the same no matter how different the activities of each group. If occasionally these bonds suffered a lapse in continuity, it was for private reasons. In more than one place in his *Notícia* Nicolau Dreys observes that on Sundays and saints' days the country inhabitants "would gather in the surrounding towns to fulfill their religious duties."* Or else it was the city dwellers who got together on racing days with the ranchers, with the overseers and foremen, the herders and the peons, and enjoyed the same moments of gaming excitement. The differences of environment and class never disturbed the fellowship and social quiet that was the habitual condition of life inside our frontiers.

Disquiet came from outside: it consisted of the eternal disputes and incidents with the Castilians. And in the face of the external enemy Rio Grande had to present a united front. From that came our respect for authority. The public sense of discipline imposed itself on each as a condition of security for all. The common necessity of defense was the political factor that preserved us from the dispersion and anarchy characteristic of the Plata.

MISLED BY THE ASSOCIATION OF IDEAS suggested by the Platine scheme, Rubens de Barcelos has attempted to discover in certain aspects of the revolutions of 1835 and 1893 something like a Rio-Grandense version of the terrible, prolonged civil convulsion that flared up on both banks of the Plata.[6]* The thesis is not without some attraction, but historical reality is against it.

The Farroupilha rebellion stands out as the act of desperation of a Province against long endured wrongs and irritations and erupted in a conspiracy in which the men of the city were not distinguished from the men of the country. The secret meetings at which it was plotted, intimately connected with the liberal ferment from which all the Brazilian agitations and revolutions of the period stemmed, took place in the capital of the Province,* in the very bosom of the Assembly and the barracks. For a whole year the focus of events was Pôrto Alegre, moving to the interior only after the first reverses. The leaders of the movement, civilians or soldiers, ranchers or not, Rio-Grandenses or Brazilians from elsewhere, all of them, because of their ideological commitments, shared a common feeling, and were unanimously fired by the preaching of the political doctrines that filled contemporary minds. The newspapers and documents of the time contain nothing that indicates the remotest glimmer of rural discrimination.

We must not lose sight of the fact that the rural population of Rio Grande do Sul never constituted, even in the earliest times, a formless and aimless group such as that of the Plata, given up to a diffuse state of anarchy

[6] That is, in both Argentina and Uruguay, which underwent the usual turbulent consequences of newly-won independence for many years thereafter. (Translators.)

and chronic rebellion. In the case of the War of the Farrapos the men of the country and the men of the city joined in the same cause. The same was true of the defenders of the Empire. The plain fact is that there was no distinction between the city and the country in the composition of the forces in conflict.

Points of contact there may be, and not a few of them, between the ideals of the Farrapos and the principles that the authors of Argentine independence attempted to set up before the fateful cycle of the caudillos. The ideological sources were indeed common. They stemmed principally from the French Revolution, from the Declaration of Independence in Philadelphia, and from the Giovine Italia,[7] all these having simultaneously infected the intellectual centers of Spanish and Portuguese America.[8]

There was one difference though and a disconcerting one. The sociological premises were not the same in both cases: the Rio-Grandense revolutionaries, after a year of

[7] The secret society of Mazzini's radicals, in the Risorgimento. It replaced the Carbonari in 1831. Garibaldi's war experiences in Rio Grande do Sul and Uruguay were occasioned by his flight from Italy after the failure of an attempted republican coup influenced by Mazzini. (Translators.)

[8] Walter Spalding took the trouble to go through the newspapers published in Pôrto Alegre from 1828 to 1836, gleaning the foreign authors from whom the political restlessness of the time was getting its nourishment. Besides several Greek and Latin classics, the following stand out among others: Benjamin Constant, Bentham, Cabanis, De Maistre, Droz, Fénelon, Guizot, Hamilton, Helvetius, Hobbes, John Jay, Jefferson, Locke, Madison, Manzoni, Mazzini, Montaigne, Montesquieu, Pascal, Raynal, Rousseau, Madame de Staël, Tocqueville, Voltaire.*

vain expectation, duped and persecuted—above all, misunderstood—finally became convinced that the monarchical institutions were responsible for the evils befalling the Province, and hurled themselves savagely against the regime. Having proclaimed the República Rio-Grandense, they fought for it for nearly nine years until they fell, defeated by force and by the prudence of Caxias.

In the Argentine revolution everything went differently. Before the growing menace of Gaucho oppression, initially polarized by Artigas, the leaders of the movement, wishing to safeguard the privileges of the city at any price, did not hesitate to break republican promises and tried anxiously to entrust the destinies of the new nation to a king, any king. The project failed only because of the collapse of the troubled negotiations carried on to that end with Carlota Joaquina[9] and the European courts. For nearly ten years the liberal chiefs of Independence clung to their monarchical dream. And the fear of disorder, of the constant caudillo menace, rose to such extremes that they seriously considered the enthronement of some intangible descendant of Atahualpa.[1] As a last resort, even the status of a colony of England would serve to cure Buenos Aires of its fears!* Zum Felde, after summarizing all this, shrugs his

[9] Daughter of Carlos IV of Spain, she married João, Prince Regent of Portugal, separated from him in 1806 because his mind was so unbalanced that she feared for her life, and became the leading spirit of the opposition to the prince's government. (Translators.)

[1] The last Inca ruler, strangled by Pizarro's orders in 1533. (Translators.)

shoulders with this contemptuous dismissal: "It is a subject for an operetta."*

If the future Uruguayans' struggle for autonomy was fostered and supported, not by the city as happened on the nether side of the Plata, but by the country, it is only that in Uruguay there was merely an inversion of positions without altering the nature of the conflict. In both cases the same separation, the same implacable dissension between the city and the country.

BUT A VITAL ELEMENT entirely alien to the Rio-Grandense crisis makes it inacceptable to attempt a comparison. That element is the autonomous presence of the rural masses combining powerfully in the shaping of the emancipationist battles fought in Argentina and Uruguay. Nothing that is peculiar to the Platine agitations could influence the revolutionary impulses that drove the Farrapos.

It is not possible to reach any other conclusion without subverting historical truth. In the contrast between these dramas one can see similarities only in a geographic sense, similar stages, the same weapons, but everything else different and antagonistic. Rio Grande do Sul never felt itself a unit per se, delimited and detached from the national body. Not even during the life of the República de Piratini.[2]

[2] "It is not possible to say," Pandiá Calógeras remarks, "that separation from the Empire was a vital point of the rebel program. Nothing

One thing indeed it was never possible to eradicate from the hearts of the Farrapos: the awareness of their status as Brazilians, a status reinforced by the presence of a frontier which for a hundred years had been bitterly disputed foot by foot. It is not paradoxical to observe that the rebels' sense of patriotism was keener than that of the men responsible for the defense of the imperial arms. While the central government did not hesitate to hire mercenaries for the army of repression, going to the extreme of seeking an alliance with Rosas against the rebelling Rio Grande,* the Farrapos preferred to lay down their arms rather than accept the aid offered them by the Argentine tyrant. And the refusal was formalized under the express and solemn declaration that their sentiments as Brazilians took precedence over any ideological considerations. All the evidence tends to the conclusion that the active commerce of the revolutionaries with the Uruguayans was confined to the purchase of horses and munitions. It is true that in the *Memória* he wrote on the Revolution of 1835, Tristão de Alencar Araripe alludes tangentially to a "small band of Uruguayan subjects" who had probably fought on the side of the republicans in a battle of 1843 against Bento Manuel.* The imputa-

---

was changed in the laws except as regards the persons whose duty it was to execute them. In the innumerable proposals made to the imperial authorities, the return to the bosom of the Empire was never called in question, but the granting of autonomy to the Province was insisted upon always. When peace was made in 1845, the common peril menacing Brazil by the Argentine Confederation stood out above all considerations. Much more federalist than separatist, the Farrapos fought for local liberties."*

tion seems unjust. At least, it was indignantly rejected by the one who had the authority to do so: José Gomes Portinho, one of the most valiant and austere soldiers of the movement.[3]

IN OUR SOCIOLOGICAL AND CULTURAL HISTORY there has been no servile imitation of the Plata. Emilio Corbiere declares that the Gaucho, "falsified by legend," seems to extend his prestige to neighboring nations where there are affinities with the Plata.* And in the field of regional literature, it is doubtless possible to find evidence that we have not been altogether impervious to contamination by that legend. Outside of literature, however, our characteristics are peculiar to the Luso-Brazilian genius, and offer sharp contrast to those of the Platine version of the Hispanic genius.

[3] This is the note that Portinho wrote in the margin of the statement by that zealous functionary of the Empire, Alencar Araripe: "It is false. The Republicans were not aided by foreign forces, not only in that battle but in any other one fought during the whole struggle. The same cannot be said for the Legality, for not only did it order soldiers hired from Europe but had Uruguayans in its pay when it attacked the Republicans at Pedras Altas. General Don Fructuoso [Rivera] himself accompanied General Bento Manuel, inasmuch as the latter praised him in an order dated February 5, 1837, at Candiota." This marginal comment, like numerous others, stands in the copy that belonged to Dr. Álvaro Gonçalves Chaves, as Alfredo Varela attests in a volume now incorporated into the Arquivo Histórico do Rio Grande do Sul.

[Bento Manuel Ribeiro fought and defeated Farrapos forces, then became a leader among the rebels, only to return finally to the imperial side. (Translators.)]

INDEED, THERE IS NOTHING IN THE EARLIEST STAGES of
Rio-Grandense civilization that resembles or is even rem-
iniscent of the country-city antinomy peculiar to the
Plata. The Rio-Grandense fields—carved into *sesmarias*
and soon dotted with cattle ranches—never came to play
the turbulent, aggressive role that fell to the lot of the
pampa on both banks of the Plata. There the territory
with its wandering hordes assumed the oppressive importance of a force in itself, constantly threatening the
standards of civilization represented by the cities and
towns. In Rio Grande the country as a political expression lacked its specific instrument of action: the caudillo.
Moreover, without opportunity to expand as an
autonomous force, our *gaúcho* accustomed himself to an
incipient social organization without the conflicts and
humiliations which the Platine Gaucho had to bear.[4]

IT IS PLAIN, then, that the Revolution of 1835 does not
lend itself to the comparison proposed by Rubens de
Barcelos. Less still does that of 1893, despite its legacy of

[4] "The machine of officialism grinds up in its gears the rebelliousness
of the Gaucho race and subjects it to the passive electoral function
under the ferule of the commissioners. In proportion as the police
authority grows stronger and extends, Gaucho freedom diminishes,
and with his freedom the primitive virtues of his character. Obliged
to choose between submission or delinquency, the Gaucho becomes
humble, *compadre* or criminal; brought to bay, he turns hypocritical
and treacherous; or else he withdraws into a reserved misanthropy,
dumbly lowing like a bull."*

crimes and persecutions. The latter's involvement with the events connected with the consolidation of the republican regime installed in 1889 is well known. The outbreak of revolution, after three years of fighting, was to be ennobled by the sacrifice of Saldanha da Gama.[5] There in letters of blood is the certificate of its national ties. And there are no grounds whatever for comparing the revolution with the type of civil wars that for so long devastated the Plata districts.

THE GEOGRAPHIC INTEGRATION of Rio Grande do Sul was completed only in the first years of the past century. Earlier, to the west we had the Seven Towns, a Spanish region under the authority of Buenos Aires, and the wide frontier belt of the Campanha, an undivided area— a no-man's land, a broad common grazing land roved by hide-hunters—where the Luso-Brazilian and Spanish vanguards had long skirmished. In the cisplatine open spaces as in the Campanha—for they were all the same plains over which the ownerless herds ranged and men

[5] Admiral Luis Filipe Saldanha da Gama, head of the Naval Academy, remained as neutral as possible for the good of the Academy, until he felt honor-bound to take sides against the dictatorial Peixoto. After numerous vicissitudes he led the rebel forces engaged near Osório by a far larger government army on June 24, 1895. In the battle the admiral was run through by a lance and killed. An official autopsy confirmed rumors that his body had been multilated by the victors— one instance of the violent blood-letting in the Revolution of 1893. Saldanha da Gama, it appears, had been convinced from the first that he was joining a losing cause, but regarded that cause as right, and so sacrificed himself to help bring about an honorable peace.* (Translators.)

engaged in the traffic of green hides—there were Indians and Gauchos of various origins and Spanish and Portuguese depredators.

This barbaric or semibarbaric population, fluctuating, rootless, aimless, attacked the wild herds with impunity, and on that activity it lived. There as in the neighboring territory it grew with the instigation of smuggling. Its habits were aggressively inimical to any kind of association, even the most rudimentary. It accommodated itself only to imitations of militia organization under caudillo tyranny, which, even under the caricature of government, was nothing but a ruthless system of pillaging and crimes.

But the progressive appropriation of a great part of that disputed area by the Luso-Brazilians did not include the indiscriminate incorporation of the restless mass of adventurers and malefactors infesting it. As the Continente grew toward the south, the conquest was gradually consolidated by means of the broad concession of *sesmarias* and their immediate occupation by the grantees.[6] The political urgency of these measures was

[6] The high tide of war, carrying away the people under arms, left as it receded, along with destruction and with some bits of land integrated into the territory, new *sesmarias* as recompense for services. After Rio Grande had been recovered and peace established with the Spanish, the population of the Campanha was greatly increased with the soldiers who requested discharge from service and settled on *sesmarias* granted by the government. At this time the fever for possession of ranches in the interior reached its peak. The grants of *sesmarias* multiplied in an astonishing and disorderly

seconded by the settlers' real hunger for lands. The lure of the plains teeming with cattle infected everybody. Oliveira Viana says that when the Paulistas grew disillusioned with the gold mines, they rushed eagerly to the herds of the southernmost region. The exodus was impressive. "Small urban and already progressive centers of the Paraná plateau, for example, fell into decay and died out, impoverished by the migration of its best men to the plains of the South."* Individuals who had rendered services, military commanders, civilians, minor officers, soldiers, even priests, all wanted their share in the division of the newly conquered lands, and the *sesmarias* went on being granted with no great ceremony, sometimes precipitately and en masse.

Thus a regime of stability unpropitious to the free play of rustic anarchy was established by the hasty scattering of ranches. Those who could not endure the discipline of the troops or the drudgery of the ranches—probably the majority of the nomad mass that formerly crossed and recrossed the region freely—sought refuge among the hordes laying waste to the cisplatine area. There everything was open to license and abuse.

The line of separation having been extended, not just between two sovereignties but between two social and political stages even then at quite different levels,[7] the

---

fashion. Shortly all the inhabitants wanted to be ranchers, and the Captaincy was cut up into extensive properties.*
[7] Let us take the deposition of General Tomás de Iriarte, who was at the time a colonel in Alvear's Uruguayan army invading Rio Grande

old hostilities provoked by cattle-hunting continued. Blows were struck by both sides. There was one difference, however: the Rio-Grandense cowboys, unlike our Uruguayan neighbors, who at that time were totally ignorant of social organization, acted in the name of the king and the interests of the ranches to which they were attached.

In Rio Grande vigilant precautions were taken against disturbing elements. Even in 1788 the correspondence of the Viceroy, Dom Luís de Vasconcelos,* furnishes news of seven Spaniards delivered up to the Montevideo government for having been caught with plunder and contraband in the Campanha of Rio Grande. Crimes were perpetrated, without a doubt, but the police were always alert to put them down. On that point the English traveler John Luccock, who was in Rio Grande from 1808 to 1813, relates that when one robbery was committed and the thieves had fled the country, they were immediately hunted by officers of the law in a fifty-mile radius in all directions, and were captured after nine days. "Affording another proof," the traveler concluded, "that under a vigilant and active Police, a desert, though of wide extent, afforded less security to criminals than a crowded city."*

---

in 1827: ". . . in our plains no settlements are so well provided with the objects that make country life comfortable, and that is because in the province of Rio Grande the populace lives better than in these lands: in this respect they have a hundred years' advantage of us: the culture is much more advanced."*

As for the protection of the herds, that was nearly always a matter of private jurisdiction, for in the suddenness of the attacks each man could count only on himself and his little clan. Not without reason were many of the ranchers military leaders or militia officers. And even those who were not military men found themselves occasionally forced to assume the command of defense or attack. Every frontiersman from peon to *sesmaria* grantee was at once herdsman and soldier. From this comes our vocation to command, and that "cult of authority" which Oliveira Viana attributes to the *gaúcho*, possibly overstating it a little. "For that populace of restless, bellicose herders," the sociologist says, "public power, with its functionaries, its generals, its troops, became for a century a condition of life, a guarantee of tranquillity and peace; in short, an organ indispensable to the survival of the social body of that distant group."*

Hostile toward the conditions of life that were being established in the Rio-Grandense area, naturally the Indians and bandits who tried entering it did not feel easy, and slipped back for good or ill to their preferred environment. There, beyond the law, feeding on the disorder of the plains, they worked up the sorry clay from which the caudillo would be shaped.

Despite all the vigilance there must have been infiltrations at this or that point of the Rio-Grandense territory simply because the pastoral community was extremely sparse. But those infiltrations, being few and sporadic, could never affect the conditions of life in Rio Grande. Here the civilizing function of the cattle ranch must be recognized. Augusto Meyer has declared in one of his magnificent essays that the granting of *sesmarias* was the least apt criterion, in the case of Rio Grande, for the settling and exploring of the land.* We think exactly the opposite. The division of the conquered areas into *sesmarias* was, at the time, imperative. Its adoption reveals the very realistic soundness of the Portuguese colonial policy. Under what other system could Portugal have combined the extent of the territory, the scarcity of settlers, the dispersion of the herds, and the necessities of defense? In the emergency what was the fate of the Azorians' attempt at small farming? Their children, and in some part they themselves, were not bound to their little farms: won over by the economic allure of the country, they too accompanied our great march to the west and southwest, ever in search of more land and more cattle.[8] From the social, economic, political, and military point of view large landholdings were the practical answer to the problems of the area and the time. If today the large landed estate presents itself as a factor of social deterioration, this is no reason to ignore the im-

---

[8]"The abuse of granting *sesmarias* too freely and the great abundance of cattle in a wild state scattered throughout the Captaincy territory at the time turned the people's activity into a new channel, from farming to the easy life of the cattle country, which furnished remunerative results with little work."*

portant historical role it played in populating and con-
solidating the conquest.

IT CAN BE SAID that the military advances carried the
settlers on the flank of their pack trains. Or else they
were components of the column itself who became
ranchers without thereby losing their status as soldiers.
Moreover, nearly all the able-bodied men of the Captaincy were members of the militia. The call to arms
might sound at any moment and they had to be alert to
the first alarm. Thus it was to be for a hundred years.
For that reason, in this out-of-the-way region, the royal
service of arms took precedence over any other activities, interests, or obligations.

The colonizing arrangements that got an early start
with Silva Pais when he established Rio Grande in 1737,
and subsequently with Gomes Freire when in 1754 he
incorporated the lands bordered on the west by the
Jacuí River, were to be repeated throughout the conquest: the appropriation of new areas and their civil
occupation were complementary operations.

As the frontier progressed, and the pastoral struggle
passed from the anarchic attacks on the wild herds to the
incipient discipline of the ranches, it was natural that the
former inhabitants should flow toward the South, rebellious, unsettled people, by instinct refractory to the
emergence of the modest standards of social stability that

gradually took root and multiplied under the Portuguese jurisdiction. Bandits who remained behind the new lines of the conquest or insinuated themselves across those lines, forming errant pockets, tended to split up, now skirting the frontier, now letting themselves eventually be absorbed. Lindolfo Cólor, who wrote a substantial book on the War of the Farrapos, points out what is least true in the usual discussions of Rio-Grandense nomadism. "The highly touted nomadism of the Brazilian *gaúchos*," he says, "thus has a quite relative meaning. They are nomadic as compared with the inhabitants of the urban centers, but in the genesis of the southern populations they represent the first, and decisive, element of social fixation, of civilization in the desert."* Indeed, there is nothing new in our own observation that "the laws of nomadism had a shorter reign here than is commonly presumed."*

The nomadic element—adventurers more or less without a country—was looked upon with great mistrust in Rio Grande, and the necessity of purging the litigious belt of that "pestilence of people" was long felt. Indeed, as early as 1780 Sebastião Francisco Betâmio, author of the classic invective against the vagrants, called for measures to prevent "men who are not known as quiet, peaceable men with no inclination to enrich themselves by means of cattle-rustling"* from staying on the frontier. This was before the great Luso-Brazilian campaign against the Campanha, when almost half of the

present Rio-Grandense territory still nominally belonged to Spain. After 1801 the high tide of settlers
fanned out, occupying the lands of the Campanha and of
the Missions under the protection of troops and militia.
Thenceforward the situation of the cattle rustlers became
untenable. Their time had passed. In any case, they
could no longer operate in the Rio Grande area as
independent gangs subject to no law but their own.

In that phase of Rio Grande's evolution due credit
must be given to the Azorians' capacity for adaptability
in displacement.[9] Hardly had they arrived in the Captaincy in 1752 when they went on to gain the recently
incorporated valley of the Jacuí, founding Santo Amaro,
Triunfo, and Taquari, besides Pôrto Alegre and river
towns. Immediately afterwards they headed toward the
Missions and the Campanha. Formerly confined in their
hard little islands, they now wanted space. Contrary to
what some scholars have asserted, not all of them were
content to stay in the urban centers or in lands adjacent
thereto, satisfied with their parcels of land, their few
agrarian implements, their seeds, their domestic animals,

[9] Adaptation to the climate of the Azores had no doubt already given
a special flexibility and malleability to that type of man. "His low
standard of living . . . permitted him all contacts, all assimilations.
. . . In Brazil they mingled without difficulty with the populations of
slaves, whether Negro or Indian. . . . In certain seaboard colonies
. . . to the south, the absorption was often reversed: the whites
retained a higher potential of assimilation than did other races and in
many places a progressive 'whitening' of the population could be
noted."*

and their scanty tillages. In fact many of them, and their descendants in greater numbers, applied for and got *sesmarias,* dived into the interior like the other pioneers, and set up ranches in all the corners of the Continente de São Pedro as the conquest spread. The easy wealth of cattle attracted people of varied origins from the Luso-Brazilian world, and the ex-islanders did not lag behind. The testimony of the archives reveals their or their children's presence everywhere.[1] In 1781 Azorians and

[1] With respect to the Azorians in Rio Grande do Sul, an authority on the subject, General José de Araújo Fabrício, member of the Instituto Histórico e Geográfico do Rio Grande do Sul and one of our most distinguished genealogists, has stated in a letter dated September 12, 1961:

"In 1749 the first Azorian couples arrived at the Presidio de Rio Grande de São Pedro, and beginning in 1752 they were sent to the Port of Viamão, afterwards named the Pôrto dos Casais [Port of the Married Couples], to Rio Pardo, Santo Amaro, Taquari, Triunfo, Conceição do Arroio, Estreito, and Mostardas, that is, on the north and east banks of the rivers Jacuí and Guaíba, and of the Lagoa dos Patos, which was the zone of the Continente de São Pedro up to that time occupied by the Portuguese. The flat lands to the south of the Jacuí were still uninhabited and open to the action of the Spanish troops, who were taking back those lands for their government. Until 1776, the year in which the Castilians were defeated and expelled from Rio Grande, the Azorians were concentrating in those little towns they had founded, or on parcels of land around those towns, devoting themselves to agriculture.

"After the victory over the Spaniards, the whole territory to the south of the Jacuí River was occupied by the Portuguese as far as the limits set in 1777 by the Treaty of San Ildefonso. *Sesmarias* were distributed throughout this area. Great landholdings were established, bestowed upon civilians and military men, Portuguese, Paulistas, Lagunistas, and also numerous Azorians and sons of Azorians, who were thus transformed from small farmers into great ranchers.

"In the books of the *Registro Geral* in the Arquivo Público, in which all the land grants are noted down, it is recorded that from

Paulistas founded Encruzilhada,* and in 1789 forty-eight couples from El-Rei started the town of Piratini in the Serra do Herval, future seat of the first government of the República Rio-Grandense.* Saint-Hilaire pointed out the numerous descendants of islanders in the extreme South, precisely in the most vulnerable zone of the boundary lines.

. . .

1780 to 1800 more than a hundred Azorians settled down with large ranches as far as the border, that is, in what are now the Municipalities of Rio Pardo, Cachoeira, São Sepé, São Gabriel, Caçapava, Encruzilhada, São Jerônimo, Camaquã, Tapes, Piratini, and Bagé, in the new lands which passed over to Portuguese control. It is certain that the number of Azorians located there would be much greater than we have succeeded in identifying.

"With the conquest of the Missions in 1801 all the lands north of the Ibicuí River were incorporated, that is, the present Mission zone, and also the rich country south of that river which contains the present frontier Municipalities of Uruguaiana, Alegrete, Quaraí, Livramento, D. Pedrito, Rosário, etc. These lands were immediately occupied and populated, and beginning with 1814 we find in the same *Registro Geral* books the concession, on a major scale, of the *sesmarias* that were already occupied, most of them. There likewise the number of ranchers born in the Azores is very great, and especially the number of their sons and grandsons.

"The Azorians accompanied the advance of our frontiers in the front line, both settling down in the new lands with their cattle ranches and serving in the military forces that conquered and defended them. They took part in the reconquest of Rio Grande, and their sons and grandsons, as soldiers and officers, some of them in high posts, participated in all the Plata campaigns, the conquest of the Misiones Orientales, and the Farroupilha Revolution."

The writers João Pinto da Silva and Augusto Meyer are thus quite wrong when, obviously without the possession of these data, they cast doubt not only on the importance of the Azorian contingent in the colonization of Rio Grande but on their capacity for expansion and adaptation to the conditions of their new environment.*

TRADITION PORTRAYS THE AZORIANS as simple folk full of resignation and humility. The picture is only partly true. Borges Fortes, who made a detailed study of the history of the "couples," reports acts of violence and depredations that they committed in reprisal for the pitiable abandonment to which they were relegated.* Nor are insurrections against the fiscal extortions imposed by the homeland foreign to the social heritage of the islanders.* Under the placidity of their customs there were such deep reserves of energy that many of them became cattle hunters and soldiers like the other settlers, at the same time when others were sowing their plots of ground and founding cities and towns. Rural occupations attracted and gradually absorbed everyone who tried them, regardless of origin, race, or color, and shortly new contingents of *gaúchos* were busily engaged in cattle rustling with the same boldness as the old hands.* Among them were the Azorians,[2] who, despite the in-

[2] It may be possible to attribute the Azorian's adaptability to the pastoral life at least in part to his experience in the Islands. Father Rambo remarks: "In the period of the reductions five great ranches took advantage of the Campanha grazing lands for the supply of meat; the heritage derived from that, *enhanced by the experience of the Azorians* (italics ours) and enriched by the introduction of new breeds and more efficient methods in the last decades, has made of the Campanha the State's richest cattle region."* The earlier experience of the Azorian in handling cattle is important for the exact discrimination of the human element that entered into the composition of our traditional type. On this matter consult also Florêncio de Abreu: "Importância da Colonização Açoriana no Rio Grande do Sul," *Jornal do Comércio*, Rio de Janeiro, June 3, 1956: "It had therefore not been hard for them to adapt to the new kind of life in Rio Grande. In the dangerous rustic chores the Azorian toughened his muscles and courage and refined his skills still further." "In the

eptitude of the first recruits,[3] whose awkwardness struck Col. Tomás Luis Osório in 1762 as "with neither heart nor courage,"* would eventually produce many of our war chiefs, beginning with Baron de Cêrro Largo, and, among the great Farrapos leaders, Souza Neto, Onofre Pires, Davi Canabarro, João Antônio da Silveira, Côrte Real, Guedes da Luz, and Paulino da Fontoura. Few were the leaders of 1835 who did not have Island blood in their veins.

Nor is it true that the Azorians had come only to sow and reap. It was impossible to exempt from armed service anyone who sought these wild and menaced

---

constant defense of his home and his land, the Azorian became at once rustic and soldier, now wielding the lance or the musket in combat, now the lasso and the hoe in the intervals between wars. He led an epic life. And with the Vicentistas and Paulistas, also colonizers of the distant *gaúcho* land, the Azorian little by little expelled the Castilian and consolidated the sacred bounds of his new fatherland."*

[3] The testimony extracted from the official correspondence of Col. Patrício Corrêa da Câmara, commandant of the Fronteira do Rio Grande, reveals rather colorfully the transition from farmer to soldier. In a letter to the Governor of the Capitania, Brig. Francisco João Róscio, dated from the camp at Piraí, December 27, 1801, he writes: "Ever since peace came to this encampment I have been much worried by not knowing how I shall be able to hold the auxiliary forces who all want to withdraw to cut their wheat and look after other crops. I have kept them here in hopes that within a few days I shall have a solution from you for the problem, reminding you that the enemy is close and his column whole and entire." By the thirty-first of the same month the difficulties seemed to have been bypassed, to judge from the colonel's next report: "The armed force opposing me, commanded by Colonel of Engineers D. Bernardo Lecoco, is powerful and has three times more men than I, which is only 450, but for all that I see the good will they all have and want to meet the enemy so that they can go attend to their harvests which are being ruined."*

frontiers. "The continual wars with the Castilians and the despotism of the governors," Alcides Lima says, "constantly forced the colonists to abandon the hoe for the sword, and the grass shack for the tent. . . . Not only did the farmers face the harsh necessity to become permanent soldiers, but they also frequently lost their crops and all their resources and their work."* Alert to the danger, the metropolitan government decreed that in each nucleus of couples a company of militia should be raised in which all the male residents, "married and single," had to enlist.* It is not known whether these orders were carried out to the letter. But proof that they were observed at least in part is furnished by Betâmio's report of "a body of troops created exemplarily with the sons of many couples in the Continente, who felt the setback in their farming for lack of the sons."* What is certain is that the Azorians responded actively to the demands and pressures of the new environment, and their sons soon merged with the first generations of all who had arrived here from different regions of the country and Portugal, shortly finding themselves, in common with the Continentinos, engaged in the chores of cowherding and in the border fighting.

From the anthropological configuration of the Rio-Grandense *gaúcho*, then, the Azorian contribution cannot be excluded. Indeed, that contribution was considerable.

. . .

WITH THE EXPANSION OF OUR TERRITORY went an affirmation of sovereignty in the form of line troops and companies of militia, and immediate civil occupation of the newly annexed areas. Another type of life was being inaugurated with the spread of cattle ranches and the consequent dying out of the cattle-raiding cycle, which was foreign to the Portuguese dominion.

The *sesmarias* were indeed landed estates. Where some were patched on to others, they created those great areas empty of people that so impressed Governor Soares de Andréia.* But even far separated from each other, the ranches served in fact to establish a spirit of neighborliness, as João Pinto da Silva has demonstrated.* The plains were no longer the scene of simple forays or refuge for vagrants, deserters, and criminals. The practice of cattle raiding continued as individual enterprise, but now conditioned by the limits of property, disciplined by the interests of an incipient pastoral organization. The time had passed for attacking the herds with impunity. The former bandits of the region, thrown back, now constituted a threat from the other side of the border. They were treated as foreign, undesirable enemies, "a pestilent people."

When Borges do Canto, carrying out orders from Rio Pardo,* then under the command of Col. Corrêa da Câmara,[4] prepared for his surprise attack on the

[4] From 1763, when the Dragoons of Rio Grande were transferred to Rio Pardo, the latter place became the most important military garrison in the Captaincy.

Misiones Orientales, his men did not spring up out of the ground like the cisplatine gangs that Zum Felde so vividly presents.* The former dragoon, now captain of militia, had once deserted and vanished into no-man's land, where he had devoted himself to adventure and smuggling. It would therefore seem natural that the Campanha, at the call of the brave soldier, would rise up and follow him. Was not that the case, as some think it was? Let us be accurate; it happened differently. Borges do Canto went to recruit his men, not among the vagrants of the wilderness but among the peons of the ranches.* Yes; it was from the ranches, as General Borges Fortes authoritatively confirmed, that the handful of *gaúchos* came who undertook the conquest of the Missions.* And why did the ex-deserter not appeal to his former companions, with whom he had been hiding out from the law? There can be only one explanation: there was no longer any place for such people inside our frontiers. The social status of the men enlisted for the assault on the Missions is further testimony to the constructive nature of the organization of Luso-Brazilian life.

Saint-Hilaire frequently distinguished the representative man of Rio Grande from the detested Gauchos, different from our cowboys in their dress as in all other ways, and coming from the other side of the border to venture unsuccessfully in the Luso-Brazilian dominions. As they could not help doing, our people sensed the difference, and it was not without vanity that they underscored the contrast. When Arsène Isabelle left Uruguay to enter Rio Grande, four countrymen joined him, and they kept saying that "we[5] had nothing to fear on Brazilian soil, either from animals or from men, but it was not so in the country that we had just traveled; they cited a number of armed highway robberies that had recently been committed there, and they maintained that we had been *fort heureux* not to have been attacked by the vagabond Indians prowling about the edge of Uruguay to pillage travelers."* But the difference was not only in regard to men and animals. On reaching Rio Grande the Frenchman's attention was caught by something unexpected, "an appearance of life and culture contrasting singularly with the desert places where we had just been."*

WHEN THE CAUDILLO, specific product of the rural or Gaucho turbulence, finally started a chain multiplication of himself in the vicinity of Rio Grande, threatening and disturbing our frontiers, the Rio-Grandenses, already taught a lesson by the presence of a traditional enemy, were aware of their political position within the Luso-Brazilian complex. They knew that the former Capitania

[5] The French traveler uses the editorial "we" (as does the author of this book), thus distinguishing himself from the four "countrymen" whom he calls "they." (Translators.)

d'El-Rei was an integral part of a vast country cour-
ageously jealous of its dominions, with a common tradition, and a culture, a language, and a destiny of its own.
The concept of life that had been evolving in the immense area forming Portuguese America made itself felt
in Rio Grande through the increasing incorporation of
elements from other parts of Brazil and from Portugal:
soldiers, settlers, priests, plain merchants. Above all, the
agents of the central government—governors, commanding officers, magistrates, civil and military functionaries—by the mere execution of their duties formed
close ties.

Physical isolation hindered but did not prevent the
constant action of those elements in the social and psychological shaping of Rio Grande do Sul. The peculiarities of the new environment were never an obstacle to
the intercourse of ideas and sentiments with the rest of
Brazil. In our literary history, for example, we sense at
every step the direct, absorbing influence of the Brazilian
master hands.* Our body of popular songs itself is quite
poor in pieces of genuinely "Gauchesque" inspiration.
Augusto Meyer, the man who has best studied it to date,
observes: "As the reader leafs through the *Cancioneiro
Gaúcho*, every time the quatrain catches his eye by its
inimitable freshness, by its beauty as of a never-wither-
ing flower, he can be certain: it is another sprig of the
Portuguese rosemary, the king of herbs, that has fallen
between the pages."* It is the same with the traditional

dances: they immediately disclose what the Rio-Grandense essayist calls the "enormous Portuguese survival."[6]

All of this indicates that we are not an island but an integral part of the immense cultural area that is Brazil. Only one unfamiliar with history can be ignorant of the active participation of our past generations in Brazilian national life. In the newspapers of the cities of Rio Grande do Sul we can see every day the local repercussion of all the events that have struck a responsive chord in Brazilian sensibility anywhere in the country.* That system so appropriate to the Portuguese genius, which Gilberto Freyre interprets and seeks to stimulate—the system of "intimate and constant interrelations between the island of each and the continent of all"*—has been active here in all the stages of our social development.

From the installation of the Captaincy the frontiersmen concentrated on watching over the quiet and integrity of the Portuguese conquest at the only point of its boundary markers disputed by arms. Exposed to perils and aggressions, Rio Grande de São Pedro represented the advance lines of the Luso-Brazilian world, and it was this world that had to be safeguarded against the unremitting fury of the enemy.

---

[6] A Portuguese citizen who has lived in Rio for more than twenty years, attending a performance of folkloric dances here, made this comment: "Since I have been in Brazil, I have never felt so much as if I were back in Portugal as I do here and now." He was visibly moved.

Brazilians from other captaincies, principally São Paulo, natives of Portugal, Azorians, refugees from the Colônia do Sacramento, and afterwards the descendants of those pioneers, would be unswervingly faithful to the mission assigned to them. And from the first they knew that they came here, or that they were born here, to confront and vanquish, at the cost of whatever risk and hardship, the difficulties and obstacles peculiar to a territory fiercely claimed by two crowns eternally at loggerheads.

Such a mission, which would burden generations on end—sometimes, as in the case of the Marques de Souza family, grandfather, son, and grandson joined in the same operations of war[7]—intensified the feeling of national pride. It was the constant presence in the Rio-Grandense mind of a greater fatherland to which they were responsible for their acts or omissions that made them resistant to caudillo contamination. So resistant, indeed, that a great part of their victories were won in the repression of caudillism and in the pursuit of caudillos, from Artigas to Rosas, and from Rosas to Solano López.

When the Farrapos laid down their arms, considering capitulation preferable to seeing Rio Grande exposed to the "iniquities" of caudillism,[8] they showed the measure

[7] This was in the battles following the taking of Montevideo by the Portuguese general Lecor in 1817.
[8] These were the words of Davi Canabarro as he stacked arms in 1845: "A foreign power (he was referring to Rosas) threatens the

of our congenital incompatibility with the institution generated by the hordes infesting the plains on the hither and yonder sides of the Plata.

Caudillism was viewed by the Rio-Grandenses as something to be feared and detested. When Bento Manuel, the indefatigable turncoat, wished to compromise Bento Gonçalves before his followers, his most telling phrase was that the chief of the Revolution was trying to make himself "a second Artigas."[9]

And yet with what frivolous facility certain orators and publicists invoke the caudillo tradition of Rio Grande even today! "Rio Grande, land of caudillos!" How much longer must we hear that ringing untruth? And it costs nothing to open the history of Rio Grande, to review its pages, however skimmingly, to examine the demeanor of its heroes, without a single exception, for us to see that our proverbial caudillo tradition is nothing but a myth.

---

integrity of the Empire; and such stolid audacity would never cease echoing in our Brazilian hearts. Rio Grande will not be the theatre of his iniquities, and we shall share in the glory of sacrificing to Brazil's future our resentments created in the frenzy of party factions."

[9] "Most Illustrious Senhor Manuel Cavalheiro de Oliveira: Considering you always as one of the good citizens of the Province, a lover of peace and order, I am emboldened to send you the enclosed proclamation for Your Grace to bring it to the attention of the gentleman your son, and to do all you can to make him abandon that anarchical party promoted by the ambitious Bento Gonçalves, who at the cost of the innocent blood of his countrymen *wishes to make himself a second Artigas.* . . . (The italics are ours.) I await your reply, and am, with esteem, etc. (signed) Bento Manuel Ribeiro. From the field, March 30, 1836."*

In the full eruption of "Artiguism," or "Artigasism," which worked unchecked on the other side of the border, we have on our side of the line the superb figure of José de Abreu, who rose from private in the Regiment of Dragoons of Rio Grande to be field marshal and holder of a title of the Empire.[1] According to Rio Branco, he fought nineteen battles against the enemy without a single defeat, acquiring the nickname of "Angel of Victory." His men, rough, brave, warlike cowboys to whom Rio Grande owes many of its heroic deeds, rendered him such homage as almost to be religious worship. An order from their chief and friend in any emergency was all that was needed for them to respond unanimously to the call without asking where they would go this time to whip the enemy once more. But as so often happens, the invincible warrior who had contributed so much to eliminate Artigas from the stage of history became the victim of a wretched, gross injustice, which deeply wounded his sense of honor. Brazil's military annals know no example of greater or more stupid ingratitude.* In reaction, did he rebel, or attempt a caudillo-like coup? No. His reaction revealed the high degree of discipline in which the hero had tempered his character. The old marshal preferred the dignity of self-

[1] After defeating the Indian forces under Col. Andresito Artigas (1816), and Uruguayans under Gen. José Gervasio Artigas (1817), Abreu lost a battle to the latter in 1819 only to beat him the next month. Abreu was promoted to field marshal in 1819, and later became Baron de Cêrro Largo. (Translators.)

imposed ostracism. He withdrew and waited for Brazil to summon him again. His wait was not in vain. Called forth once more, he refused the command of a division: a small body of his fellow countrymen, he replied, was enough. In that unit he gathered 343 volunteers, veterans of many encounters, and with them he went to die in the disastrous Battle of the Passo do Rosário, February 20, 1827. He had prophesied the end awaiting him: to the friends who applauded his reappearance he said that he was going to return to war what he had received from it alone.*

EVEN IN A STATE OF REBELLION the Rio-Grandenses managed to keep the movement from degenerating into caudillism. The dominant tendency among the Far-roupilha leaders was decidedly toward the organic forms of institutions. Despite the tremendous vicissitudes of a war that was to drag on for nearly ten years, they were always guided by the principles of civil power without losing sight of the severe ideological obligations for which they had taken up arms. The revolutionaries hastened to elect a president for the Republic of Piratini as soon as the little newborn country was proclaimed in November, 1836. (It should be noted that this act of secession was done in desperation only after a whole year had been spent in vainly trying to make the imperial government understand their cause, which to the Rio-

Grandenses was more than regional and involved not foreigners but Brazilians, "an important body of Brazilians,"* their civil rights and the stability of their economy threatened.) The choice was promptly repudiated as a governmental expedient, and an entirely civil administrative and judiciary structure was adopted. "The laws of the Empire of Brazil," a latecomer enemy of the Farrapos recognizes, "were accepted to regulate all social relations insofar as the conditions of the new governing system permitted: the minutes of the presidential election of Piratini so ordained, and in those minutes the norm of procedure was laid down for the government there inaugurated. The political Constitution of Brazil and its laws were to maintain the conditions of law and order in the new state. The existence of a new association being proclaimed, the legislation must be new: in the impossibility of building it in a trice, there could be no other prudent proposal than the one adopted, that is, to accept as provisional legislation the laws of the country from which it was seceding."*

Bento Gonçalves was elected president with the express instruction to call a Constitutional Convention, and until this could assemble, a council of procurators-general of the municipalities, created by decree dated September 18, 1836, was to be consulted by the chief executive in order that his deliberations "may appear with the seal of rectitude."* In his near-libel against the "wayward subjects" Alencar Araripe did not stray far from the truth when he declared that the Rio-Grandense Republic was nothing but an "ambulant camp." It was, indeed, but what is admirable is that in spite of the mobility which circumstances forced on the rebel government the spirit of fidelity to civil institutions never flagged among the men of 1835; that is, they maintained a vigilant repudiation of despotism, of tyranny, and of violence, all inherent in the configuration of caudillism.

Days of hopes and discouragements, of triumph and depression, of apogee and decline—they experienced it all; but nothing, not even the final defeat, sufficed to lead them into the snares of caudillism. The proud warning with which Canabarro rejected the offer by Rosas is well known: "Sir: The first of your soldiers to step over the border will furnish the blood in which we shall sign the peace of Piratini with the imperial forces, for above our love of the Republic is our self-respect as Brazilians."

All through that decade of blood and the direst of ordeals there was no caudillo,* nor was there anyone who allowed himself to be contaminated by the endemic disease of caudillism: Rio Grande's development was utterly unacquainted, then as always, with the conditions that served to generate the Plata type of caudillo. "In no American country," Ingenieros has asserted, "does economic anarchy persist such as we had from 1810 to 1830; for that reason we find nowhere the primitive, violent, inorganic kind of caudillism, the ravaging troops of mounted insurgent marauders, with no other cohesive force than love of the caudillo."* The motives and ideals that led the Rio-Grandense rebels to the republican experiment of Piratini were not compatible with the tyranny formed by historical and social conditions quite alien to our tradition.

Amid the tangle of misunderstandings on the subject, João Pinto da Silva has placed our aversion to caudillism in proper perspective: "More in contact with the Plata than with Rio de Janeiro, worked upon, in short, by various elements of separatism, Rio Grande, of whose people Brazil was demanding so many hard sacrifices, had probably thought at various opportune moments—and the whole of Rio Grande, not merely the minority as was the case in '35—of making itself autonomous,[2] *if the democratic experience of Uruguay*

[2] We do not know what basis João Pinto da Silva had for the assertion that "Rio Grande had probably thought of making itself autonomous." The imperial sources themselves say the opposite. Take for example the absolutely unassailable Alencar Araripe: "The spirit dominant in the province in a certain period was clearly favorable to rebellion: this sufficiently explains the prolongation of the war, which could be supported only by the benevolent attitude of the localities, finding resources everywhere." The qualification with which Alencar Araripe seeks to protect his position as functionary of the Empire ("in a certain period" of the struggle) is corrected by the rest of the sentence, for it clashes with the phrase "prolongation of the war." It is incomprehensible that the Empire should have had to throw against the Revolution more than half of the national army unless the rebels had the almost solid support of Rio Grande. As for the extent and depth of the support received by the Farrapos cause, let us consult a contemporary wholly above suspicion, Francisco de Sá Brito: "All through the Campanha of the province the revolution found nearly unanimous assent. The principal families, the most prosperous men, the most valiant soldiers, with rare exceptions adhered to the movement of September 20 with an enthusiasm worthy of a better cause."*

*and the anticipated expansionism of Argentina had not
made it realize that, considering the disadvantages of
imminent caudillism* (italics ours), and the risks of annexation by Buenos Aires, the most judicious thing to do
was to remain faithful to the distant and often backward
governments of Rio de Janeiro."*

The movement of '35, which had no affinity whatever to the anarchy that laid waste to the Plata, but on
the contrary was substantially and manifestly connected
with the liberal agitations that at the time shook the
nation from north to south, made very clear its incompatibility with arbitrary solutions. Diligent in the winning of their rights, the Rio-Grandenses did everything
on behalf of the preservation of law and order. Even
after they had proclaimed independence in 1836, all the
laws and provisions of the Empire, from the Constitution
down to simple official announcements, remained in
effect insofar as they did not run contrary to the new
order.

The Farrapos' military command itself took on the
character of a delegated function, since responsibility for
the fate of the cause was in the hands of patriots who did
not give up their privilege of holding and expressing
opinions and who never abdicated their right to think
for themselves and to exert unrestricted influence on the
destinies of the Republic. Criticism did not spare even
the leaders in the highest ranks. In 1841 the opposition to
Bento Gonçalves was so strong that he thought of resigning the presidency and joining the vanguard of the

rebel army as a simple soldier. As he expressed it in a letter to a friend, what he wanted, as a reply to those who were attacking him, was "to give examples of obedience" and thus show what was "the duty of a true republican."*

This was all very different from what happened in the Plata. While Rosas snatched from the timid representative bodies the legalization of his cold, bloody despotism by means of a pompous document, the *Suma del Poder Público*,* Bento Gonçalves appeared at the installation of the Rio-Grandense Constitutional Convention in 1842 and there solemnly resigned his powers.

In later years the peace of Poncho Verde was sealed. But not even the signing of that document was entrusted to the purely military will. On signing it, Canabarro stated the solemn proviso that he was acting "in obedience to the authorization of the civil magistrate."*

SEVEN YEARS AFTER THE SEPTEMBER 20TH COUP the official organ of the Revolution proclaimed its solidarity with the democratic principles defended by Benjamin Constant: "In no society founded upon the sovereignty of the people can any individual or class subject the rest to his or its particular will."* Among the rebels an active sentiment of democratic zeal unquestionably prevailed. And Bento Gonçalves himself would not defy that sentiment. While in full command of the republican forces he refused the privileges of his position and surrendered to arrest in order to make clear the motives of honor which caused his duel with Onofre Pires and the latter's death.[3] Later on, when made the object of recriminations, he did not hesitate to resign the presidency and the general command of the Revolution and submit thenceforth, until the end of the struggle, to Canabarro's leadership. Is it possibly imaginable that so critical a situation as that could have ended in such gallantry, such greatness of heart, if it had occurred in the caudillo atmosphere of the Plata?

Power never went to the revolutionaries' heads. What they wanted more than anything else was local rights and franchises. The Farrapos pledged themselves wholeheartedly, even to the final sacrifice, to set up a political system in Rio Grande that would generously embody their aspirations to autonomy. And what they wanted for themselves they wanted also for their brothers of the other provinces, counting it as certain that national unity would be re-established under the inspiration of the same ideas. Many fellow countrymen from other parts of Brazil shared their sentiments and encouraged them from a distance or directly participated in the struggle.[4]

The episode of the Rio-Grandense republic stands in

[3] The immediate cause of the duel, fought on Feb. 27, 1844, was an insult by Onofre Pires, but this was merely the culmination of friction between the two Farrapos leaders.

[4] Coelho de Souza enumerates the principal elements from other provinces of the Empire, some of them acting decisively in lending the cooperation of their enthusiasm, their intelligence, their goods, and their blood to the Farrapos cause.*

the history of Brazil as one of its noblest and most vigorous chapters. The indefatigable spirit of secession, the capacity for fighting, the bravery of the Brazilians of the extreme South—everything at that time put to the test in epic proportions—belong, surely, to the common heritage of Brazil.

The political principles animating and guiding the warriors of '35 transcended mere regional bounds. Ideologically they were influenced by the resistance to the absolutist presumption of Dom Pedro I, which ran so counter to the liberal spirit rising in all America. Such reactions were soon exacerbated by consequences of the abdication: it aroused great hopes for improved conditions, but the agents of the imperial government in their reactionary bias denied them to the Rio-Grandenses. The revolutionaries went to the extreme of secession and the republic, yet all of it was still the work of Brazilians. And precisely because of this the constitutional plan bequeathed by the Farrapos is legitimately considered as the cradle of Brazilian republican law.*

Placement of the Farrapos War in the perspective of Brazilian revolutions would alone serve to expose the extravagance of any foreign comparisons or connections. But other factors, more profound, less circumstantial, invalidate interpretations that seek to deprive the movement of its national character. Our quest for unity, incompatible with the rudimentary cantonalism of the Platine caudillos, was never extinguished in the hearts of the republicans of '35 at any instant of the struggle. That sentiment Davi Canabarro tried to translate when he invoked "our self-respect as Brazilians."

Social dispersion, absence of economic interests in common, the anarchy of the cattle country, indiscriminate hate, impulses of vengeance—these are the elements that generate the Platine type of caudillo. Disorder wearies of itself, and those who live by it, inspired by the instinct for survival, produce a chief and surrender body and soul to him. That chief is the caudillo. Now there is one law: the will of the chief. Hence the observation that the chief contains within himself the beginning and the end of political parties. When he emerges from chaos, there is no longer any trust in the efficacy of moral forces or of institutions.* Everything comes to cower at his feet in abject submission. This is the very negation of the sense of individual liberty and fidelity to principles that the Farrapos had inherited. The Revolution of '93 was equally devoid of caudillos,* although it was not devoid of violent deeds and crimes natural to a period of institutional transition, factionism, avaricious partisan monopolization, and ideological intolerance.

AND AGAIN WE ASK, why are we so often led to seek outside of our historical development what it refuses to offer? The trouble is that when we incorporated the word "caudillo" into our vocabulary we did not take care to modify its meaning, thus leaving it exposed to the most equivocal of interpretations.

In writing his notable essay on the formation of Rio Grande, Rubens de Barcelos was guilty of that slip. There is no other way to explain his insistence on the Rio-Grandense caudillism to the point of exemplifying it with the stock of the Mena Barretos, whom he enrolls among the "caudillo families" of Rio Grande. The Mena Barretos were by profession the very negation of caudillism.[5] If they can be called caudillos, it is proper to assert that Rio Grande, as public speakers often proclaim, is a land of caudillos. We can accept, by way of compromise, that any corrupt potentials for developing a caudillo here were taken away to flourish far from Rio Grande in an environment less antagonistic to the perils of caudillism. We are thinking, obviously, of Pinheiro Machado and Getúlio Vargas, who carried their dictatorial bent to perfection, each in his own way but on the federal scene.

PINHEIRO MACHADO, who controlled the destinies of so many people, had a very discreet, quite unobtrusive

[5] The record of military services by the Mena Barreto family would be extraordinary in any country. The first Mena Barreto in Brazil was a general sent by Portugal to command the Captaincy of Rio Grande in the latter seventeenth century. His descendants include seventy distinguished names in Brazilian military history, according to a list dated 1931, and the line continues unbroken since that year.

influence on the internal business of his State of origin. A
little story that is still being repeated today[6] may perhaps
exemplify the signs that warned him to be cautious in his
relations with Rio Grande. On one of his visits to his
native region he was received at the Tupanciretã station
by the highlands leader Firmino de Paula, an old political
friend, and they began chatting, a little apart from the
group of republicans crowded together on the platform.
Pinheiro, as though to see without being seen, surrep-
titiously pulled his panama down over his eyes, thus
placing his interlocutor in an awkward strategic position.
But the Cruz Alta politician, not to be put at a disad-
vantage, bluntly showed his annoyance. Completely self-
possessed, he twitched up the brim of the senator's hat
and told him: "Pinheiro! I'm not in the habit of talking
to anybody I can't look straight in the eye." The all-
powerful chief found it wise to accept the situation with
as good grace as he could muster.

Our state was certainly not an area to which Pinheiro
Machado could extend his long rampant political empire
with impunity.

[6] The story was told by Dr. José Vasconcelos Pinto, former councilman and political chief of Cruz Alta. A militant lawyer, he had been
state deputy from the Republican Party, now extinct, of Rio Grande
do Sul, and now lives in Pôrto Alegre after many years' residence in
Rio. [José Gomes Pinheiro Machado, born 1852 in Rio Grande do
Sul, became a general in the war against the revolutionaries of 1893.
He had served in the Constitutional Congress of 1891, and was
elected senator that same year. For more than twenty years he was
head of the Conservative Republican Party. He was assassinated in
1915, stabbed in the back in a Rio de Janeiro hotel. (Translators.)]

AND WHAT OF GETÚLIO VARGAS? As everyone knows, breaking the democratic pledges of the Frente Unica (the coalition resulting from his "honeymoon" with the opposition) he betook himself and his "gentle caudillo"[7] notions a long way from Rio Grande to a place he deemed more propitious for fomenting and manipulating conditions that would aid his dictatorial adventure. Immediately after the establishment of his discretionary government not only the Party of the Liberator but the Republican Party itself, both at that time in harmony with the same ideals of political regeneration, hastened to interpose warnings and to express fears. Getúlio Vargas, however, already sure of his means of action, responded with enigmatic noncommittal expressions to the admonitions from his distant province.

IT MAY BE OBJECTED that Rio Grande do Sul had a dictatorial constitution—Castilhos's positivist document of July 14, 1891—which at bottom was merely a stylized variant of caudillo tendencies. The theory is not gratuitous. In his book, which by the way is inspired by keen sympathy with Rio Grande, José Honório Rodrigues, historiographer and essayist of great competence, says

[7] "The *caudillo manso*," as Ayarragaray defines the term, "lived by plotting intrigues and planning outrages, but craftily, and even when caught red-handed in his machination he would try to wriggle out of it."*

that "it would be puerile not to see that the positivist doctrine is a superficial coating, a body of ideas which at a given moment served the type historically formed in the Continente."* But this theory collides squarely with historical and sociological truth. No bond necessarily exists between the Comtist order and the sociopolitical designs of Rio Grande. Our development is alien to the motives that led the authors of the first republican institutions to the "scientific dictatorship" attempted there. The truth is that those men, or rather Júlio de Castilhos, who absorbed them, imbibed from the exotic springs of an imported philosophy, as highly influential among us as it is indiscriminately in other centers of Brazil, through the vigorous preaching of the advocates of the positivist charter.* The liberal tendencies of Rio Grande had been so contravened by the republican leaders that the institutional diploma they bequeathed to us would in the space of three decades provoke no less than two bloody revolutions—in 1893 and in 1923—without counting the state of constant political tension implanted in us during that period, generating conflicts and dissensions. Let us not forget, either, that it was as "a permanent ally of the sword," in the words of Carlos Dante de Moraes—and "sword" here means the military cloak supplied by the Union—that Júlio de Castilhos won success for his political doctrine. The same writer synthesizes "the tremendous reactions" unleashed by the patriarch. "That mystic of order," he says, "supported by the fanaticism of his adepts, also provoked disorder. He was a great disturber through the combative force of his convictions."* Castilhos was indeed a force that launched itself against the tide. His action was classed as a challenge to the dominant tendency in Rio-Grandense political thought. Both in '93 and in '23 it was the pressure of public opinion that armed and hurled the rebel forces against the Castilhista citadel. And it was under the impact of revolutionary arms that the democratic principles guiding our tradition opened a way into the closed dictatorial texts of the old basic law of Rio Grande. Only thereafter did we begin living in an atmosphere that would permit the reconciling of the two parties in the Liberal Alliance.

BUT WE MUST NOT FORGET the positive aspects of the political cycle ended by the Pact of Pedras Altas.[8] The late Republican Party of Rio Grande succeeded in forming, in the shadow of the July 14 Charter, a government that in a certain way responded to one aspect of Rio-Grandense history. Doctrinarily it was as if someone tried to force our inclination for the organic forms of social coexistence and of government into the hard molds of so-called scientific dictatorship. The opposition

[8] The treaty ending the Revolution of 1923, signed in the Castelo de Pedras Altas, the residence of the civilian chief of the revolution, J. F. de Assis Brasil.

it stirred up because of its intolerance and sectarianism caused much bloodshed; however, it would not be absurd to admit that the habits of discipline created and developed by the action of the former military commanders, by the militia system,* and by the organization of the ranches, even though misused or carried to extremes, were of use to the regime imposed on Rio Grande by Castilhism and the powerful federal cover on which Castilhism relied.

Unfortunately the old republicans closed their minds to the liberal tradition dominating the Rio-Grandense political process. Had it not been for that grave error they would have shaped longer-lasting institutions.

It is well to recognize further—and it is not difficult to do so with the perspective of time—that the legacy of Castilhism reveals intolerance and sectarianism. In spite of that, Rio Grande owes to it, because of the austerity and asceticism of the first republican leaders, a high degree of immunity to oligarchy. While in the majority of states the exercise of power belonged to the old family clans, republican Rio Grande was successful in moving in another direction. Outrages or wrongs, persecutions or violent actions, all these are stains on the history of political parties, but it is undeniable that everything was done for the sake of the party.

The policy of hard exclusivism, of monopoly of public affairs, had a salutary effect by way of contrast: it served as a stimulus to an intrepid, tenacious opposition, the roots of which were nourished precisely on the liberal vigor of '35, which the situationist party had been so imprudent as to dismiss. That fidelity to democracy gave the Rio-Grandense opposition the vitality that permitted it to bridge the long recess imposed on partisan organizations by the Vargas dictatorship. The small Liberator Party was, in fact, the only one in the whole country that survived the devastation.

The coexistence of genuine parties that sometimes even resorted to armed violence in defense of their principles, undoubtedly gave the political life of Rio Grande do Sul an individual stamp within the Brazilian scene. Here conditions did not flourish propitious to the establishment of those vicious oligarchic forms of government installed in so many parts of Brazil by the republican regime. Just as Rio Grande was unacquainted with the military oligarchies attributed to it by Oliveira Viana,* it knew no civil oligarchies, either.

WHERE, THEN, IS THE SUPPOSED CAUDILLISM of Rio Grande? The social, economic, moral, and political conditions that originated the type in the Plata area were utterly and conspicuously foreign to us. These conditions led Ayarragaray to conclude that caudillism was the "positive constitution" of Argentina, even though party hypocrisy or the naïveté of theorists may have, as the same author observes, attempted to cover up "those congenital monstrosities"* with imported doctrines.

Much the same can be said of the tumultuous phase of Uruguayan history. It led Zum Felde to this conclusion, basically identical with Ayarragaray's dictum: "The caudillo is an economico-moral fact that cannot be abolished by any constitution."* Without those conditions the real caudillo type cannot take shape. There are no spontaneously generated caudillos. The caudillo presupposes a well-characterized social infrastructure: that condition of Gaucho anarchy unknown to Rio-Grandense history inside its frontiers. Here is how Ingenieros sums up the "fundamental premises" of caudillism:

"1.—Lack of unity of interests determines a state of economic anarchy, which is the 'substructure' of political caudillism.

"2.—The political 'superstructure' of the anarchic atmosphere is caudillism; when the action of the groups is not determined by collective interests, the personal influence of the caudillo is the sole link that makes common cause of the action.

"3.—The organization and reciprocal subordination of the caudillos constitutes a special political system: caudillism."*

In Argentina the pressure of that infrastructure made itself felt with such force that not even the cassock was immune against it. Son of a modest, respectable couple in Mendoza, Félix Aldao, despite having taken holy orders, renounced the cloth to set himself up as general and caudillo—and burden himself with crimes.*

AGAIN THE QUESTION ARISES: where and when was there any Rio-Grandense caudillism? It is surely time now to take our famous caudillo down off his equivocal pedestal. The characteristics of the representative Rio-Grandense in a position of command are different, less arrogant, less ominous. They are the characteristics evident in our traditional leaders, military or civilian, our valiant, disciplined warriors, our colonels, our figures of political influence in rural communities. In these types no mark whatever is symptomatic of the elements that engendered the genuine caudillo: social chaos, resentment of the rural populace, chronic revolt that turned the Plata Gaucho against civilization. Our "caudillo" was never certain just where the city ended and the country began. Country and city to him blended in the same interests. His actions were always within the framework of military regulations or party discipline, within a hierarchy that never granted him full autonomy of action. The constancy of war had awakened in the average citizen of Rio Grande, without distinction of rank or social class, what Oliveira Viana called "the consciousness of the necessity of governments," emphasizing at the same time that this did not happen in the Plata region "where the Gaucho was treated as an enemy and combated."*

Conditions so different, even so contrary to those that engendered the Artigas, the Quirogas, the Bustos, the Rosas, the Aldaos, the Latorres,[9] in the turbulent dependencies of the old Viceroyalty of La Plata, could not account for caudillos in Rio Grande. For want of a propitious atmosphere, certain men born here, thirsting for authoritarianism, either stir up revolutionary protest or go try their luck outside of Rio Grande. The worst of it is that occasionally they are successful.

The topographic similarity between our plains and the pampas on which the Platine Gaucho emerged is well known. Rio Grande, too, spreads out in vast open spaces —those south of the Jacuí and the Ibicuí, as far as the eye can see, and those of the old Vacaria do Pinhal, which includes the fields of Cima da Serra. On the prairies of the Campanha,[1] between routine labors and skirmishes with the Castilians, the Rio-Grandense *gaúcho* molded his individuality as a cowboy and soldier, with the attributes recorded by history and exalted by legend. But the contribution of natural factors to the psychological development of the Platine Gaucho and the Rio-Grandense *gaúcho* was very different in each case.

[9] All these are names of caudillos of Argentina and Uruguay. Artigas, Juan Facundo Quiroga, Rosas, and Aldao have been identified above, either in text or in footnotes; Bustos made himself dictator of Córdoba province in the early nineteenth century, and Latorre was dictator-president of Uruguay for more than ten years until he resigned in 1889 and went to Argentina. (Translators.)

[1] Here "Campanha" clearly refers to the southern third (and more) of the state. The two rivers named flow east and west, respectively, at the latitude of Pôrto Alegre. South of the Jacuí river basin a good deal of rather mountainous terrain interrupts the plains. (Translators.)

The pampa, which absorbed and concealed every-thing in its immensity—the stubborn resistance of the natives, the rebelliousness of the mestizos, the resentment of the displaced, and the adventurers, and the deserters, and the criminals—was the great accomplice of the Gaucho rabble that kept the provinces of the Plata in such tumult. Beyond the law, hostile to the "Goth," inimical to the city, and incompatible with any form of social organization, "the pariahs of the plains" found refuge in the desert, and there, safe from surprise at-tacks, free of police repression, they became inviolable in their aggressiveness. The endless open spaces were an invitation to all who wanted to join the natives and the human parasites in quest of impunity for their crimes, hides for smuggling, retaliation, or sheer adventure.

Nature was not limited to a purely passive role in the matter. It immediately became an accomplice of these socially negative elements and ended by throwing them against civilization. Shortly those diffuse territorial powers would find their point of crystallization in the somber figure of the caudillo. On the Luso-Brazilian side, however, it was precisely in the country region, scene of our war and pastoral labors, that a different social type emerged.

THE DIFFERENCE IS EXPLICABLE. From the earliest times of the Continente no one, not even the mightiest, felt tempted to disrespect the agents of the law. The case of Rafael Pinto Bandeira is a good illustration. Through his extraordinary feats the celebrated frontiersman, who had won his spurs "chasing off" the Spaniards, enjoyed an overwhelming prestige that enthralled the whole Captaincy, spread to the Colônia, and made a great stir at the Court itself, from which, through royal conveyances, came generous demonstrations of gratitude to him. When this hero was acrimoniously accused by Governor José Marcelino de Figueiredo, maligned and despoiled of all his property, he allowed himself to be arrested, appeared at the hearing presided over by his accuser, and, ordered to Rio de Janeiro, immediately went to defend himself against the "crimes" attributed to him by the governor.[2] The City Council of Pôrto Alegre convened in outrage and protested the innocence of the Commander of the Frontier. Other bodies, lay and religious, expressed themselves to the same effect, alleging that the hero of São Martinho and Santa Tecla, besides being the "redeemer of the Continente," was a man with "clean hands."

Public opinion was in an uproar. Nothing more than a gesture from the brave warrior would have been necessary for his enemy to be deposed and expelled from the Captaincy. Pinto Bandeira, however, considered that he

---

[2] The whole proceeding has been published in the *Revista do Museu e Arquivo do Rio Grande do Sul*, No. 23. It runs to more than five hundred pages.

should be the first to set an example of respect for the law. And so he did. And when he returned from Rio de Janeiro, fully acquitted, he was confirmed in his high post. There was no longer room in Rio Grande de São Pedro for José Marcelino de Figueiredo.*

In this manner a tradition of respect for law and order was gradually established, and that tradition, contrary to what happened in the Plata, never suffered a break in continuity here, remaining intact ever since the erection of the Presidio. With the proclamation of the Rio-Grandense Republic in 1836, authority was to divide into two parts but not to disappear. "Nothing changed in the laws," as Pandiá Calógeras says, "save in regard to the persons encharged with their execution."*

In the Platine dependencies any attempts at social organization came to grief against the benighted, vengeful fury of the turbulent rural populations.

The men of '35 broke with the Empire but remained faithful to the habits of juridical and social discipline. Further, as Wilson Martins has very accurately observed, "*gaúcho* militarism, individualistic and based on personal courage, is of an essentially civil nature, is more the affirmation of the citizen than of the soldier."* That is precisely why the Farroupilha leaders constantly sought to safeguard legal institutions. They were to lose everything in the course of ten long years of fighting—their goods, their lives, their very cause—but they never lost their zeal for the civil organization of the revolu-

tionary order. One of their first cares was the adoption
of the rights and guarantees assured by the imperial
Charter, until such time as the Constitution of the Republic could be drawn up.

IN OPPOSITION TO THE TENDENCY of the rustic populations toward dispersion and banditry, under the stimulus
of cattle rustling, we have already stressed the disciplin-
ing action of the ranch. That same action became even
more efficient in moments of danger, when the rancher,
in the King's service or guarding his own lands and
herds, gathered his men together and set himself up as
militia chief for the occasion, ready for whatever might
come.[3] The *sesmarias* soon covered the conquered areas,
quickly reaching as far as the new political boundaries.
With the banditry that once reigned there reduced, our
cowboys had their movements limited by the dominating
presence of the ranch. Our *gaúcho* knew that, no matter
how limitless the fields might seem, he would eventually
run into the Castilian frontier, that constant menace
demanding the community of all under the authority
and protection of a chief who was the first to recognize
the valor of the peons because he struggled side by side
with them in the hard work of cattle-raising and in the
battles with the enemy.

The Brazilian *gaúcho*, when one considers the

[3] "The ranches gradually advanced, and on them the combatants
found all the innumerable resources required by war—men, animals,
transportation, food."*

dominant cultural traits of his character, is less im-memorial than may appear in an imaginative examination of the facts. The foundations of his origins and descent have not yet been lost in the dust of time. It is from the stuff of pioneers that he descends. Paulistas from Laguna and from Piratininga, people from several captaincies, natives of Portugal, refugees from the Colônia do Sac-ramento, the numerous families of the prolific Azorians —these are the earliest sources of the man who took to the southern plains and became cowboy and soldier. Rem-nants of old adventurers—Indians or mestizos—who had stayed on this side of the frontier, they were also ab-sorbed and finally fused into the *gaúcho* type. The factor that imprinted shape on the rural community was not really the *galpão,* the shed for animals and imple-ments, nor the rough, isolated huts, nor the deserted plains, but the proud, authoritarian ranch, which cen-tralized all the activities of the countryside and from which the boss sallied forth for pastoral occupations or war, on a par with the *gaúchos.*

As could not fail to happen, we have also had the influence of African blood,* and not just in the narrow household environment, nor even only in the work of drying beef. Field work chores also depended on the Negro but that did not prevent his becoming a good cowboy and a good soldier. In the Farrapos War many slaves won their freedom by their heroism. One of the most gallant figures of '35, Joaquim Teixeira Nunes, had under his command a body of Negro lancers who gained renown for their mobility and the impetus of their charges.*

The indigenous blood that mingled with that of the pioneers was not sufficient to affect the Luso-Brazilian way of life. The heathen did not achieve a decisive role in the tragic antagonisms characteristic of Platine history.

If the aborigines transmitted to the pioneers some of their nomenclature and practices connected with pastoral life, they themselves were never utilized other than individually in the militias or in field work. The half-breed of white and native was undoubtedly common in rural society, but at no time were his numbers of any consequence.

It is clear that the Rio-Grandense *gaúcho* cannot at any moment of his history be confused with the barbaric or semibarbaric type of the Platine guerrilla marauders. For good or ill, politically he knew where he came from, and the constant incidents with the Castilians reminded him at every moment of his proper role on the frontier. The risks to which Brazil's boundaries on the extreme south were exposed obliged every able-bodied man, and even the women, to keep a tense, continual vigil. And for more than a hundred years the Continentinos, always under arms, were to have no rest in the rude task of watching over the conquest. Not even babies were safe from such vicissitudes. Perhaps that is the cause of the

precociously grave air which Saint-Hilaire noticed in
their faces: they did not look so much like infants as like
little old men. In sober truth there was no minimum limit
for recruitment, for the career of arms frequently com-
menced at the age of twelve! Osório, who was to be the
legendary warrior of Rio Grande, was barely seven
when he first accompanied his father on his soldiering,
and it was from military regulations, for lack of other
texts, that he learned to spell.*

DURING the whole critical period of its history, Rio
Grande do Sul was a military commandery with practically no other problems than the defense and spread of
the conquest. This situation alone would suffice for the
territory to take on a peculiar sociological function.
Despite its constituting a natural encouragement to nomadism, it would cease to be a simple no-man's-land, the
refuge of Indians, cattle raiders, criminals, or bandits. In
comparison with the conditions of life on the trans- or
cisplatine pampas, the Rio-Grandense would generate
habits only externally similar, for the strategic demands
on our side were very shortly to prevail over the ecological. "In the formation of our collective character,"
João Pinto da Silva had already remarked, "physical
geography had much less influence than political geography."* It was really political reasons that promoted
the conquest of the southern frontier of Brazil, a fact
causing the occupation of Rio Grande de São Pedro to

appear as an operation complementary to the Colônia do Sacramento. The latter in its turn was a delayed consequence of the nationalism revived by the restoration of Portugal in 1640.

BESIDES THE HABITS OF DISCIPLINE deriving from the kind of life imposed on us by circumstances, other agents of social containment made themselves felt here. The very rigidity of military authority* contributed to the acceptance of a less severe discipline created by a civilian community whose cohesion was the tighter for the assaults of an enemy greedy for lands and equally ready for fighting. We have seen the influence exerted in that respect by the great ranchers and the centers of population that were being planted throughout the Campanha, nearly always close to the military encampments.

The frontiersmen of Rio Grande, in contrast to events on the other side of the border, were immediately caught up in the full tide of national integration, which swept along in the same constructive impulse elements of the most varied origin and condition, all of them, like the old Lusitanians, still in the service of the same empire: men from Santa Catarina, from São Paulo, from Rio de Janeiro, Minas Gerais, Bahia, the Kingdom, the Colônia do Sacramento, from the Islands—and Indians, and Negroes, and half-breeds.

All contributed their share to the common task and to the elaboration of the social type in whose veins all those bloods mingled. Later on, the frontiers quiet, other people came in great masses to lend new coloration and new values to that mixture. By that time Rio Grande had already built its warrior legend.

THE CAPTAINCY GOVERNMENT, the barracks, the regular troops, the militias, were local expressions of loftier institutions whose operation went on uninterrupted. Before, in the time of the Colônia, the sovereign was a distant one but present in his authority, a king known to be attentive to the overseas reaction to the detailed instructions, letters, and admonitions that he handed down, and zealous of the conduct of his vassals. The lands conquered in his name all passed into his dominions, and only he or his agents could bestow them in small parcels or in *sesmarias*. The omnipresence of the monarch was signalized at every step by the names in vogue: Capitania d'El-Rei, Rincão d'El-Rei, Milícias d'El-Rei, Campanhas d'El-Rei, Casais d'El-Rei.[4] There were, apart from the *royal* depots, the great *royal* ranches of Bojuru and Capão Cumprido and the"*Real* Feitoria do Linho Cânhamo."[5] Military service, to which all were obligated,

[4] The first, second, and fourth are geographic names, the third is self-evident in meaning, and the last denominates the Azorian married couples sent to southern Brazil and known as "Couples of the King." (Translators.)

[5] The "Royal Hemp Establishment," installed in 1783, was an official agricultural station for growing hemp, with a ropewalk to manufacture the end product. It did not last very long. The city of São Leopoldo, north of Pôrto Alegre, stands now on the site.

was par excellence *o Serviço do Rei,* "the Service of the King," and there were things that could be done only with royal license, such as the sale of gunpowder and playing cards.

The king, through the insistent invocation of his name and royal will, thus ceased to be a remote, intangible symbol. It would not be easy to evade the injunctions of his laws or the enormous sense of unity of the Lusitanian empire. Rafael Pinto Bandeira, the "intrepid and determined" warrior who had stirred the Continente with his exploits, did not consider himself exempt from going to the Courts at Lisbon, there to receive from the very hands of Dona Maria I the medals he had merited, besides tributes never before given to any Brazilian.* How justly proud he must have been as he returned to his Continente! The valiant commander of the frontier, conscious of his vassalage, had been personally received by the ruler of the immense Luso-Brazilian and other more distant worlds.[6]

With the coming of Dom João VI to Brazil in 1807 and with the subsequent reigns of Dom Pedro I (1821–31) and Dom Pedro II (1840–89, after Regency 1831–40), the monarch's geographic proximity en-

[6] "Colonialism gave a permanent, organic character to the accidental fact of the discovery. And it also gave the transoceanic spirit that characterizes the rulers, the governors, the explorers, those who came with the desire not to stay, and also those who came to stay, like the missionaries, for they all turned to the great cities as though to the seat of a superior culture, the sole refuge, however uncertain and distant, of the intellectual elements of formation and for that reason of emancipation."*

hanced the centralizing fascination of his power and majesty. Acquaintance with the evolution of Farroupilha thinking suffices to make us sense the profound respect which the rebels themselves held for the institutions of the Empire. It was the power of this tradition that tempered them, moderating their outbursts of rebelliousness. A minimum of comprehension on the part of the Regency, and all wrongs would have been forgotten, and the Revolution would have gone no further than the armed protest of September 20, 1835. Along this same line, there is no ignoring the powerful influence exerted on the minds of the Farrapos by the proclamation of the child-emperor's majority in 1840. From that point, with the political genius of Caxias at the forefront of events, the disarming of aroused minds began smoothing the way toward pacification. How symptomatic in its touching sincerity is the heartfelt sigh of Canabarro as arms were stacked: "At last we are Brazilians again."

The process of Rio-Grandense development at any of its stages invariably underwent the catalytic action of the capital. No one who has ever thumbed through the testimonies of our past, whether of history, politics, economy, folklore, journalism, literature, or theater,[7]

[7] With regard to the Rio-Grandense theater, João Pinto da Silva denies it any importance, and as for the "typically regional," he says, "there is nothing, in fact, in our theater. . . . In that as in many other things, we have been and continue to be tributaries of the Plata."* Nothing could be less true. Athos Damasceno has delved painstakingly into our archives, going through all the newspapers and

can fail to sense the preëminence of the common bonds
of nationality over the complex of regional life. Proof of
our centripetism is evident in the work of figures such as
Joaquim Caetano da Silva, Araújo Pôrto Alegre, Mauá,
Gaspar Martins, Plácido de Castro, Assis Brasil,[8] and so

---

magazines of the past century in a study that lasted years on end, and
out of the meticulous inventory resulting from his researches there is
nothing, not a shadow of anything at all, that can justify Pinto da
Silva's statement. As far as the last part of the above quotation is
concerned, the present chapter, like the rest of this book, seeks to
demonstrate and to document the contrary. Our subordination to the
Plata is merely an unfounded surmise. In the field of the local theater
the Luso-Brazilian character is an invariable constant.*

[8] All Rio-Grandenses, these men contributed to Brazil in many fields:
J. C. da Silva (1810–73), educated in France, taught in Rio de Janeiro;
was appointed chargé d'affaires in the Netherlands, where he did
research on the Treaty of Utrecht; wrote books on the Brazil-French
Guiana boundary and on the Amazon; served as Director of Public
Education, and of the National Archives.

Manuel de Araújo Pôrto-Alegre, Baron Santo Ângelo (1806–79),
educated in Europe, a musicologist and poet, founded the Conserva-
tory of Dramatic Art and the Imperial Academy of Opera.

Irineu Evangelista de Sousa, Baron Mauá (1813–89), organized
Bank of Brazil (1851), and Brazil's first railway (1854); he headed the
largest shipyards in South America, an illuminating gas company, and
the Amazon Navigation Company.

Gaspar da Silveira Martins (1835–1901), was successively municipal judge, national deputy, Minister of Treasury, and national
senator.

José Plácido de Castro (1873–1908), a rebellious spirit from military school days, joined rebels in Revolution of 1893 and became a
major. Refused amnesty in 1895. Engaged in rubber production in
Acre 1899, he was put in command of Brazilian forces in the 1902
move to annex that territory, and defeated Bolivian army. Retiring to
private life, he was assassinated by political enemies.

Joaquim Francisco de Assis Brasil (1857–1938), minister plenipo-
tentiary to Argentina, Portugal, and the U.S., member of the Constitutional Assembly, president of Rio Grande do Sul, and author of a
number of books. (Translators.)

many others, not to mention current examples, or the enormous and decisive military participation by Rio Grande, inside and outside its borders, in the defense of the honor and the territorial integrity of Brazil. As for our contribution in blood, could it be necessary to remember that thirty per cent of the Brazilian forces sent against López[9] in 1865 came from our rolling hills, a scant twenty years after the Peace of Poncho Verde had been signed? It was not without reason that Joaquim Nabuco declared that the Rio-Grandenses had given Brazil *at least* half of her military legends.*

Our own revolutions, whether through their ideologies, or through their political ties, and even through the geographic direction of their plans and onslaughts, have always been animated by consciousness of belonging to the nation.

This national inclination for unity is one of the legacies we owe to the agglutinating genius of the Portuguese, the genius that never ceased acting decisively in the formation of Brazil, often in spite of the errors or the unreasonableness of Lisbon and its functionaries. In the Plata, as Ayarragaray shows,* the evolution from family to village, from village to district, from district to province, took place among convulsions, and would be

[9] Francisco Solano López (1827–70), after serving Paraguay in high diplomatic posts, succeeded his father as president in 1862. He invaded and occupied Mato Grosso in 1864, invaded Rio Grande do Sul and declared war on Argentina in 1865. Brazil, Argentina, and Uruguay finally conquered and killed him in 1870. (Translators.)

consolidated in successive stages only after the devastating cycle of caudillism had been overcome. In Rio Grande do Sul, precisely because we did not experience resistance from the nomad forces of the Platine plains and deserts against the march of conquest, the social and political process of incorporation was entirely different. The town of Rio Grande once initiated was subsequently enlarged with its "continent," that is, with the lands adjacent to it,* and afterwards with the lands occupied peacefully or won by arms. And once new frontiers were attained, the areas embraced therein passed without internal resistance to the jurisdiction of the new town founded by Silva Pais. The hostilities came from the outside, and their effect was to alert the vigilance of the pioneers and to tighten their bonds. According to João Pinto da Silva, "It was the frontier that gave historical physiognomy to Rio Grande."*

When the word "Gaucho," which appears to be of Quechua origin, crossed the Rio Grande border to take root here and spread, the mutation it underwent was not limited to the abrupt shift of syllable stress. Indeed, the appellative "*gaúcho*" was fitted to another social type, one with a different ethnic and psychological composition, a different historical orientation, and political commitments rigorously subordinated to those of Brazil as a whole.

VI

The Frontier &
the Language

WE SAW in the Introduction to these chapters that
the poet Humberto de Campos, even though spe-
cifically ill-informed on the historical and social background of Rio Grande do Sul, nevertheless felt not the
least constraint in declaring that the language spoken here
is not really Portuguese. Years later Afonso Arinos said
exactly the contrary. Writing about a Rio-Grandense
book,* he emphasized that as far as language is concerned we are the most conservative writers in Brazil
today.

The Minas Gerais essayist begins by bringing out
certain aspects of the problem of style as an expression
of provincial or antiprovincial expression in its regional

incidences, and the better to accentuate or characterize the divergence between the two types of style—which he compares, respectively, to the baroque and the classic —he contrasts the northeastern writers and those of the extreme South.

The celebrated critic, as we understand it, thinks that the literature of the Northeast, revolting against the conventional molds of the language, seeks its new measures in the natural forces of the land. In his virgin communion with things the writer once more finds himself encountering the sources of instinct itself. Hence from that world can emerge only crudely baroque, anticlassical forms. Everything agitated, then, but in that germinative ferment in which great phenomena rise. It is therefore hoped that in that steaming mixture of humus and human vigor, formless, powerful, the gestation of the word that is to come is working, being shaped—the "new, pure style."

While things in the Northeast appear thus to Afonso Arinos, he observes quite the contrary in the notable authors of current Rio-Grandense literature: faithful to the traditional standards of the language, they accommodate themselves within a style that is actually, because of its urban, conservative expression, the very negation of the regional. The critic recognizes that Creole[1] subjects still occupy the major place in our literary produc-

---

[1] Here the author seems to narrow the meaning of "Creole" to "southern Brazilian," or even to "Rio-Grandense." (Translators.)

tions, but he remarks that we treat local themes with more intelligence than creative emotion. The material offered us by the environment is dominated, absorbed, by a vigilant art animated by a power of concentration that opposes the free influence of telluric forces.

Contrasts are always fascinating. It even seems that the very snares they set for us are seductive. One, perhaps the greatest, of those pitfalls is simplifying to undue extremes the values we are dealing with. The reciprocal simplification, called for by the opposition seeking to exhibit itself, leads to operations that do not always offset each other and for that reason often misrepresent or at least strain the reality of the terms placed in divergence. How can one ignore, for example, the vigorously classic frame of a Graciliano Ramos[2] in weighing the typical or representative literature of the Northeast? Deprived of one of its substantial expressions, the picture would certainly be incomplete.

However that may be, it is incontestable that among the Rio-Grandense writers, contemporary or past, the conservativism pointed out by Afonso Arinos prevails, as regards language. Whether the authors are of Portuguese or other racial extractions, the literature being created here—fiction, poetry, or essay—all but invari-

[2] Considered one of the masters of Brazilian prose style (1892–1953), his best novels are *Angústia* and *Vidas Sêcas*, but his masterpiece is the four-volume *Memórias do Cárcere* (Prison Memoirs), product of his unjust sentence to the penal colony of Ilha Grande in the 1930's.* (Translators.)

ably relies upon the fundamental structure of the language, which moreover serves to prove that that structure is much more plastic than the purists suppose. To demonstrate it there is the same group of writers cited by the critic—Alcides Maya, Augusto Meyer, João Pinto da Silva, Erico Verissimo, Viana Moog, André Carrazoni, Dionélio Machado, Athos Damasceno[3]—and to that group could be added the names of other Rio-Grandense novelists, poets, and essayists of the old generation and the new. It is curious that the formal zeal for the language among the descendants of old immigrants is even greater, if such a thing is possible, than among those of pure Lusitanian stock. When they win recognition in literature or in journalism they do not bring with them the slightest accent of foreign origin. Some carry devotion to their adoptive language to such a degree that the archaic odor of old texts can be scented in some of them.

The tendency to observe, substantially, the vernacular tradition is revealed even in the strict field of regionalism, if we discount the *arriviste* sub-literature, which tries to pass by dint of impertinent Castilianisms. Simões Lopes Neto, the greatest, the most genuine of our regionalists, has not escaped the rule. In spite of his Hispanicisms, so many of them needless, in spite of the satiety of idioms to which he resorts, he still leaves clear

---

[3] All these men are Rio-Grandense novelists, poets, essayists, historians, and critics of literature, most of them still active. (Translators.)

and clean the "classic savor" that Aurélio Buarque de Holanda saw in the *Contos Gauchescos* and in the *Lendas do Sul*. With the same insight Augusto Meyer studied the preliminary drafts of our great rustic rhapsody, *Antônio Chimango*, and in his lucid analysis he makes this observation: "Every emendation, little by little, must contribute to the balance of poetic expression, in a very personal encounter between the language of the pastoral countryside and the canonical habits of controlled style." Thus the Rio-Grandense essayist sees Ramiro Barcelos's compromise between milieu and tradition, giving us the most delightful satiric poem of Brazil.* As for Alcides Maya, he resorts to dialectal vocabulary with palpable constraint; it is enough to say that in his crisp prose local words frequently appear in italics or within quotation marks. His baroque, which in Afonso Arinos's classification ought to identify him with the forces and inspirations of the land, shows no telluric influence whatever: he is of purely cultural extraction. Darcy Azambuja and Ciro Martins are two who without artifice harmonize regional coloring with the permanent standards of the language. In this sense the work of both is exemplary, constituting, moreover, by their fidelity to the accents of their home district, a source of valuable contributions to the Brazilian lexicon. That shows that our "classicism," even though corruption of the language is repugnant to it, does not keep its windows closed to the renovating breeze of time and environment.

Take the case of Mário Quintana. I know of none of today's great poets of Brazil better qualified to circulate freely throughout the country, precisely because of the purity of his language. And let it not be said that Mário Quintana has been insensible to the legitimate exigencies of contemporary poetry.

This deep-rooted fidelity to the language reveals unforeseen aspects. As is well known, Gumercindo Saraiva, although born in Rio Grande, grew up in Uruguay and there forgot the language of his own people. Well, as one story about him goes, in the Revolution of '93 one of his companions asked him one day why he did not speak Portuguese instead of Spanish. To which the great Maragato[4] leader retorted with sardonic humor: "If I've got to mistreat a language, I prefer to mistreat somebody else's."

At first sight there seems to be a certain contradiction between the care for the preservation of the language and the singularity of Rio Grande's development within the national framework. Considering the near-isolation of the old Luso-Brazilian groups that came to this distant region as settlers and soldiers, was it not to be expected that we should break away from our cultural inheritance and that the language should end by falling apart into the most remote regional subdialect?

Put that way, the question is not framed in its proper

[4] Term applied to the federalists of Rio Grande who rebelled against the republicans in power in 1893. Saraiva led the first federalist invasion of Rio Grande in February, 1893, and despite inadequate

terms, of course. The physical isolation of Rio Grande was considerably mitigated by the political imperative of its conquest and settlement. That circumstance required a constant link with the rest of the Viceroyalty. The bonds established from the beginning never suffered a rupture or break in continuity, having withstood even the temporary separatism of the Farrapos War.

Afonso Arinos shows us the key to the problem of our language in suggesting that the politico-geographic position of Rio Grande upholds the fact that "today the 'Gaúchos'[5] are the most conservative writers of Brazil, as far as language is concerned." Although he dwells on the interpretation of that fact no longer than necessary for a fleeting aside, without a doubt it contains the profound reason, less deliberate than involuntary, for our writers' conservative, or organic, tendencies. We are situated, as Arinos so well observes, on the "corruptible frontiers of the language," and this seems to clarify everything. In art, as in all else, every explanation of Rio Grande must depend upon the position of vigilance and discipline that have been rigidly imposed on us for so long. The tensions and conflicts that we as frontiersmen have had to endure have not permitted us more leisurely transactions with natural forces. We are therefore very untelluric. From the beginning we have been involved

---

supplies, including munitions, fought for his native state until he was mortally wounded in August, 1894.* (Translators.)

[5] Here the term means Rio-Grandenses, of course. (Translators).

and drawn together less by the physical conditions of our surroundings than by the active presence of man himself—friend or enemy.

The Brazilian of the extreme South is entirely unacquainted with what Graça Aranha called, in his habitual imposing style, "the cosmic terror." Nature neither frightens nor depresses him. On the contrary, he is imbued with a tranquil sense of dominion over the elements. The representative nature of Rio Grande, the nature that was its epic legend, conceals no surprises, does not enclose itself in mysteries. Its perspectives are ample, clean, unimpeded. The land, as in a feminine act of surrender, stoops to man's feet, stretching itself out in submissive curves and humbly dragging itself on to vanish in the distance of the horizon. It was on that smooth, broad stage that the figure of the "monarch"[6] rose up, lord of the green knolls. The mountain, the bristling sierras, the forest, made themselves felt only after the sociological maturing of the son of Rio Grande, who, whatever the topographical accidents surrounding him may be, except for the old Campanha, will always bear within him the landscape that witnessed the action of the old fighter-toilers. The countryside, the broad green prairies drenched with sky and sun—"light of God on all sides," as the old scout Blau Nunes put it—

[6] *Monarca* (besides its usual obvious sense) is a local term for the *gaúcho* who sits his horse with especially proud bearing and skill. (Translators.)

the clear light which night itself, falling slowly, seems to respect—all this is inside each one of us, and is what has conspired with the frequency of frontier combat to awaken in the *gaúcho* his feeling of security within his native landscape.

On the other hand, the submissiveness of nature to man awakens in him a certain tender sentiment for the physical environment, a feeling so well translated by the word "querência," in wide use among us.[7] This sentimental reaction is one of the constants in the Rio-Grandense psyche. When General Flôres da Cunha, back from the 1930 march on Rio de Janeiro, addressed the crowd acclaiming him in Pôrto Alegre, he divested himself of his habitual scowl and poured all his emotion into this phrase, pregnant with loving resonance: "Sweet land of Rio Grande!"

During its early history Rio Grande had to cope with great difficulty of communications, intercepted to the north by the virgin forest and to the east by an extensive, desolate seaboard fringe of pure sand without the slightest vestige of security against the sea, offering by way of access only a troubled, treacherous bar, known as "the devil's bar" before the protective breakwaters were constructed. The south and west sides, bounded by Uruguay and Argentina, were exposed to

---

[7] *Querência:* a term full of connotations, meaning beloved homeland, one's old home, the place where one was born, or lived, and for which he feels the deepest sentimental attachment. (Translators.)

the aggression of foreign cultures. Here, as we have stressed so many times in the preceding chapters, is where the critical confrontations of nationality took place, and the blood so often shed in them awakened the lively sense of affirmation that has preserved us against the tyranny of telluric influences.

With our boundaries established and consolidated, not just borders of a political sovereignty but a perfectly defined cultural complex confronting the Hispanic-American world, it was necessary to defend not only the eternally threatened territory but also the national cultural institutions, one of the most noble and distinctive among them being our language.

As if the long bellicose contact with neighboring peoples were not enough, heavy successive masses of German and Italian immigrants came afterwards, practically segregated from the "pure" Lusitanian community in uncultivated areas.[8] They contributed materially to diversifying and enriching our economy and our human and cultural landscape, but at the same time they created new "corruptible frontiers of the language," this time inside the gates, potentially aggravating the dangers threatening from outside. Those groups represented as many different ways of possible deterioration of the national language simply because as a rule they spoke

---

[8] People of other stocks also came to Rio Grande, in more recent times, but with the exception of some groups of Poles they have merged into the general mass of the populace.

numerous simple dialects—or rather, subdialects—whose deformities poorly recalled the refined matrices of origin.[9]

Thus besieged externally and internally by agents of linguistic corruption, how could we orient ourselves, even instinctively, by any other tendency than that of the preservation and defense of the language brought by the conquistadores of the Continente de São Pedro as part of their cultural baggage? It was unquestionably necessary to resist disfiguring influences, and this would not be possible if we left Portuguese abandoned to

[9] A fact that precipitated the expansion and increasing dominion of our language in those areas was the total nationalization of primary and secondary education. This measure, responsible also for expediting the acculturative process of the immigrant groups installed there, was put into effect under J. P. Coelho de Souza, when he headed the Secretaria da Educação e Cultura (1937-44). Thanks to his determination, energy, and prudence, the law was carried out without serious resistance in spite of the grave obstacles created by the criminal outrages of the police of that time against Brazilian citizens because of their German or Italian names, all on the pretext that Brazil, at war with the Axis powers, found herself menaced by the Hitlerite Fifth Column. The results of the nationalization of education are tangible and continue to multiply, all the more so because other factors came into play toward the same end: the development of the highway network, permitting an intensive interchange of persons and interests, wider and faster distribution of the newspapers of the capital, radio, television, and the surprising proliferation of Centros de Tradição Gaúcha in the old areas of colonization. Today, the scheming leaders who fought for the "peaceful" coexistence of several languages in Rio Grande are preaching in the desert. Nobody any longer gives ear to their harangues. And yet the problem used to be quite serious. The schools run by Germans or descendants of Germans, schools in which Portuguese was less than a dead language, rose to more than two thousand. Gilberto Freyre has duly analyzed other aspects of the gravity of the problem.*

spontaneous disintegration into weak forms, without even the power to impose itself in the new immigrant areas.

Any experiment of literary renovation based on the softening of the skeletal framework of the language, whether through genuine preoccupation with the soil and its people (of which Afonso Arinos expects so much) or purely artificial like that which resulted in the frustration of Mário de Andrade's *Macunaíma*[1]—such experiments are simply not viable among us. Less viable still in all probability was the one attempted with so much flamboyance by Guimarães Rosa. Barricaded among the retorts and alembics of his stylistic laboratory, manipulating with exhaustive patience the ingredients that he picks over in a kind of cultural subworld heaped with the minute detritus of a language in a flagrant state of decomposition, the painstaking artificer of *Grande Sertão: Veredas* would find here in Rio Grande only factors of discouragement for his cryptic literary arrangements, despite certain less incommunicable, even impressive, pages of notable dramatic power

[1] Mário Raul de Morais Andrade (1893–1945), poet, novelist, folklorist, critic and historian of music, art, and literature, wrote "to make Brazilians 100 per cent Brazilian, to nationalize a nation yet so lacking in national characteristics," as he said. Bandeira remarks of him: "Naturally language was one of his first preoccupations. . . . From 1924 on, he composed . . . in an artifically 'Brazilian' language—a highly personal literary synthesis and systematization of idioms gathered from the four corners of the country."* This explains the "frustration" of his novel *Macunaíma*. (Translators.)

and sundry patches that afford a glimpse of keen poetic sensibility.[2]

Let us accept the historically obvious fact that the Portuguese language is very far from being organically incompatible with changes caused by shifting it in space and time. Outside of certain already discredited academic circles it is difficult to find anyone who seriously believes that permanence of grammatical norms is an argument against the natural evolution of the spoken or written language.

It is not that any programmatic intent impels the Rio-Grandense writer to shun experiments of renovation, but rather the underlying need, stimulated by historical and sociological tensions, to keep watch over the cultural legacy of the language, guarding its flanks against harmful infiltrations. To us, with our pioneer instinct, the traditional canons of the language we speak—which have nothing to do with academic finickiness—like the factors that inspired and conducted the struggles of old, are vitally related to national appeals and demands.

Because of the intense, harsh history of our life in this distant region, experience has hammered into our very flesh the lesson that the language, in its traditional, fluent and communicative expression, bulks large among the factors that make us an integral part of the Brazilian

[2] João Guimarães Rosa (1908–   ), author of *Sagarana, Corpo de Baile,* and *Grande Sertão: Veredas,* all prose fiction. The author's critique is meant to reflect Guimarães Rosa's elaborate style. (Translators.)

entity. A powerful, decisive instrument of community and unity, that language will be classic, as Afonso Arinos wishes, if our writers demonstrate an active sense of propriety receptive to changing conditions, and constantly seek the organic and up-to-date balance between matter and form. That balance will be achieved, naturally, only if the capacity for incorporation and assimilation of new values is one of the factors from which it results. This is precisely the kind of renovation to which Barbosa Lima Sobrinho refers in his long, substantial essay, characterizing it as "a permanent force in the life and transformation of languages."*

It will be said that the refusal by Rio-Grandense writers in general to weaken the characteristic virtues of the language is strictly cultural in nature, without popular influences. It will not be amiss, however, to remark that in literature as in other arts the most authentic influences of the collective unconscious can hide under the forms selected by the keenest consciousness. It seems clear that our "classicism" has its roots in history. The unity of the language on the basis of a fundamental, common structure is what we achieve, first by instinct of defense and cultural affirmation, and then by habit. As a condition and instrument of national cohesion and in the form mutually comprehensible by all Brazilians, bridging the immense blank spaces interrupting our scanty human geography, the language has not yet lost, for us, the old Lusitanian sense of empire and determination that together with the other weapons wielded by the old fighters, aided us so much in the struggles of old. The fact is that the writer cannot escape from the laws and inspirations of his milieu just because he is a writer. Whatever his idiosyncrasies or individual peculiarities, he will always be a sociological unit bearing the ballast of tradition and history that completes his status as man.

BIBLIOGRAPHY

Abreu, Capistrano de: *Correspondência*. Rio de Janeiro: Inst. Nacional do Livro; 1954.

———: *Ensaios e Estudos*, 2nd and 3rd Series. Rio: Livr. Briguiet; 1937–8.

Abreu e Silva, Florêncio de: "Retrospecto Econômico e Financeiro do Estado do Rio Grande do Sul," *Revista do Arquivo Público do Rio Grande do Sul*, No. 8 (1922), pp. 25ff.

———: "Aspectos do Desenvolvimento Econômico e Financeiro do RGS,*" in *Comemorações do Centenário da Independência do Brasil*. Pôrto Alegre: Ofic. Gráf. da Federação; 1922.

———: "Importância da Colonização Açoriana no RGS,"

* Since the name "Rio Grande do Sul" occurs many times in these entries, hereafter the current abbreviation of "RGS" is used. (Translators.)

Jornal do Comércio (Rio), June 3, 1956.

Alcântara Machado: *Vida e Morte do Bandeirante*. São Paulo: Livr. Martins Edit.; 1943.

Alencar Araripe, Tristão de: *Guerra Civil no RGS*. Rio: Tip. Universal de E. & Laemmert; 1881.

Almanaque do RGS, 1888, 1891, 1893.

O Americano (Alegrete), 1842. Reprinted by Museu e Arquivo Histórico do RGS, 1935.

Amoroso Lima, Alceu: *Europa e América–Duas Culturas*. Rio: Agir; 1962.

Arinos de Melo Franco, Afonso: *Terra do Brasil*. São Paulo: Cía. Edit. Nacional; 1930.

———: "Um Citadino," *O Jornal* (Rio de Janeiro).

Arquivo Público do RGS: "Documentos Relativos à Incorporação das Missões ao Domínio Português," *Rev. do Arquivo Público do RGS*, Vol. I (1921). Pôrto Alegre: Oficinas Gráficas de A Federação; 1921.

Assis Brasil, J. F. de: *História da República Rio-Grandense*. Rio: Tip. Leutzinger & Filho; 1882.

Assis Brasil, Gen. Ptolomeu: *Batalha de Caiboaté*. Pôrto Alegre: Globo; 1935.

Austregésilo, Míriam Élis: "Estudo sôbre Alguns Tipos de Transportes do Brasil Colonial," *Rev. de Hist.*, No. 4 (1950).

Ayarragaray, Lucas: *La anarquía argentina y el caudillismo*. Buenos Aires: J. Lajuane & Cía.; 1925.

Azarola Gil, Luis Enrique: *La epopeya de D. Manuel Lobo*. Buenos Aires: Cía. Ibero-Americana de Publicaciones, S.A.; 1931.

Bandeira, Manuel: *Brief History of Brazilian Literature*, trans., intro., and notes by Ralph Edward Dimmick. Washington: Pan American Union; 1958.

Barbosa Lima Sobrinho: *A Língua Portuguêsa e a Unidade do Brasil*. Rio: José Olympio Editôra; 1958.

Barcelos, Rubens de: *Estudos Rio-Grandenses*. Pôrto Alegre: Globo; 1955.

Barreto, Abeillar: "A Livraria de Silva Pais," *Província de São Pedro*, No. 15 (1951).

Bello, José Maria: *A History of Modern Brazil, 1889–1964*, trans. by James L. Taylor, with new concluding chapter by Rollie E. Poppino. Stanford: Stanford University Press; 1966.

Beltrão, Romeu: *Cronología Histórica de Santa Maria e do Extinto Município de São Martinho*. Santa Maria: Livr. Editôra Paloti; 1958.

Bernardi, Mansueto: "Bandeira Nacional e Bandeiras Estaduais," *Rev. do Inst. Hist. e Geogr. do RGS*, Nos. 3 and 4 (1923).

———: *O Primeiro Caudilho Rio-Grandense*. Pôrto Alegre: Globo; 1957.

Betâmio, Sebastião Francisco: "Notícia Particular do Continente do RGS," *Rev. do Inst. Hist. e Geogr. do Brasil*, Vol. XVI.

Blanco Fombona, Rufino: *El conquistador español del siglo XVI*. Madrid: Edit. Mundo Latino; n.d.

Bonfim, Manuel: *O Brasil na História*. Rio: Livr. Francisco Alves; 1931.

Borges Fortes, Gen. João: "O Brigadeiro José da Silva Pais e a Fundação do RGS," *Rev. do Inst. Hist. e Geogr. do RGS*, 1933.

———: *Rio Grande de São Pedro*. Rio: Gráficas Bloch; 1941.

———: *Cristóvão Pereira*. Pôrto Alegre: Tip. do Centro; 1932.

———: *Casais*. Rio: Edição do Centenário Farroupilha; 1932.

————: *A Estância*. Rio: Tip. do Ministério da Agricultura; 1931.

Bougainville, L. A. de: *Viaje alrededor del mundo*, 2nd Spanish edn. Buenos Aires–México: Espasa-Calpe Argentina, S.A.; 1946.

Buarque de Holanda, Sérgio: *História Geral da Civilização Brasileira*. São Paulo: Difusão Européia do Livro; 1960.

Bunge, Carlos Octavio: *Nuestra América*. Buenos Aires: Casa Vaccaro; 1918.

Calmon, Pedro: *História do Brasil*. Rio: José Olympio Edit.; 1945.

Calógeras, J. Pandiá: *A Política Exterior do Império*. Rio: Impr. Nacional; 1937.

————: *A Política Externa do Império*. Rio: Impr. Nacional; 1927.

————: *Formação Histórica do Brasil*. São Paulo: Cía. Edit. Nacional; 1957.

Campos, Humberto de: *Crítica*, 1st Series. Rio: Livr. Edit. Marisa; 1933.

Carneiro de Mendonça, Marcos: *A Amazônia na Era Pombalina*. Rio: Inst. Hist. e Geogr. Bras.; 1961.

César, Guilhermino: *História da Literatura do RGS*. Pôrto Alegre: Globo; 1956.

Coelho de Souza, J. P.: *O Sentido e o Espírito da Revolução Farroupilha*. Pôrto Alegre: Globo; 1945.

————: "Diretivas Políticas do RGS," *Província de São Pedro*, No. 2 (1945).

Cólor, Lindolfo: *Garibaldi e a Guerra dos Farrapos*, 2nd edn. Pôrto Alegre: Globo; 1958.

Corbiere, Emilio: *El gaucho*. Buenos Aires: Talleres Gráficos L. J. Rosso; 1929.

Cortesão, Jaime: *A Fundação de São Paulo, Capital Geográfica do Brasil*. Rio: Livros de Portugal; 1955.

————: *Raposo Tavares e a Formação Territorial do Brasil.* Rio: Min. da Educação e Cultura; 1958.

————: *Alexandre de Gusmão e o Tratado de Madrid.* Rio: Min. das Relações Exteriores; 1956.

————: *Jesuítas e Bandeirantes no Guaíra.* Rio: Biblioteca Nacional; 1951.

————, ed.: *Manuscritos da Coleção de Angelis.* Rio: Biblioteca Nacional; 1954.

Costa Brochado: *D. Sebastião o Desejado.* Lisbon: Editorial Império Ltda.; 1941.

Costa Franco, Sérgio: "Oliveira Viana e a Revolução Farroupilha," *Correio do Povo,* June 14, 1949.

Cruz, Alcides: *Vida de Rafael Pinto Bandeira.* Pôrto Alegre: Livr. Americana; 1906.

Damasceno, Athos: *Palco, Salão e Picadeiro em Pôrto Alegre no Século XIX.* Pôrto Alegre: Globo; 1956.

Deffontaines, Pierre: "Geografia Humana do Brasil," *Rev. Bras. de Geogr.,* Vol. I, Nos .1, 2, 3.

Dreys, Nicolau: *Notícia Descritiva da Província do RGS.* Pôrto Alegre: Livr. Americana; 1927.

Élis Júnior, Alfredo: *Feijó e a Primeira Metade do Século XIX.* São Paulo: Cía. Edit. Nac.; 1940.

————: *Resumo da História de São Paulo.* São Paulo: Tip. Brasil; 1942.

————: "O Ciclo do Muar," *Rev. de Hist.,* No. 1 (1950).

————: *Raposo Tavares e Sua Época.* Rio: José Olympio Edit.; 1944.

————: *Cartas Avulsas.* Rio: Acad. Bras. de Letras; 1931.

Ferreira, Tito Lívio: *Gênese Social da Gente Bandeirante.* São Paulo: Cía. Edit. Nac.; 1944.

Ferreira Filho, Artur: *História Geral do RGS.* Pôrto Alegre: Globo; 1958.

Ferreira Rodrigues, Alfredo: "Os Espanhóis no Rio Grande," *Almanaque do RGS*, 1896.

Fontoura, Edgar: *Escôrço Biográfico de José da Silva Pais*. Pôrto Alegre: Globo; 1937.

Fragoso, Tasso: *A Batalha do Passo do Rosário*. Rio: Impr. Militar; 1922.

Freire, Felisbelo: *História Constitucional da República dos Estados Unidos do Brasil*. Rio: Tip. Moreira Maximino, Chagas e Cía.; 1894.

Freyre, Gilberto: *Brazil: An Interpretation*. New York: Alfred A. Knopf; 1945.

——: *Interpretação do Brasil*. Rio: José Olympio Edit.; 1947.

——: *The Masters and the Slaves*, 2nd edn. New York: Alfred A. Knopf; 1966.

——: *Continente e Ilha*. Rio: Casa do Estudante do Brasil; 1943.

——: *Uma Cultura Ameaçada: a Luso-Brasileira*, 2nd edn. Rio: Casa do Estudante do Brasil; 1942.

Gay, Cônego Pedro: *História da República Jesuítica do Paraguai*. Rio: Impr. Oficial; 1942.

González, Manuel Pedro: *Trayectoria del gaucho y su cultura*. Havana: Úcar García y Cía.; 1943.

Goulart, José Alípio: *Tropas e Tropeiros na Formação do Brasil*. Rio: Conquista; 1961.

Handelmann, Heinrich: *História do Brasil*, trans. by the Institute. Rio: Inst. Hist. e Geogr. Bras.; 1931.

Hansel, José: "Sepé Tiaraju," *Estudos*, Vol. XV, Nos. 3 and 4, 1955.

Harney, Martin P., S.J.: *The Jesuits in History: The Society of Jesus through Four Centuries*. Chicago: Loyola University Press; 1962.

Harnisch, Wolfgang Hoffmann: *O Rio Grande do Sul—A Terra e o Homem.* Pôrto Alegre: Globo; 1941.

Hernández, Pablo, S.J.: *Organización social de las doctrinas guaraníes de la Compañía de Jesús.* Barcelona: Gustavo Gil; 1913.

Ingenieros, José: *Sociología argentina.* Buenos Aires: Losada; 1946.

Isabelle, Arsène: *Voyage à Buenos-Ayres et à Porto-Alègre.* Le Havre: Impr. Morlent; 1835.

———: *Viagem ao Rio da Prata e ao RGS*, trans. by Teodemiro Tostes. Rio: Livr. Zélio Valverde; 1949.

———: *Emigração e Colonização*, trans. by Belfort de Oliveira. Rio: Gráfica Edit. Souza; 1950.

Jaeger, Luiz Gonzaga, S.J.: *Os Heróis de Caapó e Pirapó.* Pôrto Alegre: Globo; 1940.

———: *As Invasões Bandeirantes ao RGS.* Pôrto Alegre: Tip. do Centro; n.d.

Kirkpatrick, F. A.: *The Spanish Conquistadors.* London: A. & C. Black; 1934.

Laytano, Dante de: *O Negro no RGS.* Pôrto Alegre: Tip. Champagnat; 1958.

Leite, Serafim, S.J.: *História da Companhia de Jesus no Brasil.* Rio: Impr. Nac.; 1943. (Also Lisbon: Livr. Portugália; 1938.)

———: *Novas Cartas Jesuíticas.* São Paulo: Cía. Edit. Nac.; 1940.

Lima, Alcides: *História Popular do RGS*, 2nd edn. Pôrto Alegre: Globo; 1935.

Lins, Ivan: *Aspectos do P. Antônio Vieira.* Rio: Livr. São José; 1956.

Luccock, John: *Notes on Rio de Janeiro, and the Southern Parts of Brazil.* London: Samuel Leigh; 1820.

Martínez Estrada, Ezequiel: *Radiografía de la pampa*. Buenos Aires: Losada; 1946.

Meireles, Cecília: "Folclore Guasca e Açoriano," *Província de São Pedro*, No. 6 (1946).

———: "Notas de Folclore Gaúcho-Açoriano," ibid., No. 8 (1947).

O Mensageiro, reprinted by Museu e Arquivo Hist. do RGS, 1930.

Mesquita Filho, Júlio de: *Ensaios Sul-Americanos*. São Paulo: Livr. Martins Edit.; 1946.

Meyer, Augusto: "Salve-se o Lunar de Sepé," *Correio do Povo* (Pôrto Alegre), Dec. 15, 1956.

———: *Prosa dos Pagos*. Rio: Livr. São José; 1960.

———: Preface to Teodemiro Tostes's trans. of Arsène Isabelle's *Viagem ao Rio da Prata e ao RGS*, q.v.

———: *Cancioneiro Gaúcho*. Pôrto Alegre: Globo; 1950.

———: *Estudo Crítico em "Antônio Chimango" de Amaro Juvenal*, 3rd edn., rev. Pôrto Alegre: Globo; 1961.

Monteiro, Mário: *Aleixo Garcia*. Lisbon: Livr. Central; 1923.

Moraes, Carlos Dante de: *Figuras e Ciclos da História Rio-Grandense*. Pôrto Alegre: Globo; 1959.

Muratori, Lodovico Antonio: *Il Cristianesimo Felice delle Missione dei Padri della Compagnia di Gesú nel Paraguai*. Venice: Giambattista Pasquali; 1743.

Nabuco, Joaquim: *Escritos e Discursos Literários*. Rio: Livr. Garnier; 1919.

Nichols, Madaline Wallis: *The Gaucho*. Durham, N.C.: Duke University Press; 1942.

Nóbrega, Manuel da, S.J.: *Cartas do Brasil*. Rio: Acadêmia Brasileira de Letras; 1931.

———: *Cartas Jesuíticas*. Rio: Acadêmia Bras. de Letras; 1931.

Oliveira Martins: *O Brasil e as Colônias Portuguêsas*. Lisboa: Guimarães & Cía.; 1953.

Oliveira Viana, F. J.: *Instituições Políticas Brasileiras*. Rio: José Olympio Edit.; 1949.

————: *Populações Meridionais do Brasil. Vol. II, O Campeador Rio-Grandense*. Rio: José Olympio Edit.; 1952.

Ornelas, Manoelito de: *Tiaraju*. Pôrto Alegre: Globo; 1945.

Petit Muñoz, Eugenio: *Interpretaciones esquemáticas sobre la Conquista y la colonización española en América*. Montevideo: Edit. La Cruz del Sur; 1927.

Pinto da Silva, João: *A Província de São Pedro*. Pôrto Alegre: Globo; 1930.

————: *História Literária do RGS*. Pôrto Alegre: Globo; 1924.

Pôrto, Aurélio: "Antecedentes Históricos do Povoamento do Sul," *Terra Farroupilha* (Vol. Comemorativo do Segundo Centenário da Fundação do RGS, 1737–1937), 1937.

————: *História das Missões Orientais*. Rio: Impr. Nacional; 1943.

————: "Presídio do Rio Grande de São Pedro," *Terra Farroupilha*.

————: "Continente do Rio Grande," *Almanaque do Correio do Povo* (Pôrto Alegre), 1959.

Pôrto Alegre, Apolinário: *Cancioneiro da Revolução de 1835*. Pôrto Alegre: Globo; 1935.

Prado Júnior, Caio: *Formação do Brasil Contemporâneo*. São Paulo: Livr. Martins Edit.; 1942.

Prado, Paulo: *Paulística*. Rio: Ariel; 1934.

Rambo, Balduíno, S.J.: *A Fisionomia do RGS*, 2nd edn. Pôrto Alegre: Livr. Selbach; 1956.

————: "Os Índios Rio-Grandenses Modernos," *Província de São Pedro*, No. 10.

Rêgo Monteiro, J. da C.: *A Colônia do Sacramento*. Pôrto Alegre: Globo; 1933.

Ribeiro, João: *História do Brasil*, 5th edn. Rio: Livr. Francisco Alves; 1914.

Ribeiro de Almeida, Gabriel: "Memória sôbre a Tomada dos Sete Povos das Missões da América Espanhola," in Veloso da Silveira, q.v.

Ricardo, Cassiano: *Marcha para Oeste*. Rio: José Olympio Edit.; 1942.

Rio Branco, Barão do: *Questão de Limites*. Rio: Min. das Relações Exteriores; 1945.

———: *Biografias*. Rio: Min. das Rel. Ext.; 1947.

Rocha Pombo: *História do Brasil*. Rio: W. M. Jackson Inc.; 1942.

Rodrigues, Alfredo F.: "General Osório," *Almanaque do RGS*, 1888.

Rodrigues, Eurico: "Um Fantasma na História Rio-Grandense," in *A Defesa Nacional*. Rio: Min. da Guerra; 1957.

Rodrigues, José Honório: *O Continente do Rio Grande*. Rio: Edições São José; 1954.

Rosa, Othelo: "Causas da Revolução Farroupilha," *Província de São Pedro*, No. 2 (1945).

———: "A Formação do RGS," in *Fundamentos da Cultura Rio-Grandense*. Pôrto Alegre: Faculdade de Filosofia da Universidade do RGS; 2nd Series, 1957.

———: *Vultos da Epopéia Farroupilha*. Pôrto Alegre: Globo; 1935.

———: "O Conteúdo Político da Revolução Farroupilha," *Província de São Pedro*, No. 16.

———: "As Missões Jesuíticas e a Consciência da Juventude," ibid., No. 14.

———: "Sugestão sôbre um Monumento a Sepé Tiaraju," ibid., No. 21.

Rourke, Thomas: *Man of Glory: Simon Bólivar.* New York: William Morrow & Co.; 1939.

Sá Brito, Francisco de: *Memória da Guerra dos Farrapos.* Preface, Introduction, and Explanatory Notes by Paulino Jacques. Rio: Gráfica Editôra Souza; 1950.

Saint-Hilaire, Auguste: *Viagem ao RGS,* trans. by Leonam de Azevedo Pena. Rio: Ariel; 1935.

Salis Goulart, J.: *A Formação do RGS.* Pelotas: Globo; 1927.

Sanmartin, Olinto: *Bandeirantes no Sul do Brasil.* Pôrto Alegre: Tip. do Centro; 1949.

São Leopoldo, Visconde de: *Anais da Província de São Pedro.* Rio: Impr. Nac.; 1946.

Sarmiento, Domingo F.: *Facundo.* Buenos Aires: La Cultura Argentina; 1923.

———: *Los caudillos.* Buenos Aires: W. M. Jackson Inc.; n.d.

Sepp, Antônio, S.J.: *Viagem às Missões Jesuíticas e Trabalhos Apostólicos.* São Paulo: Livr. Martins Edit.; 1943.

Souza Doca, E. F. de: *O Sentido Brasileiro da Revolução Farroupilha.* Pôrto Alegre: Globo; 1935.

———: *História do RGS.* Rio: Organização Simões; 1954.

———: "O Brasil no Prata," *Rev. do Inst. Hist. e Geogr. do RGS,* No. 1 (1931).

———: "Vocábulos Indígenas na Geografia do RGS," ibid., Vol. V, Nos. 1 and 2.

———: "O Porquê da Brasilidade da Revolução Farroupilha," *Província de São Pedro,* No. 2 (1945).

Spalding, Walter: *A Revolução Farroupilha.* São Paulo: Cía. Edit. Nac.; 1939.

———: *A Epopéia Farroupilha.* Rio: Biblioteca do Exército; 1963.

Taunay, Afonso de E.: *História Geral das Bandeiras Paulistas*. São Paulo: Tip. Ideal; 1925.

———, ed.: *Relatos Sertanistas*. São Paulo: Livr. Martins Ed.; 1953.

Teixeira Soares: *Diplomacia do Império no Rio da Prata*. Rio: Edit. Brand Ltda.; 1955.

Teschauer, Carlos, S.J.: "Poranduba Rio-Grandense," *Anuário do RGS*, 1902.

———: *História do RGS nos Dois Primeiros Séculos*. Pôrto Alegre: Livr. Selbach; 1922.

Varela, Alfredo: *História da Grande Revolução*. Pôrto Alegre: Globo; 1933.

Vargas Neto: *Tropilha Crioula e Gado Chucro*. Pôrto Alegre: Globo; 1955.

Vasconcelos, Dom Luís de: *Correspondência. Arquivo Nacional—Publicações VI*. Rio: Impr. Nac.; 1907.

Vellinho, Moysés: *Letras da Província*. Pôrto Alegre: Globo; 1944.

Veloso da Silveira, Hemetério: *As Missões Orientais*. Pôrto Alegre: Livr. Universal de Carlos Echenique; 1909.

Veríssimo, Inácio José: *Pombal, os Jesuítas e o Brasil*. Rio: Impr. do Exército; 1961.

Veríssimo, José: "Impressões do Sul," *Jornal do Comércio* (Rio), July 21, 1912.

Washington Luíz: *Na Capitania de São Vicente*. São Paulo: Livr. Martins Ed.: 1956.

Zorrilla de San Martín, Juan: *La epopeya de Artigas*. Montevideo: Impr. Nac. Colorada; 1950.

Zum Felde, Alberto: *Proceso histórico del Uruguay*. Montevideo: Maximino García; n.d.

NOTES

4 : 10 Alfredo Varela: *História da Grande Revolução* (Pôrto Alegre: Livraria do Globo; 1933).

5 : 18 Mansueto Bernardi: "Bandeira Nacional e Bandeiras Estaduais," *Rev. do Inst. Hist. e Geogr. do R. G. do S.*, Nos. 3 and 4 (1923); Jorge Salis Goulart: *A Formação do Rio Grande do Sul* (Pelotas: Globo; 1927); Souza Doca: *O Sentido Brasileiro da Revolução Farroupilha* [*farroupilha* is merely a variant form of Farrapos, used as adjective] (Pôrto Alegre: Globo; 1935) and "O Porquê da *Brasilidade da Revolução Farroupilha*," a lecture delivered at the Centro Gaúcho de São Paulo, Sept. 20, 1936; Othelo Rosa: "Causas da Revolução Farroupilha," *Província de São Pedro* [a leading literary periodical, not to be confused with the same name in a geographic context, as in the next title below], No. 2 (1945); João Pinto da Silva: *A Província de São Pedro* (Pôrto Alegre: Globo; 1930); J. P. Coelho de Souza: *O Sentido e o Espírito da Revolução Farroupilha* (Pôrto Alegre:

Globo; 1945) and "Diretivas Políticas do Rio Grande do Sul," *Província de São Pedro*, No. 2 (1945); Rubens de Barcelos: *Estudos Rio-Grandenses* (Pôrto Alegre: Globo; 1955); Walter Spalding: *A Revolução Farroupilha* (São Paulo: Editôra Nacional; 1939).

8 : 25 José Veríssimo: "Impressões do Sul," *Jornal do Comércio* (Rio de Janeiro), July 21, 1912.

9 : 13 Paulo Prado: *Paulística* (2nd edn.; Rio de Janeiro: Ariel; 1934), p. xvi. Let us quote Gilberto Freyre: ". . . Brazil is not simply one natural and cultural region; inside the almost continental immensity of that part of America, Nature and culture have their own subdivisions. Therefore Brazil needs to defend itself permanently against its own enemies of its organic regionalism which is in keeping with it and is essential to its development or to its creativity." (*Brazil: An Interpretation* [New York: Alfred A. Knopf; 1945], p. 73.) The last clause is translated from the Brazilian translation, *Interpretação do Brasil* (Rio: Olympio Editôra; 1947), pp. 49–50.

10 : 3 Auguste Saint-Hilaire: *Viagem ao Rio Grande do Sul*, trans. by Leonam de Azevedo Pena (Rio: Ariel; 1935), pp. 95–6.

10 : 26 P. Balduíno Rambo, S.J.: *A Fisionomia do Rio Grande do Sul* (2nd edn., rev.; Pôrto Alegre: Livraria Selbach; 1956), p. 53.

12 : 7 Humberto de Campos: *Crítica* (Rio: Livr. Edit. Marisa; 1935), 1st Series, p. 285.

12 : 19 General João Borges Fortes: "O Brigadeiro José da Silva Pais e a Fundação do Rio Grande," *Rev. do Inst. Hist. e Geogr. do R. G. do S.* (1933), p. 111; Edgar Fontoura: *Escôrço Biográfico de José da Silva Pais* (Pôrto Alegre: Globo; 1937), p. 24.

13 : 9 Alfredo Élis Júnior: *Feijó e a Primeira Metade do*

Século XIX (São Paulo: Companhia Edit. Nacional; 1940), pp. 439–40.

15 : 2 Othelo Rosa: "O Conteúdo Político da Revolução Farroupilha," *Província de São Pedro*, No. 16, pp. 59 ff.

15 : 18 João Capistrano de Abreu: *Ensaios e Estudos* (Rio: Livr. Briguiet; 1937–8), 3rd Series, p. 86.

15 : 19 ――――: *Correspondência de Capistrano de Abreu* (Rio: Inst. Nacional do Livro; 1954), I, 113.

16 : 13 ――――: *Ensaios*, 2nd Series, p. 24.

17 : 9 Jaime Cortesão: *A Fundação de São Paulo, Capital Geográfica do Brasil* (Rio: Livros de Portugal; 1955), and *Raposo Tavares e a Formação Territorial do Brasil* (Rio: Ministério da Educação e Cultura; 1958).

17 : 14 João Ribeiro: *História do Brasil* (Rio: Livr. Francisco Alves; 1914), pp. 163–4.

18 : 3 F. J. Oliveira Vianna: *Instituições Políticas Brasileiras* (Rio: Livr. José Olympio Editôra; 1949), p. 198.

18 : 8 Rosa: "O Conteúdo Político," p. 59.

18 : 9 Sérgio Costa Franco: "Oliveira Viana e a Revolução Farroupilha," *Correio do Povo* (Pôrto Alegre), June 14, 1949.

18 : 11 F. J. Oliveira Viana: *Populações Meridionais do Brasil* (Rio: José Olympio Edit.; 1952).

19 : 19 Barcelos: *Estudos Rio-Grandenses*, p. 145.

CHAPTER ONE

22 : 1 J. da C. Rêgo Monteiro: *A Colônia do Sacramento* (Pôrto Alegre: Livr. do Globo; 1933), I, 46, *n.* 29.

23 : 14 P. Manuel da Nóbrega, S.J.: *Cartas do Brasil* (Rio: Publicação da Academia Brasileira de Letras; 1931), p. 124.

23 : 23 Ibid., p. 145, *n.* 2.

24 : 2 Ibid., p. 116.

24 : 4 Ibid., p. 81.

24 : 21 Prado: *Paulística*, p. 60.

24 : 24 Appointed successively by Martim Afonso de Souza and
Tomé de Souza as commander-in-chief in the field and
captain of the town of Santo André, João Ramalho
came to be elected also as city councilman of the latter
place. (Alfredo Élis Júnior: *Resumo da História de
São Paulo* [São Paulo: Tip. Brasil; 1942], p. 68; *Cartas
Avulsas* [Rio: Publ. da Academia Bras. de Letras;
1931], p. 93, *n.* 42; Tito Lívio Ferreira: *Gênese Social
da Gente Bandeirante* [São Paulo: Comp. Edit. Nac.;
1944], p. 92.)

24 : 28 In a letter dated 1612 Diogo de Vasconcelos informed
the King that without the native women "it would be
difficult to control or settle so large a coast." (Gilberto Freyre: *The Masters and the Slaves* [2nd edn.;
New York: Alfred A. Knopf; 1966], p. 84.)

26 : 25 Rêgo Monteiro: *A Colônia*, p. 39, *n.* 15.

26 : 26 Serafim Leite, S.J.: *História da Companhia de Jesus no
Brasil* (Rio: Impr. Nac.; 1943), p. 254.

27 : 14 Pandiá Calógeras: *A Política Exterior do Império* (Rio:
Impr. Nac.; 1937), p. 201.

28 : 13 Aurélio Pôrto: "Antecedentes Históricos do Povoa-
mento do Sul," *Terra Farroupilha* (Pôrto Alegre:
Segundo Centenário da Fundação do Rio Grande do
Sul; 1937), p. 111.

28 : 30 Calógeras: *A Política Exterior*, pp. 173–4.

29 : 18 Heinrich Handelmann: *História do Brasil* (Rio: Trad.
do Inst. Hist. e Geogr. Bras.; 1931), p. 668.

29 : 31 Leite: *História da Companhia*, VI, 550.

31 : 11 Aurélio Pôrto: *História das Missões Orientais* (Rio:
Impr. Nac.; 1943), pp. 25–6 and 80; E. F. de Souza
Doca: *História do Rio Grande do Sul* (Rio: Organi-
zacão Simões; 1954), p. 36.

31 : 19 P. Carlos Teschauer, S.J.: "Poranduba Rio-Grandense,"

Anuário do Rio Grande do Sul, 1902, p. 177; Leite: *História da Companhia,* Vol. VI, Book V, Chaps. iii and iv.

32 : 8 Alfonso de E. Taunay: *História Geral das Bandeiras Paulistas* (São Paulo: Tip. Ideal; 1925), II, 170.

34 : 23 Martin P. Harney, S.J.: *The Jesuits in History: The Society of Jesus through Four Centuries* (Chicago: Loyola Univ. Press; 1962), p. 241.

35 : 4 Taunay: *História Geral,* II, 79.

36 : 7 Cassiano Ricardo: *Marcha para Oeste* (Rio: José Olympio Edit.; 1942).

36 : 29 Taunay: *História Geral,* II, 91.

37 : 5 João Capistrano de Abreu: *Ensaios,* pp. 68–9.

38 : 12 Rêgo Monteiro: *A Colônia,* II, 5–16.

38 : 27 Barão do Rio Branco: *Questão de Limites* (Rio: Ministério das Relações Exteriores; 1945), I, 27.

39 : 24 Visconde de São Leopoldo: *Anais da Província de São Pedro* (Rio: Impr. Nac.; 1946), p. 10.

40 : 13 Mário Monteiro: *Aleixo Garcia* (Lisbon: Livr. Central; 1923); Cortesão: *A Fundação de São Paulo.*

40 : 28 Leite: *História da Companhia,* VI, 537; Pôrto: "Presídio do Rio Grande de São Pedro," *Terra Farroupilha,* p. 176.

40 : 29 Jaime Cortesão: *Alexandre de Gusmão e o Tratado de Madrid* (Rio: Min. das Relações Exteriores; 1956), Part I, Vol. II, p. 55.

42 : 21 L. E. Azarola Gil: *La epopeya de D. Manuel Lobo* (Buenos Aires: Cía. Ibero-Americana de Publicaciones, S.A.; 1931).

43 : 11 Leite: *História da Companhia,* VI, 535.

43 : 13 Handelmann: *História do Brasil,* p. 662.

43 : 19 João Capistrano de Abreu: *Ensaios,* pp. 75–6.

44 : 2 Cortesão: *Alexandre de Gusmão,* p. 39.

44 : 14 Ibid., pp. 30–1.

44 : 29 Ibid., Part III, Vol. I, pp. 304–16.

46 : 4 Azarola Gil: *La epopeya*, p. 25.

46 : 16 Manuel Bonfim: *O Brasil na História* (Rio: Livr. Francisco Alves; 1931), pp. 370 ff.

48 : 17 Alfredo Élis Júnior: "O Ciclo do Muar," *Revista de História* (São Paulo), No. 1 (1950); Míriam Élis Autsregésilo: "Estudo sôbre Alguns Tipos de Transportes do Brasil Colonial," ibid., No. 4 (1950); Afonso Arinos de Melo Franco: *Terra do Brasil* (São Paulo: Comp. Edit. Nac.; 1930), p. 149; José Alípio Goulart: *Tropas e Tropeiros na Formacão do Brasil* (Rio: Conquista; 1961).

49 : 16 Calógeras: *A Política Exterior*, I, 228.

52 : 12 Oliveira Martins: *O Brasil e as Colônias Portuguêsas* (Lisbon: Guimarães & Cia. Editôres; 1953), p. 86.

52 : 18 Cortesão: *Alexandre de Gusmão*, p. 51.

52 : 27 Élis Júnior: "O Ciclo do Muar."

53 : 28 Pedro Calmon: *História do Brasil* (Rio: José Olympio Edit.; 1945), IV, 1202.

54 : 4 Rocha Pombo: *História do Brasil* (Rio: W. M. Jackson Inc.; 1942), II, 392.

54 : 17 Manoel Cardozo: "The Dependency, 1500–1808," in Lawrence F. Hill, ed.: *Brazil* (Berkeley: Univ. of California Press; 1947), p. 11.

CHAPTER TWO

56 : 11 L. A. Muratori: *Il Cristianesimo Felice delle Missione de' Padri della Compagnia di Gesù nel Paraguai* (Venice: Giambattista Pasquali; 1743), p. 55.

56 : 18 L. A. de Bougainville: *Viaje alrededor del mundo* (2nd Spanish edn.; Buenos Aires–México: Espasa-Calpe Argentina, S.A.; 1946), p. 106.

56 : 26 Cortesão: *Raposo Tavares*, p. 128.

57 : 14 Bougainville: *Viaje*, pp. 108–11.

58 : 4   Caio Prado Júnior: *Formação do Brasil Contemporâneo* (São Paulo: Livr. Martins Edit.; 1942).

58 : 5   Júlio de Mesquita Filho: *Ensaios Sul-Americanos* (São Paulo: Livr. Martins Edit.; 1946).

58 : 14 Cortesão: *Raposo Tavares*, p. 137.

58 : 24 P. Manuel da Nóbrega, S.J.: *Cartas Jesuíticas* (Rio: Acad. Brasileira; 1931), I, 81.

60 : 4   Thomas Rourke: *Man of Glory: Simón Bolívar* (New York: William Morrow & Co.; 1939), p. 36.

60 : 9   Prado Júnior: *Formação do Brasil Contemporâneo*, p. 92.

61 : 4   Costa Brochado: *Dom Sebastião o Desejado* (Lisbon: Edit. Império Ltda.; 1941), pp. 39 ff.

61 : 11 Leite: *História da Companhia*, VI, 535.

61 : 22 Serafim Leite, S.J.: *Novas Cartas Jesuíticas* (São Paulo: Comp. Edit. Nac.; 1940), p. 290.

62 : 23 Pôrto: *História das Missões Orientais*, p. 80.

62 : 26 Cortesão: *Raposo Tavares*, p. 121.

63 : 4   *Manuscritos da Coleção De Angelis*, compiled by Jaime Cortesão (Rio: Bibl. Nac.; 1954).

63 : 10 Leite: *História da Companhia*, VI, 471–523.

64 : 9   Oliveira Martins: *O Brasil*, p. 135.

64 : 29 P. Pablo Hernández, S.J.: *Organización social de las doctrinas guaraníes de la Compañía de Jesús* (Barcelona: Gustavo Gil; 1913), II, 9.

65 : 4   Hernández: *Organización*, II, 634–5.

65 : 27 Ibid., I, 352, 393.

66 : 26 Marcos Carneiro de Mendonça: *A Amazônia na Era Pombalina* (Rio: Ed. do Inst. Hist. e Geogr. Brasileiro; 1961), p. 79. See also pp. 133, 143–7, 152, and 157.

66 : 31 Inácio José Veríssimo: *Pombal, os Jesuítas e o Brasil* (Rio: Impr. do Exército; 1961), p. 44, n. 51a.

67 : 1   Ivan Lins: *Aspectos do P. Antônio Vieira* (Rio: Livr. São José; 1956), p. 76.

67 : 3   Mesquita Filho: *Ensaios Sul-Americanos*, p. 251.

67 : 29 Cortesão: *Raposo Tavares*, p. 78.

69 : 34 Ibid., p. 147. See also Pôrto: *História das Missões Orientais*, p. 51.

70 : 11 Rambo: *A Fisionomia*, p. 151. On the incursions of the *bandeirantes* into Rio Grande, see, in addition to Aurélio Pôrto's study, Olinto Sanmartin: *Bandeirantes no Sul do Brasil* (Pôrto Alegre: Tip. do Centro; 1949).

70 : 24 Calógeras: *A Política Exterior*, I, 164 and 174.

71 : 2 Pôrto: "Antecedentes Históricos," p. 110.

72 : 5 Alcântara Machado: *Vida e Morte do Bandeirante* (São Paulo: Livr. Martins Edit.; 1943), p. 66.

72 : 31 Cortesão: *A Fundação de São Paulo*, p. 62.

73 : 2 Mesquita Filho, *Ensaios Sul-Americanos*, p. 201.

73 : 33 Freyre: *The Masters and the Slaves*, p. 108; Sérgio Buarque de Holanda: *História Geral da Civilização Brasileira* (São Paulo: Difusão Européia do Livro; 1960), I, 84.

74 : 13 Washington Luíz: *Na Capitania de São Vicente* (São Paulo: Livr. Martins Edit.; 1956), p. 75.

74 : 24 Cortesão: *Raposo Tavares*, p. 135.

75 : 1 Alfredo Élis Júnior: *Raposo Tavares e Sua Época* (Rio: José Olympio Edit.; 1944), p. 87.

75 : 30 Sérgio Milliet: preface to *Vida et Morte do Bandeirante* of Alcântara Machado (São Paulo: Livr. Martins Edit.; 1943).

76 : 23 Pôrto: *História das Missões Orientais*, pp. 303, 304, 306–8, 398.

76 : 27 Cortesão: *Raposo Tavares*, p. 221.

77 : 29 Leite: *Novas Cartas Jesuíticas*, p. 111; Carneiro de Mendonça: *A Amazônia*, pp. 85, 89, 212–13.

78 : 11 The parts enclosed in quotation marks in this paragraph have been transcribed (and translated) from Father Leite's *História da Companhia*, II, 194–235.

78 : 16 Oliveira Martins: *O Brasil*, pp. 25–6; Inácio José Veríssimo: *Pombal*, p. 126.

78 : 26 Lins: *Aspectos do P. Antônio Vieira*, p. 287.

80 : 2 Washington Luíz: *Na Capitania*, p. 305. See also Hernández: *Organización*, II, 630–1, 637.

80 : 28 Rambo: *A Fisionomia*, pp. 151, 414.

81 : 28 Hernández: *Organización*, II, 656.

83 : 6 P. Antônio Sepp: *Viagem ás Missões Jesuíticas e Trabalhos Apostólicos* (São Paulo: Livr. Martins Edit.; 1943), pp. 209, 232, 234.

83 : 17 Ibid., pp. 196, 214.

84 : 9 Cortesão, ed.: *Manuscritos da Coleção De Angelis*, V, 306–23; Hernández: *Organización*, II, 544.

84 : 15 Pôrto: *História das Missões Orientais*, pp. 155–6; Mesquita Filho: *Ensaios*, p. 260.

84 : 23 Sepp: *Viagem*, p. 92.

85 : 6 Hernández: *Organización*, II, 47.

86 : 6 Ibid., I, 374, and II, 458.

86 : 30 Cortesão, ed.: *Manuscritos da Coleção De Angelis*, p. 138.

87 : 12 Leite: *Novas Cartas Jesuíticas*, p. 85.

87 : 14 Hernández: *Organización*, I, 65.

87 : 28 Ibid., I, 401.

88 : 27 Ibid., II, 490.

89 : 4 Ibid., II, 558.

89 : 15 Lins: *Aspectos do P. Antônio Vieira*, p. 286.

89 : 24 Hernández: *Organización*, I, 245, 251.

90 : 1 Mesquita Filho: *Ensaios*, p. 305.

90 : 7 Cortesão, ed.: *Manuscritos da Coleção De Angelis*, V, 256–328.

91 : 28 Ibid., V, 329–33.

92 : 9 J. F. de Assis Brasil: *História da República Rio-Grandense* (Rio: Tip. Leutzinger & Filho; 1882), p. 18 *n.*

92 : 16 Saint-Hilaire: *Viagem*, pp. 95–6.

94 : 8 Hernández: *Organización*, I, 284.

94 : 13 Hemetério Veloso da Silveira: *As Missões Orientais* (Pôrto Alegre: Livr. Universal de Carlos Echenique; 1909), p. 283.

94 : 32 Cônego Pedro Gay: *História da República Jesuítica do Paraguay* (Rio: Impr. Oficial; 1942), *n.* xxx, de Rodolfo Garcia, pp. 28–9.

95 : 13 Pôrto: *História das Missões Orientais*, p. 187.

95 : 15 Ibid., pp. 327, 330.

95 : 29 Freyre: *The Masters and the Slaves*, p. 173. Also, Souza Doca: *História do Rio Grande do Sul*, p. 44; and Francisco Xavier de Mendonça Furtado, in Carneiro de Mendonça: *A Amazônia*, pp. 70, 74, 147, 212–13.

96 : 18 General João Borges Fortes: *Rio Grande de São Pedro* (Rio: Biblioteca Militar; 1941), p. 77; *Cristóvão Pereira* (Pôrto Alegre: Tip. do Centro; 1932), p. 16.

97 : 4 Oliveira Martins: *O Brasil*, p. 69.

97 : 22 Hernández: *Organización*, II, 536, 610.

98 : 26 Ibid., II, 239–40.

98 : 29 Leite: *Novas Cartas Jesuíticas*, p. 134.

100 : 2 Pôrto: *História das Missões Orientais*, p. 546.

100 : 4 Alcides Lima: *História Popular do Rio Grande do Sul* (2nd edn.; Pôrto Alegre: Globo; 1935), p. 119.

100 : 12 Veloso da Silveira: *As Missões Orientais*, p. 240.

100 : 13 Ibid., p. 263.

CHAPTER THREE

102 : 5 Vargas Neto: *Tropilha Crioula e Gado Chucro* (Pôrto Alegre: Globo; 1955), p. 88.

104 : 16 P. Carlos Teschauer, S.J.: *História do Rio Grande do Sul nos Dois Primeiros Séculos* (3 vols.; Pôrto Alegre: Livr. Selbach; 1921–2).

105 : 2 Augusto Meyer: "Salve-se o Lunar de Sepé," *Correio do Povo* (Pôrto Alegre), Dec. 15, 1956.

108 : 14 Hernández: *Organización*, II, 405.

110 : 12 Teschauer: *História do Rio Grande*, II, 15.

112 : 25 Oliveira Viana: *Populações Meridionais*, II, 100.

116 : 10 Eurico Rodrigues: "Um Fantasma na História Rio-

Grandense," *A Defesa Nacional* (Rio: Ministério da Guerra; 1957), No. 510, pp. 67–74.

116 : 23 Othelo Rosa: "As Missões Jesuíticas e a Consciência da Juventude," *Província de São Pedro*, No. 14, pp. 170–2; "Sugestão sôbre um Monumento a Sepé Tiaraju," ibid., No. 21, pp. 228–231. (Othelo Rosa reported both opinions.)

117 : 6 Manoelito de Ornellas: *Tiaraju* (Pôrto Alegre: Globo; 1945). Other references on Sepé Tiaraju are General Ptolomeu Assis Brasil: *Batalha de Caiboaté* and Mansueto Bernardi: *O Primeiro Caudilho Rio-Grandense* (both Pôrto Alegre: Globo; 1935 and 1957, respectively). Although we disagree completely with the learned author of this last book, we cannot fail to recognize the importance of his role in the polemic re-examination of the subject.

117 : 27 General Ptolomeu Assis Brasil: *Batalha de Caiboaté*, p. 92. See also Father Teschauer: *História do Rio Grande*, II, 261.

118 : 8 Hernández: *Organización*, II, 215.

121 : 10 José Hansel: "Sepé Tiaraju," *Estudos* (Pôrto Alegre), Vol. XV, Nos. 3 and 4 (1955).

CHAPTER FOUR

124 : 7 Souza Doca: *História do Rio Grande do Sul*, p. 58.

124 : 22 W. H. Harnisch: *O Rio Grande do Sul—A Terra e o Homem* (Pôrto Alegre: Globo; 1941).

125 : 12 Ibid., pp. 17, 67.

125 : 22 Pôrto: *História das Missões Orientais*, pp. 353–70.

125 : 23 Borges Fortes: *Cristóvão Pereira*, p. 3.

126 : 27 Luís de Camões: *The Lusiads*, trans. by Leonard Bacon (New York: The Hispanic Society of America; 1950), p. 163, note on Book IV, stanza 14, line 2.

127 : 2 Cortesão: *Alexandre de Gusmão*, Part I, Vol. II, p. 39.

127 : 12 Ibid., p. 42.

128 : 28 Élis Júnior: "O Ciclo do Muar"; Austregésilo: "Estudo sôbre Alguns Tipos"; Melo Franco: *Terra do Brasil,* p. 149; José Alípio Goulart: *Tropas e Tropeiros.*

130 : 14 José Alípio Goulart: *Tropas e Tropeiros,* p. 44.

131 : 12 Afonso de E. Taunay, ed.: *Relatos Sertanistas* (São Paulo: Livr. Martins Edit.; 1953), VII, 158.

131 : 20 Élis Júnior: "O Ciclo do Muar," p. 76.

132 : 3 Borges Fortes: *Cristóvão Pereira,* pp. 13–14.

132 : 19 Taunay: *Relatos Sertanistas,* p. 230.

133 : 9 Ibid., pp. 158–9.

134 : 11 Borges Fortes: *Cristóvão Pereira,* p. 15.

135 : 12 Pôrto: *História das Missões Orientais,* p. 362.

136 : 10 Ibid., p. 373

137 : 3 Borges Fortes: *Cristóvão Pereira,* p. 24.

CHAPTER FIVE

139 : 20 Lucas Ayarragaray: *La anarquía argentina y el caudillismo* (Buenos Aires: J. Lajuane & Cía.; 1925), p. 19.

140 : 8 Cortesão: *Alexandre de Gusmão,* Part I, Vol. II, p. 55; Teixeira Soares: *Diplomacia do Império no Rio da Prata* (Rio: Edit. Brand Ltda.; 1955), pp. 14–15.

140 : 17 Madaline Wallis Nichols: *The Gaucho* (Durham, N.C.: Duke University Press; 1942), p. 52.

141 : 3 Emilio Corbiere: *El gaucho* (Buenos Aires: Talleres Gráficos Argentinos L. J. Rosso; 1929), p. 13.

141 : 5 Ayarragaray: *La anarquía,* p. 85.

141 : 11 Domingo F. Sarmiento: *Facundo* (Buenos Aires: La Cultura Argentina; 1923), p. 264.

141 : 20 Corbiere: *El gaucho,* p. 35.

142 : 5 Ezequiel Martínez Estrada: *Radiografía de la Pampa* (Buenos Aires: Edit. Losada, S.A.; 1946), I, 41.

142 : 9 José Ingenieros: *Sociología argentina* (Buenos Aires: Losada; 1946), p. 450.

142 : 16 Nichols: *The Gaucho*, p. 17, *n.* 14.

142 : 29 Arsène Isabelle: *Voyage à Buenos-Ayres et à Porto-Alègre* (Le Havre: Impr. de Morlent; 1835), pp. 166–7. See also Corbiere: *El gaucho*, pp. 36–7; Ayarragaray: *La anarquía*, p. 232.

143 : 3 Ayarragaray: *La anarquía*, p. 235.

143 : 6 Martínez Estrada: *Radiografía*, I, 34.

143 : 11 Corbiere: *El gaucho*, pp. 53–4.

144 : 3 Ibid., p. 229.

144 : 9 Martínez Estrada: *Radiografía*, p. 44.

144 : 11 Quoted by Ingenieros: *Sociología*, p. 124.

144 : 15 R. Blanco Fombona: *El conquistador español del siglo XVI* (Madrid: Edit. Mundo Latino; n. d.), p. 274.

144 : 20 Alberto Zum Felde: *Proceso histórico del Uruguay* (Montevideo: Maximino García; n. d.), pp. 42–3.

144 : 27 Nichols: *The Gaucho*, p. 44.

145 : 11 Sarmiento: *Facundo*, p. 299.

145 : 18 Carlos Octavio Bunge: *Nuestra América* (Buenos Aires: Casa Vaccaro; 1918), p. 13.

145 : 25 F. A. Kirkpatrick: *The Spanish Conquistadors* (London: A. & C. Black; 1934), p. 334. Also: "In the seventeenth century, already falling into irremediable decadence, Spanish arrogance, which is not occasional but congenital, astonished travelers. With one particularity: that haughty arrogance is not found only in the classes favored by birth or politics or wealth; it extends to all. One can see it in the insolence of a powerful favorite, . . . but also can glimpse it in the bearing of the farmer and under the rags of the beggar." (Blanco Fombona: *El conquistador*, pp. 38–9.)

145 : 29 Hernández: *Organización*, II, 546.

146 : 17 Ingenieros: *Sociología*, pp. 155 ff.

146 : 30 Blanco Fombona: *El conquistador*, p. 268.

147 : 1 Ayarragaray: *La anarquía*, p. 19.

147 : 10 Bunge: *Nuestra América*, p. 69.

147 : 16 Eugenio Petit Muñoz: *Interpretaciones esquemáticas sobre la Conquista y la colonización española en América* (Montevideo: Edit. La Cruz del Sur; 1927), p. 87.

147 : 26 Ingenieros: *Sociología*, p. 452.

148 : 2 Ibid., p. 179.

148 : 19 Ayarragaray: *La anarquía*, p. 2.

149 : 2 Ingenieros: *Sociología*, p. 462.

149 : 21 Corbiere: *El gaucho*, p. 27.

149 : 26 Ibid., pp. 98, 107.

149 : 28 Sarmiento: *Facundo*, p. 160.

150 : 6 Manuel Pedro González: *Trayectoria del gaucho y su cultura* (Havana: Úcar García & Cía.; 1943), p. 31.

150 : 18 Corbiere: *El gaucho*, pp. 56–7, 61–2.

151 : 26 Quoted by Souza Doca: "O Brasil no Prata," *Rev. do Inst. Hist. e Geogr. do Rio Grande do Sul*, No.1 (1931), p. 73.

152 : 1 Zum Felde: *Proceso*, pp. 30, 141.

152 : 20 Ingenieros: *Sociología*, p. 184.

153 : 14 Abeillar Barreto: "A Livraria de Silva Pais," *Província de São Pedro*, No. 15, pp. 178 ff.

154 : 19 P. Luíz Gonzaga Jaeger, S.J.: *As Invasões Bandeirantes ao Rio Grande do Sul* (Pôrto Alegre: Tip. do Centro; n. d.), p. 58; Hernández: *Organización*, II, 140.

155 : *n.* 9 Quoted by Muratori: *Il Cristianesimo Felice*, p. 161.

157 : 3 Artur Ferreira Filho: *História Geral do Rio Grande do Sul* (Pôrto Alegre: Globo; 1958), p. 52.

157 : 17 Zum Felde: *Proceso*, pp. 28–9.

157 : 20 Hernández: *Organización*, II, 257–8. Consult also Florêncio de Abreu: "Retrospecto Econômico e Financeiro do Estado do Rio Grande do Sul," *Rev. do Arquivo Público do Rio Grande do Sul*, No. 8 (1922), pp. 25 ff.

158 : 7 Veloso da Silveira: *As Missões Orientais*, p. 399, *n.* 2, and p. 438.

158 : 17 Pinto da Silva: *A Província*, pp. 42, 48. "In the eighteenth century," Father Rambo informs us, "the Azorian immigration and the consequent clash with the Spanish expelled the Indians from all the southern half of the State." ("Os Índios Rio-Grandenses Modernos," *Província de São Pedro*, No. 10, p. 81.)

160 : 3 Apolinário Pôrto Alegre: *Cancioneiro da Revolução de 1835* (Pôrto Alegre: Globo; 1935), p. 58.

160 : 13 Borges Fortes: "O Brigadeiro José da Silva Pais," p. 49.

162 : 3 *O Mensageiro* (Pôrto Alegre: Reprinted by, Museu e Arquivo Hist. do Rio Grande do Sul; 1930), II, 55.

164 : 3 Nichols: *The Gaucho*, p. 41.

164 : 11 Hernández: *Organización*, II, 239.

165 : 16 Ingenieros: *Sociología*, pp. 375 ff.

165 : 22 Juan Zorrilla de San Martín: *La epopeya de Artigas* (Montevideo: Impr. Nacional Colorada; 1950), p. 111.

167 : 7 Nicolau Dreys: *Notícia Descritiva da Província do Rio Grande do Sul* (Pôrto Alegre: Livr. Americana; 1927), pp. 103, 125.

168 : 2 Barcelos: *Estudos Rio-Grandenses*, pp. 20 ff.

168 : 12 Jorge Salis Goulart: *A Formação*, p. 152; Pinto da Silva: *A Província*, pp. 81, 103.

169 : 33 Walter Spalding: *A Epopéia Farroupilha* (Rio: Biblioteca do Exército; 1963), pp. 45-59.

170 : 24 Souza Doca: "O Brasil no Prata," pp. 49-51, 57; Tasso Fragoso: *A Batalha do Passo do Rosário* (Rio: Impr. Militar; 1922), pp. 105-6.

171 : 2 Zum Felde: *Proceso*, p. 79.

172 : 11 Teixeira Soares: *Diplomacia*, pp. 93, 101, 112, 274.

172 : 23 Tristão de Alencar Araripe: *Guerra Civil no Rio Grande do Sul* (Rio: Tip. Universal de E. & Laemmert; 1881), p. 140.

172 : 31 Pandiá Calógeras: *Formação Histórica do Brasil* (São Paulo: Comp. Edit. Nac.; 1957), p. 177.

173 : 9 Corbiere: *El gaucho*, p. 191.

174 : 28 Zum Felde: *Proceso*, p. 199.

175 : 30 José Maria Bello: *A History of Modern Brazil*, trans. by James L. Taylor (Stanford: Stanford Univ. Press; 1966), pp. 107–48.

177 : 9 Oliveira Viana: *Populações Meridionais*, II, 100.

177 : 27 General João Borges Fortes: *Rio Grande de São Pedro* (Rio: Gráficos Bloch; 1941), pp. 95, 101; Barcelos: *Estudos Rio-Grandenses*, p. 27; Lima: *História Popular*, p. 99.

178 : 10 *Arquivo Nacional—Publicações VI* (Rio: Impr. Nacional; 1907), p. 335.

178 : 24 John Luccock: *Notes on Rio de Janeiro, and the Southern Parts of Brazil* (London: Samuel Leigh; 1820), pp. 178–9.

178 : 29 General Tomás de Iriarte: *Rivadavia, Monroe y la Guerre Argentino-Brasileña* (Buenos Aires: Grandes Obras Argentinas S.I.A.; 1945), p. 412.

179 : 18 Oliveira Viana: *Populações Meridionais*, p. 260.

180 : 7 Augusto Meyer: *Prosa dos Pagos* (Rio: Livr. São José; 1960), p. 26.

180 : 29 Florêncio de Abreu: "Aspectos do Desenvolvimento Econômico e Financeiro do Rio Grande do Sul," *Comemorações em Honra do Cent. da Independ. do Brasil* (Pôrto Alegre: Ofic. Gráf. da Federação; 1922), p. 67.

182 : 14 Lindolfo Cólor: *Garibaldi e a Guerra dos Farrapos* (2nd edn.; Pôrto Alegre: Globo; 1958), p. 117.

182 : 17 Moysés Vellinho: *Letras da Província* (Pôrto Alegre: Globo; 1944), p. 28.

182 : 26 Sebastião Francisco Betâmio: "Notícia Particular do Continente do Rio Grande do Sul," *Rev. do Inst. Hist. e Geogr. do Brasil*, XVI, 187–242.

183 : 30 Pierre Deffontaines: *Geografia Humana do Brasil*, separata da *Rev. Bras. de Geografia*, Vol. I, Nos. 1–3, p. 66.

185 : 1 Othelo Rosa: "A Formação do Rio Grande do Sul,"

Fundamentos da Cultura Rio-Grandense (Pôrto Alegre: Faculdade de Filosofia da Universidade do Rio Grande do Sul; 2nd Series, 1957), p. 19.

185 : 4 *Almanaque do Rio Grande do Sul,* 1893, p. 89; Souza Doca: "Vocábulos Indígenas na Geografia do Rio Grande do Sul," *Rev. do Inst. Hist. e Geogr. do R. G. do S.,* Vol. V, Nos. 1 and 2, p. 150.

185 : 36 Pinto da Silva: *A Província,* pp. 55–6; Augusto Meyer: preface to the translation (by Teodemiro Tostes) of *Viagem ao Rio da Prata e ao Rio Grande do Sul* of Arsène Isabelle (Rio: Livr. Zélio Valverde; 1949), p. 11. See also on this point Othelo Rosa: "A Formação do Rio Grande do Sul," pp. 15–16.

186 : 6 General João Borges Fortes: *Casais* (Rio: Edição do Centenário Farroupilha; 1932), pp. 132–3.

186 : 8 Varela: *História da Grande Revolução,* I, 62.

186 : 17 Alcides Cruz: *Vida de Rafael Pinto Bandeira* (Pôrto Alegre: Livr. Americana; 1906), p. 37.

186 : 26 Rambo: *A Fisionomia,* p. 153.

187 : 3 Quoted by Oliveira Viana: *Populações Meridionais,* p. 180. See also Alfredo Ferreira Rodrigues: "Os Espanhóis no Rio Grande," *Almanaque do Rio Grande do Sul,* 1896, p. 232, *n.* 19.

187 : 18 Pôrto: *História das Missões Orientais,* p. 390.

187 : 36 *Rev. do Arquivo Público do Rio Grande do Sul,* No. 1 (1921), pp. 64–5, 67.

188 : 7 Lima: *História Popular,* p. 98.

188 : 11 Borges Fortes: *Casais,* pp. 50, 91, 111.

188 : 16 Betâmio: "Notícia Particular," p. 264.

189 : 11 See Arsène Isabelle: *Emigração e Colonização,* trans. by Belfort de Oliveira (Rio: Gráfica Edit. Souza; 1950), p. 35.

189 : 13 Pinto da Silva: *A Província,* p. 77.

189 : 25 "Documentos Relativos à Incorporação do Território

das Missões ao Domínio Português," *Rev. do Arquivo Público do Rio Grande do Sul*, I (1921).

190 : 3 Zum Felde: *Proceso*, p. 52.

190 : 12 Gabriel Ribeiro de Almeida: "Memória sôbre a Tomada dos Sete Povos das Missões da América Espanhola," in Veloso da Silveira: *As Missões Orientais*, pp. 87–110.

190 : 15 General João Borges Fortes: *A Estância* (Rio: Tip. do Ministério da Agricultura; 1931), p. 20.

191 : 11 Isabelle: *Emigração*, p. 377.

191 : 16 Ibid., p. 375.

192 : 20 Guilhermino César: *História da Literatura do Rio Grande do Sul* (Pôrto Alegre: Globo; 1956), p. 190. Our comments on this book: "Part of a whole, and of a whole as poor in literature as is Brazil, Rio Grande do Sul does not show what can be called literary autonomy. . . . Literarily, as historically, politically, and culturally, we are satellites of the Brazilian communion, we live in terms of it as one of its active organs, and it is for that reason that the Rio-Grandense literary process could not fail to consist of parallel, simply complementary or reflex expressions or movements. Such expressions or movements, constantly faithful to suggestion from the common sources of irradiation, will not always be continuous or synchronous with those of the center, and will often fructify far from the point of origin. . . . The aesthetic significance, nearly always slight, of the copious material having been meditated upon, its spirit and its tendencies compared with the social inspirations of the period having been assimilated, the conclusion—which the author does not leave for the final chapter of his book because it is deduced from every chapter—is that Rio Grande, intimately polarized by the foci of irradiation of the country, has always been present in all the movements

that form the history of Brazilian literary thought.
. . . Therefore it is plain that Guilhermino César's
book, through painstaking analysis of our literary testimonies, has banished once and for all the persistent
and unfounded refrain of Rio Grande's cultural affili-
ation to the Plata. The truth is that in literature as in
all else we form a single body with Brazil. Regionalism
itself, which Guilhermino César traces with rare critical sagacity from its birth through its development,
must be considered in its instinctive impulse and mo-
tivation, as a successful effort to integrate the southern
border into the culture of the Brazilian nation." (Vellinho: *Letras da Província*, pp. 245–6.)

192 : 28 Augusto Meyer: *Cancioneiro Gaúcho* (Pôrto Alegre:
Globo; 1950), p. 7. Also consult Cecília Meireles:
"Folclore Guasca e Açoriano," *Província de São
Pedro*, No. 6 (1946), pp. 7–10; and her "Notas de
Folclore Gaúcho-Açoriano," ibid., No. 8, pp. 67–71.

193 : 11 Romeu Beltrão: *Cronologia Histórica de Santa Maria
e do Extinto Município de São Martinho* (Santa Maria:
Livr. Edit. Paloti; 1958).

193 : 15 Gilberto Freyre: *Continente e Ilha* (Rio: Edição da
Casa do Estudante do Brasil; 1943).

195 : 32 *Almanaque do Rio Grande do Sul*, 1891, p. 158.

196 : 21 Barão do Rio Branco: *Biografias* (Rio: Ministério das
Relações Exteriores; 1947), pp. 15–86.

197 : 11 Fragoso: *A Batalha do Passo*, p. 263.

198 : 3 *O Mensageiro*, Dec. 1, 1836.

198 : 20 Alencar Araripe: *Guerra Civil*, p. 47.

198 : 27 Ibid., p. 150.

199 : 19 Coelho de Souza: *O Sentido*, pp. 69 ff.

200 : 1 Ingenieros: *Sociología*, p. 184.

200 : 35 Francisco de Sá Brito: *Memória da Guerra dos Farrapos*
(Rio: Gráfica Edit. Souza; 1950), p. 121.

201 : 6 Pinto da Silva: *A Província*, pp. 38–9.

202 : 5 Alencar Araripe: *Guerra Civil*, p. 193.

202 : 10 Bunge: *Nuestra América*, p. 279.

202 : 17 Alencar Araripe: *Guerra Civil*, p. 178.

202 : 23 *O Americano*, Sept. 28, 1842. (Reprinted by Museu e Arquivo Histórico do Rio Grande do Sul, 1933, p. 197. The paper was then being published in Alegrete, third capital of the Revolution.)

203 : 31 Coelho de Souza: *O Sentido*, pp. 59–66.

204 : 20 Felisbelo Freire: *História Constitucional da República dos Estados Unidos do Brasil* (Rio: Tip. Moreira Maximino, Chagas & Cia.; 1894), I, 314.

205 : 15 Ayarragaray: *La anarquía*, pp. 129–30.

205 : 19 Pinto da Silva: *A Província*, p. 94.

208 : 26 Ayarragaray: *La anarquía*, p. 148.

209 : 4 J. H. Rodrigues: *O Continente do Rio Grande* (Rio: Edições São José; 1954), p. 53.

209 : 15 César: *História da Literatura*, p. 345.

210 : 3 Carlos Dante de Moraes: *Figuras e Ciclos da História Rio-Grandense* (Pôrto Alegre: Globo; 1959), p. 174.

211 : 5 Borges Fortes: *Rio Grande de São Pedro*, pp. 101–2; Coelho de Souza: "Diretivas Políticas," p. 140.

212 : 18 Oliveira Viana: *Populações Meridionais*.

212 : 27 Ayarragaray: *La anarquía*, p. 68.

213 : 5 Zum Felde: *Proceso*, p. 126.

213 : 23 Ingenieros: *Sociología*, p. 182.

213 : 29 Domingo F. Sarmiento: *Los caudillos* (Buenos Aires: W. M. Jackson, Inc.; n. d.), pp. 11–67.

214 : 25 Oliveira Viana: *Populações Meridionais*, p. 255.

218 : 5 Cruz: *Vida de Rafael Pinto Bandeira*, p. 86.

218 : 14 Calógeras: *Formação Histórica*, p. 177.

218 : 23 Wilson Martins's critical commentary, published in *Estado de São Paulo*, April 18, 1959, on Vol. I of *Memórias*, by João Neves da Fontoura.

219 : 28 Borges Fortes: *Rio Grande de São Pedro*, p. 160. See also Souza Doca: *História do Rio Grande do Sul*, p. 131.

220 : 22 Florêncio de Abreu: "Importância," *Comemorações em Honra do Cent. da Independ. do Brasil*, p. 26; Dante de Laytano: *O Negro no Rio Grande do Sul* (Pôrto Alegre: Tip. Champagnat; 1958).

221 : 3 Othelo Rosa: *Vultos da Epopéia Farroupilha* (Pôrto Alegre: Globo; 1935), pp. 195–7; Jorge Salis Goulart alludes to "the intrepid Negro lancers of Canabarro" in *A Formação*, p. 97.

222 : 9 Alfredo F. Rodrigues: "General Osório," *Almanaque do Rio Grande do Sul*, 1888, p. 7.

222 : 25 Pinto da Silva: *A Província*, p. 26.

223 : 8 Moraes: *Figuras e Ciclos*, pp. 128 ff.

225 : 15 Cruz: *Vida de Rafael Pinto Bandeira*, p. 98.

225 : 31 Alceu Amoroso Lima: *Europa e América—Duas Culturas* (Rio: Agir; 1962), p.35.

226 : 28 João Pinto da Silva: *História Literária do Rio Grande do Sul* (Pôrto Alegre: Globo; 1924), pp. 173–4.

227 : 13 Athos Damasceno: *Palco, Salão e Picadeiro em Pôrto Alegre no Século XIX* (Pôrto Alegre: Globo; 1956).

228 : 11 Joaquim Nabuco: *Escritos e Discursos Literários* (Rio: Livr. Garnier; 1919), p. 110.

228 : 22 Ayarragaray: *La anarquía*, p. 31.

229 : 9 Aurélio Pôrto: "Continente do Rio Grande," *Almanaque do Correio do Povo* (Pôrto Alegre), 1959, pp. 46–7. In this study the author clarifies perfectly the exact idea of "continente."

229 : 17 Pinto da Silva: *A Província*, p. 9; Jorge Salis Goulart: *A Formação*, p. 38. Father Rambo picks up the same thought: "In short, the secular struggle for the frontier, joined with the nature of the land, forged the character of the *gaúcho* in the purest sense of the term; in the course of the last hundred years to the present, the Campanha has revealed itself as the fecund cradle of men and ideas, *determining the political*

physiognomy of Rio Grande." (Italics ours.) (*A Fisionomia*, p. 152.)

CHAPTER SIX

230 : 8 Afonso Arinos: "Um Citadino," *O Jornal* (Rio de Janeiro).

232 : 28 Manuel Bandeira: *Brief History of Brazilian Literature*, trans., intro., and notes by Ralph Edward Dimmick (Washington, D.C.: Pan American Union; 1958), pp. 152–3.

234 : 13 Augusto Meyer: *Estudo Crítico em Antônio Chimango, de Amaro Juvenal* (3rd edn., rev.; Pôrto Alegre: Globo; 1961), p. 30. [The same firm published J. Simões Lopes Neto: *Contos Gauchescos e Lendas do Sul*, and Amaro Juvenal (pseudonym of Ramiro Barcelos): *Antônio Chimango*, as Vols. 1 and 5 of the *Coleção Província*. (Translators)].

236 : 27 Bello: *A History of Modern Brazil*, pp. 117, 135.

240 : 36 Gilberto Freyre: *Uma Cultura Ameaçada: a Luso-Brasileira* (2nd edn.; Rio: Casa do Estudante do Brazil; 1942).

241 : 29 Bandeira: *Brief History of Brazilian Literature*, pp. 143–4.

243 : 12 Barbosa Lima Sobrinho: *A Língua Portuguêsa e a Unidade do Brasil* (Rio: José Olympio Edit.; 1958), p. 130.

INDEX

(Italicized references in the form *oo : oo* indicate mention of the subject of the entry in the Notes section preceding the Index.)

A NOTE ABOUT THE AUTHOR

MOYSÉS VELLINHO was born in Santa Maria, Rio Grande do Sul, Brazil, in 1901. He studied at the Colégios Anchieta e Júlio de Castilhos in Pôrto Alegre and took a degree in juridical and social sciences at the Universidade Federal do Rio Grande do Sul in 1926. Mr. Vellinho served as district attorney for Caxias do Sul and Jaguarão in 1926-7; as chief of the cabinet, Department of the Interior, from 1928 to 1930; and as a cabinet official in the Ministry of Justice in 1931. From 1935 to 1937 he was a deputy in the state assembly and from 1938 to 1964 minister of the State Court of Accounts. He is an active associate of the Instituto Histórico e Geográfico do Rio Grande do Sul and a member of the Academia Internacional da Cultura Portuguêsa in Lisbon and the Conselho Federal de Cultura in Rio de Janeiro. His publications include *Letras da Província* (1944), *Simões Lopes Neto* (1957), and *Machado de Assis* (1960). Mr. Vellinho lives in Pôrto Alegre, Rio Grande do Sul, and is currently working on another historical study of the region.

A NOTE ON THE TYPE

The text of this book was set on the Linotype in Janson, a re-
cutting made direct from type cast from matrices long thought
to have been made by the Dutchman Anton Janson, who was a
practicing type founder in Leipzig during the years 1668–87.
However, it has been conclusively demonstrated that these types
are actually the work of Nicholas Kis (1650–1702), a Hungarian,
who most probably learned his trade from the master Dutch
type founder Kirk Voskens. The type is an excellent example
of the influential and sturdy Dutch types that prevailed in England up to the time William Caslon developed his own incomparable designs from these Dutch faces.

*The book was composed, printed, and bound
by American Book–Stratford Press, Inc., New York, N.Y.*

Typography and binding design by
GUY FLEMING

Moysés Vellinho was born in Santa Maria, Rio Grande do Sul, Brazil, in 1901. He studied at the Colégios Anchieta e Júlio de Castilhos in Pôrto Alegre and took a degree in juridical and social sciences at the Universidade Federal do Rio Grande do Sul in 1926. Mr. Vellinho served as district attorney for Caxias do Sul and Jaguarão in 1926–7; as Chief of the Cabinet, Department of the Interior from 1928 to 1930; and as a cabinet official in the Ministry of Justice in 1931. From 1935 to 1937 he was a deputy in the state assembly and from 1938 to 1964 minister of the State Court of Accounts. He is an active associate of the Instituto Histórico e Geográfico do Rio Grande do Sul and a member of the Academia Internacional da Cultura Portuguêsa in Lisbon and the Conselho Federal de Cultura in Rio de Janeiro. His publications include *Letras da Província* (1944), *Simões Lopes Neto* (1957), and *Machado de Assis* (1960). Mr. Vellinho lives in Pôrto Alegre, Rio Grande do Sul, and is currently working on another historical study of the region.